A PASSIONATE BALANCE

TRADITIONS OF CHRISTIAN SPIRITUALITY SERIES

A PASSIONATE BALANCE

The Anglican Tradition

Alan Bartlett

SERIES EDITOR:
Philip Sheldrake

ORBIS BOOKS

Maryknoll, New York 10545

Founded in 1970, Orbis Books endeavors to publish works that enlighten the mind, nourish the spirit, and challenge the conscience. The publishing arm of the Maryknoll Fathers and Brothers, Orbis seeks to explore the global dimensions of the Christian faith and mission, to invite dialogue with diverse cultures and religious traditions, and to serve the cause of reconciliation and peace. The books published reflect the views of their authors and do not represent the official position of the Maryknoll Society. To learn more about Maryknoll and Orbis Books, please visit our website at www.maryknoll.org.

First published in Great Britain in 2007 by
Darton, Longman and Todd Ltd
1 Spencer Court
140-142 Wandsworth High Street
London SW18 4JJ
Great Britain

First published in the USA in 2007 by
Orbis Books
P.O. Box 308
Maryknoll, New York 10545-0308
U.S.A.

FSC
Mixed Sources
Product group from well-managed
forests and other controlled sources
Cert no. SGS-COC-2953
www.fsc.org
© 1996 Forest Stewardship Council

Printed and bound in Great Britain.

Library of Congress Cataloging-in-Publication Data

Bartlett, Alan, 1958-
  A passionate balance : the Anglican tradition / Alan Bartlett.
    p. cm. -- (Traditions of Christian spirituality)
  ISBN 978-1-57075-677-1
  1. Spirituality--Anglican Communion. I. Title.
  BX5005.B37 2007
  283--dc22
                                2007016615

CONTENTS

PREFACE TO THE SERIES

Nowadays, in the Western world, there is a widespread hunger for spirituality in all its forms. This is not confined to traditional religious people, let alone to regular churchgoers. The desire for resources to sustain the spiritual quest has led many people to seek wisdom in unfamiliar places. Some have turned to cultures other than their own. The fascination with Native American or Aboriginal Australian spiritualities is a case in point. Other people have been attracted by the religions of India and Tibet or the Jewish Kabbalah and Sufi mysticism. One problem is that, in comparison to other religions, Christianity is not always associated in people's minds with 'spirituality'. The exceptions are a few figures from the past who have achieved almost cult status such as Hildegard of Bingen or Meister Eckhart. This is a great pity, for Christianity East and West over two thousand years has given birth to an immense range of spiritual wisdom. Many traditions continue to be active today. Others that were forgotten are being rediscovered and reinterpreted.

It is a long time since an extended series of introductions to Christian spiritual traditions has been available in English. Given the present climate, it is an opportune moment for a new series which will help more people to be aware of the great spiritual riches available within the Christian traditions.

The overall purpose of the series is to make selected spiritual traditions available to a contemporary readership. The books seek to provide accurate and balanced historical and thematic treatments of their subjects. The authors are also conscious of the need to make connections with contemporary experience and values without being artificial or reducing a tradition to one dimension. The authors are well versed in reliable scholarship about the traditions they describe. However, their intention is that the books should be fresh in style and accessible to the general reader.

One problem that such a series inevitably faces is the word 'spirituality'. For example, it is increasingly used beyond religious circles and does not necessarily imply a faith tradition. Again, it could mean substantially different things for a Christian and a Buddhist. Within Christianity itself, the word in its modern sense is relatively recent. The reality that it stands for differs subtly in the different contexts of time and place. Historically, 'spirituality' covers a breadth of human experience and a wide range of values and practices.

No single definition of 'spirituality' has been imposed on the authors in this series. Yet, despite the breadth of the series there is a sense of a common core in the writers themselves and in the traditions they describe. All Christian spiritual traditions have their source in three things. First, while drawing on ordinary experience and even religious insights from elsewhere, Christian spiritualities are rooted in the Scriptures and particularly in the Gospels. Second, spiritual traditions are not derived from abstract theory but from attempts to live out gospel values in a positive yet critical way within specific historical and cultural contexts. Third, the experiences and insights of individuals and groups are not isolated but are related to the wider Christian tradition of beliefs, practices and community life. From a Christian perspective, spirituality is not just concerned with prayer or even with narrowly religious activities. It concerns the whole of human life, viewed in terms of a conscious relationship with God, in Jesus Christ, through the indwelling of the Holy Spirit and within a community of believers.

The series as a whole includes traditions that probably would not have appeared twenty years ago. The authors themselves have been encouraged to challenge, where appropriate, inaccurate assumptions about their particular tradition. While conscious of their own biases, authors have none the less sought to correct the imbalances of the past. Previous understandings of what is mainstream or 'orthodox' sometimes need to be questioned. People or practices that became marginal demand to be re-examined. Studies of spirituality in the past frequently underestimated or ignored the role of women. Sometimes the treatments of spiritual traditions were culturally one-sided because they were written from an uncritical Western European or North Atlantic perspective.

However, any series is necessarily selective. It cannot hope to do full justice to the extraordinary variety of Christian spiritual traditions. The principles of selection are inevitably open to question. I hope that an appropriate balance has been maintained between a sense of the likely readership on the one hand and the dangers of narrowness on the other. In the end, choices had to be made and the result is inevitably weighted in favour of traditions that have achieved 'classic' status or which seem to capture the contemporary imagination. Within these limits, I trust that the series will offer a reasonably balanced account of what the Christian spiritual tradition has to offer.

As editor of the series I would like to thank all the authors who agreed to contribute and for the stimulating conversations and correspondence that sometimes resulted. I am especially grateful for the high quality of their work which made my task so much easier. Editing such a series is a complex undertaking. I have worked closely throughout with the editorial team of Darton, Longman and Todd and Robert Ellsberg of Orbis Books. I am immensely grateful to them for their friendly support and judicious advice. Without them this series would never have come together.

PHILIP SHELDRAKE
University of Durham

PREFACE

This book is, like most books, setting out to make a case. I introduce Anglican spirituality by offering my particular perspective on it. But, I hope, there is enough breadth of material in the book about Anglicanism to make it useful as an introduction, whether readers accept my overall argument or not.

The book was written against the backdrop of a renewed crisis in the Anglican Communion. Whilst I have attempted to find some distance from this, it is the inescapable context within which I have been teaching and writing for many years. I believe in the Anglican values and spirituality which this book expresses and think that if Anglicans allowed themselves to be shaped more deeply by their heritage, then we would be in a better place now. All this means that the book varies its tone from 'objective' descriptions of Anglican spirituality to passionate passages of more personal argument. You have been forewarned !

I am very grateful to Philip Sheldrake for the invitation to write this and for his patient support in its gestation; and to Brendan Walsh at DLT for some robust editing and insightful feedback.

The people behind the anonymous types in the Introductory Chapter are the Revd Ken Morgan, Vicar of St Mary's, Shalford (Guildford), where I was a choirboy; Canon Ted Roberts of St James', Bermondsey (Southwark), and the Revd 'Snowy' Davoll of the Cambridge University Mission in Bermondsey, where I took the first steps towards ordained ministry; and Canon Michael Webb of Holy Cross, Fenham (Newcastle) where I served my curacy. I am deeply fortunate to have seen such deeply committed parish clergy at work. In an era when parochial ministry is under more strain than for 150 years, their example sustains my confidence in the value of this form of ministry in the Church of England.

Others who deserve special thanks include Georgina and Leslie Morley for the generous use of their cottage in beautiful Upper Teesdale where one balmy autumn the guts of the book was written.

And the book would have been *impossible* without the emotional and practical support of Helen, Ben and Anna. *Thank you.*

The book itself is dedicated to the staff and students of Cranmer Hall, St John's College in Durham, where I was trained and have taught for over ten years. I was employed to teach, amongst other things, 'Anglican Studies', a new post in an English theological college. This revealed a seriousness about Anglicanism which is part of the genetic make-up of the place. I am deeply grateful to College for the opportunity to study and teach Anglicanism (and for a period of study leave to write this book); for the rich stimulus of sympathetic as well as sceptical colleagues (Anglican *and,* with deep affection, non-Anglican) and for generations of students who have responded with such enthusiasm to Anglican theology and spirituality. It is invidious to name colleagues individually, but I remember with respect Michael Vasey, who in a series of 'church teaching seminars' first set me off on the quest into Anglicanism. More recent colleagues to be thanked by name include: Bob Fyall (a wise Conservative Evangelical Scottish Presbyterian) for revealing to me that I love 'balance'; Stephen Sykes for stimulating conversations about Anglicanism; Stephen Hampton, Walter Moberly, George Morley, Judith Walker-Hutchinson who each read some chapters and Gavin Wakefield who enthusiastically read and commented in detail on the whole book; and to Jane Ghosh, librarian, for getting hold of books at such speed. They have all made the book much better. I, of course, remain responsible for any inaccuracy or infelicity.

Style

To keep the main text as fluent as possible, the endnotes include the more specialist arguments. Otherwise they are bibliographical. The endnotes include abbreviated references to the key books in the select bibliography. Otherwise the first citation of a book in each chapter is in full and abbreviated thereafter. Spelling has only been modernised for the Prayer Book, or where it has been modernised in the cited text. I cite the Articles from the final 1571 version but note earlier differences where significant. For ease of identification, even if ungrammatically, I capitalise Scripture, Reason and Tradition whenever I refer to this method of doing theology. For the same reason, I have also consistently capitalised ecclesiastical adjectives such as Protestant or Catholic, Liberal or Evangelical.

INTRODUCTION: PASSIONATE BALANCING

Who Am I?

One of my colleagues specialised in asking interviewees, 'Where is your heartland?' It was an effective way of inviting them to expose their spiritual and theological convictions. But it always left me feeling inadequate. What was my heartland? I would once have known. I had been (almost) a cradle Anglican, a Charismatic, a Conservative, then an Open Evangelical. But now? One day, I had one of those corridor conversations. As he wandered away, Bob lobbed back in my direction, 'I suppose for some people, balance is their heartland.' I stood there, transfixed. That was me. I was passionate about balance and that was, in part, why I had chosen to be and still am an Anglican. That is why this book is called *A Passionate Balance.*

A further word of explanation about myself will help readers understand this book. When teaching something as contentious as Anglicanism, it is only right to enable hearers to know where you are coming from. I am Irish but a long-term immigrant to England. Baptised a Methodist, I became a choirboy at a typical Church of England parish church led by one of those exemplary parish priests to whom anyone in the village felt they could go for care and wisdom. Confirmation at fourteen was a spiritual milestone but was followed at fifteen by 'conversion' during a mission led by a wild American travelling evangelist. I put this in inverted commas not out of disrespect but because I was already a Christian. Nonetheless it marked a significant change in the intimacy of my walk with God. There followed several adolescent years in a vibrant youth group at a Charismatic Baptist church followed by the, perhaps inevitable, loss of faith when confronted by the harsh realities of life. Then came recovery of faith in a university Christian Union, under-girded by the preaching at one of the Church of England's famous Conservative Evangelical churches.

Faith renewed, I headed off to the inner city and work in a dynamic Christian youth club and a creative local Evangelical parish church. Slowly, it dawned on me that there were Christians around whom I respected deeply for their Christ-like qualities but who did not share my convictions about the inerrancy of Scripture or the nature of salvation. This started a long theological and spiritual journey, which continued through theological college and a curacy in a middle-of-the-road/Liberal Catholic parish with an excellent training incumbent, to being a convinced Anglican. This has been confirmed by ten years of teaching Anglicanism to ordinands, postgraduates, curates, readers, lay groups, Methodists, Roman Catholics, Lutherans and Orthodox.

Apart from self-advertisement, why am I sharing these facts? Because my *experience* has led me to believe that the truth of God is not the monopoly of any of the 'tribes' within Anglicanism. Alongside the passionate advocacy and embodiment of our own theological convictions, I have discovered that we must pay careful attention to others. Not to find the lowest common denominator, but because the humble, surprising and wise Christ whom we follow finds a home and voice amongst widely differing people. It is in dialogue, argument and even compromise that we hear Christ. The truth of God is found in a dynamic balancing of different perspectives.

Anglican Method

This life experience is now under-girded by theological convictions. Anglicans claim to use the famous 'three-stranded cord' in theology and spirituality: 'Scripture, Reason and Tradition'. Traditionally, they have linked this to the image of the three-stranded cord in Ecclesiastes 4:12. This book will argue that there is still life in this method.[1] It is crucial both in itself and for what it embodies: the conviction that the truth about God is not to be found in an exclusive focus on any of these aspects but in a disciplined dialogue between them – with a carefully managed primacy given to Scripture – leading to a state of dynamic balance. For those with a visual imagination, picture a three-stranded cord with one of the strands larger than the others; but *the strands are inextricably linked.*

I think this method is best exemplified in the treasures of Classic Anglicanism (from the Reformation to, very roughly, the 1660s).[2] So we give most space in this book to selected (*not* comprehensive) expressions of Anglican faith from this period: the depth of Cranmer's prayer books; the wisdom of Elizabeth; the passion of Donne; the simplicity of Herbert; the joy of Traherne.[3] We will also meet a few of those who came later and, because of the long-running current crisis, we will study some important modern documents. Within this rich company, both because he is almost universally regarded as the founder of Anglicanism and because his ideas are still crucial for the welfare of modern Anglicanism, much space will be devoted to Richard Hooker, the great theologian of Elizabeth I.

The 'three-stranded cord' method has received greater prominence and bite in the Church of England in the last generation through the Declaration of Assent. This is the promise about faith which everyone who receives an English bishop's licence (lay and ordained) is required to make. It is worth quoting here in full because we shall often refer to it:

> The Church of England is part of the one, holy, Catholic and apostolic Church worshipping the one true God, Father, Son and Holy Spirit. It professes the faith *uniquely revealed* in the Holy Scriptures and *set forth* in the Catholic creeds, which faith the Church is called upon *to proclaim afresh* in each generation. Led by the Holy

Spirit, it has *borne witness* to Christian truth in its *historic formularies*, the Thirty-nine Articles of Religion, the Book of Common Prayer, and the Ordering of Bishops, Priests and Deacons.[4]

This is an English, rather than global, Anglican statement of faith but it has deep roots in Anglicanism. It reminds us that Anglicans are clearly Trinitarian and believe themselves to be part of the ancient Catholic Church.

The Declaration takes us to the heart of Anglican theological methodology. Notice the verbs. Anglicans are here required to state their belief in the faith which is *uniquely revealed* in Scripture. Scripture has primacy (chapter 3). The faith is then *set forth* – articulated, made visible, proclaimed – in the great Catholic creeds. But as was made clear during the Reformation, this setting forth is dependent on the primary authority of Scripture. Anglicans do believe that Scripture ranks above Tradition, though they are *never* to be separated (chapters 3 and 4). In comparison to this, Anglican faith in the *historic formularies* is much less,[5] although they are not to be disregarded. Anglicans believe that the Holy Spirit was at work in guiding the Church when they were compiled – more formally, that the formularies are not 'repugnant to the Word of God' (Canons A2, 3, 4) – but Anglicans are not required simply to accept their authority, because they are so clearly limited documents from a particular period.[6] Finally, the faith is not just repeated in each generation. There are various interpretations given to the phrase *to proclaim afresh* but, at least, it means the duty to engage seriously with the social and cultural patterns of each context and age (chapters 2 and 5).

The story of the composition of the Declaration is a window into the nature of Anglicanism which this book celebrates. By the 1960s it was again clear that the traditional declarations of faith required of English Anglican clergy were causing angst and bringing the Church into disrepute. Therefore one of the first tasks of the reconstituted Doctrine Commission was to draw up a new form of assent. This was, inevitably, a messy process and included the sort of haggling in the corridors of synods that appears to show the Church in a very poor light. What has the Holy Spirit to do with ecclesiastical politics like this? And yet, out of this very human process, a form of words emerged which is good and life-giving and commands very wide assent. Paul Avis describes it as 'superb'.[7] This example speaks to me about Anglican faith in God at work *through* the mess of human life, not above it (chapter 1).

History and Wisdom

There is a second cluster of justifications for giving priority to looking back to Classic Anglicanism. This period was hugely formative for Anglicans. They almost all consciously trace their ancestry back into these centuries. Anglicans also believe that history is a good teacher of wisdom. More than learning lessons from the past, there is a theological conviction that as we reflect on the history of the Church (and the world), we are exploring God's interaction with human beings and that is, potentially, a source of wisdom (chapter 1). To reflect theologically on this rich formative period of Anglicanism enables us to move from the descriptive work which is historical theology to constructive theology,which commends a way of being Christian *now*. One of the key insights is the wisdom of balance.

Modesty

As well as balance and history, there is a third important component in this conversation about Anglicanism – modesty (chapter 2). There is a strong persistent strand in Classic Anglicanism which stresses the need for human beings to be 'modest', that is, restrained and self-aware, as they talk of God. This modesty also requires Anglicans to attend to other conversation partners because human grasp on the truth of God is always limited and so, to use another metaphor, they need to check out their position by taking as many bearings as possible.

In keeping with this modesty, a crucial bearing is always critical reflection within the current context. Notwithstanding my delight in the treasures of Classic Anglicanism, Anglican method reminds us of the contextualised nature even of these majestic expressions of Anglican faith.[8] Honest historical work shows that Anglicanism has changed, sometimes profoundly, over the course of its lifetime, because human beings always live in changing contexts. As Euan Cameron, a distinguished church historian and an Anglican reminds us:

> Historical change is not an option, a political or theological choice for the churches and for individual Christians. It is their inescapable predicament.[9]

Part of the sub-text of this book is to identify and then *evaluate* some changes in Anglicanism. Change is inevitable. What is changed is arguable. In other words, another essential balance in Anglicanism is between the classic expressions of Anglican Christianity and the varied re-workings of that which have arisen in different contexts, and rightly and inevitably are arising in our own day. A crucial aspect of Anglican modesty is the 'vernacular' – inculturating Christian faith. Nonetheless, the spiritual benefit of this must be balanced by an alertness to the risk of the loss of faithful continuity.

Anglicans are called 'to proclaim afresh' the faith in each generation. The *Windsor Report* expresses the tensions of this clearly:

> Virtually all Christians agree on the necessity for theological development, and on the fact that the Holy Spirit enables the church to undertake such development ... Healthy theological development normally takes place within the missionary imperative to articulate the faith afresh in different cultures ... [but] ... how is the line between faithful inculturation and false accommodation to the world's ways of thinking ... to be discerned and

determined? ... The church therefore always needs pro-
cedures for discussing, sifting, evaluating and deciding
upon proposed developments... [10]

We must note here that these are inextricable theological *and*
ecclesiastical questions. Just as theological modesty will lead
to caution about rigid theological boundaries, even more so
will modesty about church authority lead to caution about
enforcing ecclesiastical boundaries (chapter 4).

The Modern Crisis

In some ways modern Anglican conflicts are rooted in this
complex, dynamic way of trying to discover the truth of God:
though other less reputable causes include insufficient attention to Anglican history and some, frankly, fantastical interpretations of what it is to be an 'Anglican'.

There have been wonderful celebrations of Anglicanism,
especially its apparent ability to allow Evangelicals, Liberals
and Catholics – Scripture, Reason and Tradition – to co-exist
in the same Church. A typical gem was:

> [Anglicans] are heirs of the Reformation as well as of
> Catholic tradition; and they hold together in a single fel-
> lowship of worship and witness those whose chief
> attachment is to each of these, and also those whose
> attitude to the distinctively Christian tradition is most
> deeply affected by the tradition of a free and liberal cul-
> ture which is historically the bequest of the Greek spirit
> and was recovered for Western Europe at the
> Renaissance.[11]

However, we must face the reality that modern historians are
questioning this cosy self-perception of Anglicans and that real
Anglican life often falls short of this respectful trialogue.
Indeed, as Aidan Nichols (an English Roman Catholic theologian) has waspishly observed, Anglicanism is often characterised not by conversation but by a 'trialogue of the deaf'.[12]

The very idea that a claim is being made for some sort of 'Anglican identity' will strike many as laughable. Talking with people about this book produced the old joke: 'That'll be a short book, then!' I often begin a teaching session on Anglicanism by asking participants, 'What is an Anglican?' This frequently becomes group therapy as people pour out a mass of frustrations. Western Anglicanism has become synonymous with unprincipled compromise and the lazy acceptance of intellectual contradictions, with wishy-washy attitudes to faith and morals, with liturgy performed without connection to its original meaning, with boredom and élitism. Whilst we need to nail the tendency to use the word 'Anglican' as a term of mockery, there is truth behind these clichés.

Another way to explore this is in terms of modern arguments within Anglicanism. What is the core of Anglicanism? Is it – as some Anglicans argue – tolerance, inclusivity and a lack of definability?[13] A minimum content for the faith[14] with light institutional support – 'Bonds of Affection'? There is modesty in this approach. But I believe it to be deeply flawed, and that the easy language of tolerance is a fatal weakness in recent Anglican thinking. As an overarching rhetoric it is founded on a fallacy because even the most tolerant of Anglicans retains deep boundaries, for example about moral issues such as apartheid. Worse, tolerance had become a way of avoiding the hard work of really talking with each other. (Anglican ecumenical conversations sometimes have an unreal quality because everyone knows that the real question is whether the Anglicans can agree amongst themselves about what they are officially signing.[15]) In a context where the conflict is about whether Anglican Christians can stay together in one visible body, 'tolerance' as a value lacks the strength to hold them together. Anglicans need a richer account of their theology and spirituality to do this.[16]

The report *Faithful Cities* criticises the secular language of tolerance and commends hospitality as the key Christian concept when confronted by the 'other'.[17] Anglican life would be hugely enriched if Anglicans treated each other with hospitality rather than with the indifference of tolerance. So we will expound (chapter 4) a positive account of Anglican hospitality – comprehension – which is another way of living out balance.

Generous Orthodoxy

The opposite perspective to the idea that the core of Anglicanism is tolerance is the view that Anglicanism remains committed to the articulation and inculturation of the essence of classic Christianity. It is a 'generous orthodoxy'.[18] Again, in the interests of transparency, let me declare that this is my own view. Archbishop Rowan Williams has expressed this brilliantly in a recent book. His working summary of Anglicanism is worth quoting in full:

> I have simply taken it as referring to the sort of Reformed Christian thinking that was done by those (in Britain first, then far more widely) who were content to settle with a church order grounded in the historic ministry of bishops, priests and deacons, and the classical early Christian formulations of doctrine about God and Jesus Christ – the Nicene Creed and the Definition of Chalcedon. It is certainly *Reformed* thinking, and we should not let the deep and pervasive echoes of the Middle Ages mislead us: it assumes the governing authority of the Bible, made available in the vernacular, and repudiates the necessity of a central executive authority in the Church's hierarchy. It is committed to a radical criticism of any theology that sanctions the hope that human activity can contribute to the winning of God's favour, and so is suspicious of organised asceticism (as opposed to the free expression of devotion to God which may indeed be profoundly ascetic in its form) and of a theology of the sacraments which appears to bind God too closely to material transactions (as opposed to seeing the free activity of God sustaining and transforming certain human actions done in Christ's name).[19]

Much of my book is written in dialogue with this definition.

The deep point of Williams' summary is that, whilst Anglicanism includes the protection of appropriate diversity and an openness to be changed, it is under-pinned by the conviction that there are fundamental continuities between modern Anglicanism and previous expressions of Christianity, especially in the Patristic and Classic Anglican periods. I believe Anglicanism is at its healthiest when it holds these theological riches together, along with an honesty about the deep intellectual and social changes which world and Church have experienced since the mid seventeenth century. Deleting the insights of *any* of these formative influences on modern Anglicanism results in a crucial loss of the balance for which this book is arguing. This is the theological basis for Anglican stability and cohesion.

As part of this general case, I will also argue that, contrary to some perspectives, there are sufficient continuities and a sufficient core to the term 'Anglicanism' to warrant its use to describe a particular way of being Christian and being Church, stretching back to the earliest years of the English Reformation. There is a sustained continuous Anglican ethos (theological approach, values, instincts, spirituality).

All this rests on the deepest conviction, which is that classic Christianity, even when refined to its essentials, and allowing for the gulf between human vocabulary and divine reality, can be put into translatable and sustainable words. In that respect, I am in complete agreement with Bishop Stephen Sykes when he argues that there is a core of identifiable belief in Anglicanism, and that the core doctrine for Anglicans is the Incarnation (see chapter 2).[20] (By Incarnation here I mean the *whole* that is the life, death and resurrection of Christ as the apogee of the self-revelation and self-giving of God.) I would add to this the crucial theological (including Anglican) insight that the triune God is active in creation *and* redemption simultaneously, that God inseparably holds these two activities together.[21] Bradshaw, weaving together Barth, Irenaeus and Michael Ramsey, puts this vividly:

God can reveal himself through a blossoming shrub, a summer's day, a Mozart concerto or a dead dog ... and we do well to listen if he does; but *the Church is founded on the unique act of God in Christ ... Ontologically ... there is a central Christology,* while we also know that the Word works secretly in many and various ways in the world.[22]

Anglicanism is not free-floating.[23] Anglicans are anchored in God in Christ.

At this point it is helpful to put on the table another lump of Anglican granite. In 1888 the Lambeth Conference approved the 'Lambeth Quadrilateral', which was a refinement of the 'Chicago Quadrilateral' earlier drawn up by the American Anglican bishops as the basis for ecumenical conversation. It is one of American Anglicanism's greatest gifts to the Anglican Communion. It lists the following principles:

1   The Holy Scriptures of the Old and New Testaments as 'containing all things necessary to salvation', and as being the rule and ultimate standard of faith.

2   The Apostles' Creed as the Baptismal Symbol; and the Nicene Creed, as the sufficient statement of the Christian Faith.

3   The two sacraments ordained by Christ himself – Baptism and the Supper of the Lord – ministered with unfailing use of Christ's Words of Institution, and of the elements ordained by him.

4   The Historic Episcopate, locally adapted in the methods of its administration to the varying needs of the nations and peoples called of God into the unity of his Church.[24]

We will return to this text frequently but here simply note again the primacy of Scripture, the commitment to the ecumenical creeds, and the clear place of sacramental and ordered ministry: Protestant and Catholic inextricably combined. But notice how the *Windsor Report* summarises it:

The Lambeth Quadrilateral commits Anglicans to 'a series of normative practices: scripture is *read*, tradition is *received*, sacramental worship is *practised*, and the historic character of apostolic leadership is *retained*'.[25]

This is a tight balance but it is a balance of *doing* as much as a balance of conceptual beliefs. This sense that Anglicanism is about 'doing the faith' more than 'defining the faith' is strong, with its corollaries of modest statements of faith held alongside disciplined practices.

Balance Again

There is a core ethos to Anglicanism: a balanced, modest, generous orthodoxy. This moderates, in an Anglican direction, the different traditions within Anglicanism. (In other words there are distinctively Anglican expressions of Evangelicalism, Catholicism and Liberalism.) Further, this structural holding-together in one visible body of three of the great traditions of Christianity is the fundamental example of balance which we will explore (chapter 1). This takes us back to where our Introduction started. No one tribe has a monopoly of truth in Anglicanism. It is only together that we will discover and live the truth of God. So this book really is about balance; but it is the pressing seriousness of these issues and the potential of Anglicanism for good that produces the *passion* which drives me as I teach and try to live Anglican Christianity.

All this is a long way of saying that the deep structure of this book is to begin with theology, methodology and history and increasingly to draw out the consequences of these for Anglican spiritual life. The persistent lack of clarity about Anglicanism justifies this theology-led approach to spirituality. And on a personal note, the study and teaching of the treasures of Anglicanism has been for me life-giving and liberating. If this book at times has an old-fashioned feel to it, it is partly out of conviction but also because if readers are encouraged to delve for themselves into these treasures, the book will have been worth the writing.

Global Anglicanism

Whilst this book starts with Classic Anglicanism, it does not remain there and the wisdom of modern Anglicans from around the world will also feature, as it has joyfully in my own experience.[26] I have been privileged to share worship not just with Anglicans who have come from all over the world to study at Cranmer Hall, but also with Anglicans in their own contexts in Africa, the Far East and North America. Indeed the growth of a worldwide Anglican Communion has fundamentally changed what it is to talk of being an Anglican.

Once upon a time, it was (almost) enough to be English to be an Anglican. In Hooker's mind, the Church and the Common-wealth (the Tudor state) were two different ways of describing the same people.[27] This was not fully true even in Hooker's day and, after civil war and legal toleration, by the late seventeenth century it was no longer true. But (almost) all Anglicans were still subjects of the British crown and episcopate. Two factors transformed this practically *and* conceptually. First, after the American War of Independence there were clearly Anglicans who were no longer subjects of the crown. This meant that for some Anglicans, to be an Anglican was to be, not a member of a British state church, but a 'Protestant Episcopalian'. This is a *theological*, not a national, statement of identity and marked a significant moment of change.

Second, Anglicanism away from England grew rapidly in the nineteenth and twentieth centuries, initially as a byproduct of the British Empire but then much more dynamically as the new churches developed their own lives.[28] In the early twenty-first century, the typical Anglican is a young African woman. But this makes the question of explaining what *now* is the character of this Communion more urgent. If 'Englishness' is not enough – as it is not – how does Anglicanism define itself alongside the other great worldwide churches?

Several years ago I spent a weekend in Geneva thinking about Anglicanism with the (Anglican) Archdeaconry of Switzerland, a legacy of Victorian rest cures in the Alps. These good people knew exactly who they were. Switzerland is divided between Reformed Protestantism of a variety of types and Roman Catholicism. The Anglicans share with the Reformed a modified Protestant soteriology and a non-papal church order. They share with the Roman Catholics a eucharistically focused worship and a traditionally ordered ministry. They have deep common ground with both traditions but are also distinctive. They describe themselves as 'reformed Catholics'. They are not monochrome but they have clarity about their identity including a strong sense of the Anglican *via media*. This clear sense of Anglican identity is something I have often seen across the Anglican Communion. That little phrase, 'reformed Catholic', is the most valuable two-word summary of Anglicanism and we will return often to this gift from the worldwide Anglican Communion.

So What?

But by this stage of this Introduction a sensitive reader may be feeling that this is all rather introverted. So what if the Anglican Communion can live a balanced and modest life? So what if it learns from its past and tries to embed itself into new cultural contexts? For whose benefit is all this?

Anglicans believe that it is in the renewal of human lives in worship, in relationship with God, that good human communities are nurtured and the earth is sustained, because these are the purposes of God. Whilst the Five Marks of Mission to which the Anglican Communion is committed begin with the duty 'to proclaim the Good News of the Kingdom' and to 'teach, baptise and nurture new believers', they move on to the duty to 'respond to human need by loving service'. They also include as *integral* to Christian life the responsibilities to seek to 'transform unjust structures of society' and to strive to 'safeguard the integrity of creation'.[29] It is a big vision. As Bishop Tom

Wright has passionately reminded us, God's purposes are nothing less than the bringing back of the whole of creation to its 'intended harmony'.[30]

These values are present from the earliest days of Anglicanism. There is often an unspoken 'so that' in the middle of Cranmer's prayers and collects. The beginning section of a collect is a combination of worship and teaching and then, in the traditional style (though Cranmer was particularly gifted in composing collects), the congregation are moved to pray for a change in their own way of living. This can be an individual change but often it is communal. So the call to confession, at the pivot point of the Prayer Book communion service, reads (*italics mine*):

> Ye that do truly and earnestly repent you of your sins, and are *in love and charity with your neighbours,* and *intend to lead a new life, following the commandments of God, and walking from henceforth in his holy ways:* Draw near and take this holy Sacrament to your comfort: make your humble confession to Almighty God, *before this congregation* here gathered together in his holy name, meekly kneeling upon your knees...

Note that the sinner is not allowed to repent unless they are truly intending to live differently. This is not the 'cheap grace' with which later Anglican generations have become familiar, but thorough, action-filled repentance. Note the (entirely biblical) requirement to be in good relationships with those around us and that the purpose of confession is to lead a holy (and communal) new life. Note in passing the deep sacramental spirituality at work here – that it is in right receipt of the sacrament that we are most truly strengthened for new life. This is outward-looking, community-transforming spirituality.[31]

One last comment: it is all too easy when teaching about a particular expression of Christianity to slip into a form of ecclesiastical self-superiority and indeed imperialism, so that one's own well-loved tradition becomes not just better than all the rest, but whatever is good in the others is colonised. So, such and such a wise practice in another church is 'really Anglican'. We can say two simple things here. First, the obvious point that we must distinguish between those things which are distinctive about Anglicanism – unique, specific, particular, defining – and those things which are commonly found amongst Anglicans, but which may very often be shared with many other Christians and others.

Second, and more importantly, I am committed to the exposition of Anglican theology and values but in no sense is this to undermine the primary unity and value which is to be found in the whole Body of Christ. 'Christian first, Anglican second': at its best, Anglicanism has joyfully proclaimed this. Anglican modesty stresses that the focus on living with Christ in the world is so primary that all else is secondary. But if this book has a justification, it is that Anglicanism has insights which if articulated and lived, may be of benefit to the whole Body of Christ and indeed to Christ's world. It is in that spirit that this book is written.

1 'NO MONOPOLIES HERE': THE BALANCING DIALOGUES OF ANGLICANISM

Rowan Williams has reminded us of the dangers of the religious world in which we live. He describes this as:

> an age when the theological debate so readily polarises between one or other variety of positivism [definitive knowing] (biblically fundamentalist, ecclesiastically authoritarian, or whatever) and a liberalism without critical or self-critical edge.[1]

In an era of insecurity, especially but far from exclusively in the Western Church, it is tempting to retreat to apparent certainties. The growing aggressive conservatism (or liberalism) of groups across the churches indicates that this is a popular option. It has many problematic consequences, but above all it will tear the Church apart again; yet more schisms in the Body of Christ. The Church needs to identify and proclaim ideas and mechanisms which will preserve her from these dangers. Anglican 'balance' is just such an idea and mechanism. To help us to understand this sense of balance, we will look for its roots in the history of Anglicanism.

Theology and History

History can be seen as 'one damn thing after another'. Amongst Christians this manifests itself as a wilful ignoring of the realities of history in favour of ahistorical theologising. In other words, we ignore what has really happened and so our theology becomes abstract and detached. Conversely, I believe, for example, we should not do ecclesiology (thinking theologically about the Church), without giving weight to the reality of the Church as it has been in history. For me, study of church history has resulted in strong convictions about the fallibility of the Church. To quote the wise and humorous Gavin White: 'I believe in one, Holy, Catholic, Apostolic and Scruffy Church.'[2] But it is possible to go further than this.

Significant theologians of different traditions within Anglicanism (Hooker, Newman[3]) argued that study of the historical development of doctrine or of church order can help the Church to discern the guidance of God, including on these specific issues. This should not be surprising. As David Brown argues:

> It seems odd to postulate a God without revelatory impact upon the history of the Church when that history is not significantly different in fallibility and conditionedness from the history of the biblical community itself.[4]

As we undertake theological reflection on Anglican history, we may begin to identify the revelation of God which has come through that history, as a way of exploring the roots and values of Anglican spirituality.

Another way of discussing this is to use the language of wisdom. Because God is, and is in, wisdom, to grow in wisdom is to come nearer to God. As we grow wise through our study of church history, we may experience something akin to revelation. The wisdom which results from this work is located in two inter-connected places. First, there is the evolving wisdom of the Church, which it has been able to identify and name: to coin a phrase, *ecclesial evolution as revelatory*. (I am using the word 'evolution' here in a loose sense to mean organic change but avoiding the word 'development' because of its connotations.) Second, there is *wisdom within ourselves* as we think and pray. For example: whilst I would not want to argue that God was straightforwardly sovereign in generating the chaos of the English Reformation and the chequered history of Anglicanism then and thereafter, I suggest that Anglicans have learned wisdom through this experience. One of these wisdoms is a deep caution about believing that any particular tribe has a monopoly of truth. For ourselves, we may come to discern that Christ is heard to speak in unexpected places.[5]

This approach is rooted theologically in convictions about the collaborative way in which God relates to humankind.[6] Rowan Williams has expressed this point beautifully:

> Bishop Westcott ... said that God had revealed himself in such a way as not to spare us *labour*; God speaks in a manner that insists we continue to grow in order to hear... [7]

God intends us to grow in wisdom by using raw ingredients rather than providing us with ready-made meals. We have to work at extracting wisdom from church history, and here are some guidelines to follow as we do this.

First: we must not project back on to the past our own beliefs, cherry-picking examples which confirm our prejudices. 'The past is a foreign country', and it is only as we let it be itself that we will find ourselves on at least semi-solid ground when we draw conclusions. Part of this discipline is to be honest about those aspects of the past which we choose to ignore. I make much use of Hooker's ideas later, but some of his defences of the sixteenth-century Church of England are toe-curlingly biased and I simply ignore them. Another part is to be honest when we are advocating interpretations with which the contemporary participants would have disagreed. Candidly, I doubt if Cranmer would accept all of my exposition of Anglicanism![8]

Second: we are often not as similar to our spiritual ancestors as we like to imagine. One of the benefits of careful attention to the past is to alert us to profound differences between then and now. So as well as tracing our roots in the past, we are also forced to confront the often unacknowledged reality of change. For example, notwithstanding his Protestantism, Cranmer would not have embraced modern Evangelicalism's strongly conversionist operative theology. Cranmer believed too deeply in the Church's authority, the role of the sacraments, and above all in predestination to be a revivalist preacher.

Third: some people do not accept that ideas that made sense in one era have to be carefully and deeply translated if they are to make sense in a different one and so they become 'living fossils'– not a very attractive image! (There *can* be a strange benefit to the Church of 'living fossils'. Sometimes they preserve theologies and spiritualities which are the source of revival at some later date, even if always in a renewed form. Anglicanism has evolved into an organism – a 'modest' Church – which is ineffective at eradicating the ideas of those whose time has gone, but this has the merit of preserving some of this fossilised material.)

Fourth: there is hard wisdom to be learned when a theological tendency is side-lined by the wider Church. Some theological traditions which have failed to sustain their dominance in the Church did so *because* they lost credibility. My own view is that key elements of Puritanism are theologically and pastorally very problematic, for example its beliefs about predestination. When such a belief is firmly rejected by the mainstream of the Church, is this ecclesial evolutionary wisdom at work?

Fifth: we should pay particular attention to the expertise of professional historians. The Church has to be careful not to react too easily as it does this, because historians make their living from being revisionists. The pendulum swings and today's historical orthodoxy is tomorrow's old hat. But modern historiography has real strengths. For example, historians remind us that we must not listen only to the voices of the winners – whose voice was excluded or who has been forgotten or misinterpreted? (One of the reasons for the bitterness of modern Anglican disputes is that telling the story in certain ways intentionally pushes out other Anglicans.) At the very least, real history complicates our simplistic stories.

Sixth: 'accidents' may have deep implications. In this book we explore some historical accidents which *hindsight* enables us to use as a basis for principled theological reflection and action, but which were, when they happened, just accidents. Arguably, the Church of England is an accident shaped by the health of four monarchs!

Seventh: we must be explicit that we go back to the past with our own convictions. There is no Olympian other way. (By 'Olympian' I mean the perspective one might have from sitting on top of Mount Olympus – i.e. as a god standing outside time and history with a perfect perspective. We only have to describe this to realise that we are more like people stuck in a traffic jam who can see a little way in front and behind.) As long as we are explicit about this then it can be properly evaluated by others. Above all, this reminds us that *we never speak simply from God's point of view.*[9]

Eighth: real people cause continuity. For example, it is clear that despite the huge efforts of the sixteenth-century reformers, traditional attitudes persisted. Of course they did, because the people persisted. One of the dangers of dividing history into periods is that we forget that real lives don't coincide with chapters in textbooks. An epiphany moment in my own studies was reading Eamon Duffy's beautiful book *The Voices of Morebath,*[10] which tells the story of a Devon village and its priest from the 1530s till the 1570s. The same man was priest through Henry's Reformation (destroyed monasteries, Henry as 'pope' and an English Bible in his church), the clearly Protestant Reformation of Edward VI and Cranmer (destroyed stone altars and the first English Prayer Books, against which the priest supported armed rebellion) and Mary's Counter-Reformation, when all was not quite well again. He then became a convinced Protestant and a licensed preacher (very unusual) under Elizabeth's Settlement. From one perspective, so much had changed. From another, so little. He was still priest to his people, pastoring them as he had always done.

Ninth: the final discipline is that the past may sometimes be right. This assertion functions on two levels. Part of my conviction that Anglicanism is 'orthodoxy generously conceived' is precisely that there is a *givenness* about Christian faith. We do not invent it anew. We always stand at least in dialogue with the past and mostly we look back with reverence. As Rowan Williams reminds us, we are '... better to trust our history where it does not appear actively to mislead us ... the accumulation of historical precedent has real intellectual weight, in the light of our ineradicable folly, selfishness and slowness as human thinkers... '[11] More positively, theology is not a discipline where God is just an object for discussion. This is a dialogical discipline. God speaks with us. We must not forget that 'the language of classical doctrine originated in the sense of a gift of transformation or conversion'.[12] Above all, when reflecting theologically on church history, we know that 'God's self-consistency is to be relied on'.[13]

So, having noted these guidelines, we continue this chapter with some episodes in the history of Anglicanism which we will use as the basis for explorations into Anglican theology and spirituality. We will be looking especially at issues to do with balance; both in terms of balance between different traditions in the Church and balance as a method of thinking theologically.

'No Monopolies Here'

The following diagram is a simplistic way of demonstrating something of the nature of Anglicanism. Firstly, if we trace the family trees of the different tribes of Anglicanism, we find early and long continuities; all the Anglican tribes belong. Secondly, this also demonstrates that Anglicanism has had to learn how to balance itself from its very earliest days. This next section will interweave these two types of observation.

We can, for example, trace a Protestant/Evangelical family tree back to the 1520s. (I am simply asserting a basic fact and sense of continuity, not that Evangelicals are identical across these centuries.) Crudely speaking, we might say that this shows that Anglican Evangelicalism obviously belongs within Anglicanism.[14] *But*, whilst modern Evangelicals rightly cite many texts in the formularies which are robustly Protestant,

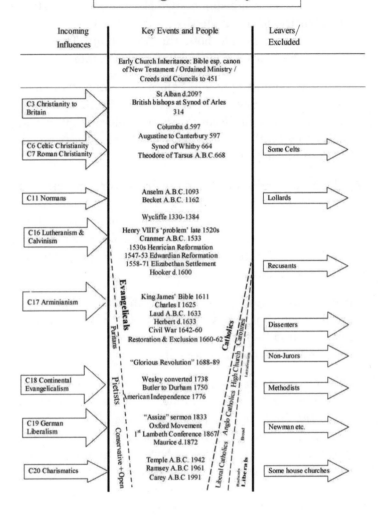

Anglican History

Incoming Influences	Key Events and People	Leavers/ Excluded
	Early Church Inheritance: Bible esp. canon of New Testament / Ordained Ministry / Creeds and Councils to 451	
C3 Christianity to Britain	St Alban d.209? British bishops at Synod of Arles 314	
C6 Celtic Christianity C7 Roman Christianity	Columba d.597 Augustine to Canterbury 597 Synod of Whitby 664 Theodore of Tarsus A.B.C.668	Some Celts
C11 Normans	Anselm A.B.C.1093 Becket A.B.C. 1162	Lollards
C16 Lutheranism & Calvinism	Wycliffe 1330-1384 Henry VIII's 'problem' late 1520s Cranmer A.B.C. 1533 1530s Henrician Reformation 1547-53 Edwardian Reformation 1558-71 Elizabethan Settlement Hooker d.1600	Recusants
C17 Arminianism	King James' Bible 1611 Charles I 1625 Laud A.B.C. 1633 Herbert d.1633 Civil War 1642-60 Restoration & Exclusion 1660-62	Dissenters
	"Glorious Revolution" 1688-89	Non-Jurors
C18 Continental Evangelicalism	Wesley converted 1738 Butler to Durham 1750 American Independence 1776	Methodists
C19 German Liberalism	"Assize" sermon 1833 Oxford Movement 1st Lambeth Conference 1867 Maurice d.1872	Newman etc.
C20 Charismatics	Temple A.B.C. 1942 Ramsey A.B.C 1961 Carey A.B.C 1991	Some house churches

this must be held in balance with the significant aspects of sixteenth-century Anglicanism which retained a strong Catholic identity, for example the issue of orders.

The formularies include both the 'Protestant' Thirty-nine Articles and the 'Catholic' Ordinal. Article 11 states:

> We are accounted righteous before God, only for the merit of our Lord and Saviour Jesus Christ by Faith, and not for our own works or deservings: Wherefore, that we are justified by Faith only is a most wholesome Doctrine, and very full of comfort...

So Anglicans are indeed justified (by grace) through faith. But who announces and manages this good news of justification? It is the Catholic clergy, standing in the chain of hands, so it was thought, back to Christ and the Apostles. Cranmer *inserted* into the Ordinal the following sentence to be prayed at the moment of ordination:

> Receive the Holy Ghost: whose sins thou dost forgive, they are forgiven: and whose sins thou dost retain, they are retained: and be thou a faithful dispenser of the Word of God, and of his holy Sacraments...

This latter passage needs careful handling because, in common with other Protestants, Cranmer emphasised reading and preaching the Bible as the primary means of accessing forgiveness. But on the other hand, Cranmer had deliberately modified the Protestant ordinal he borrowed from Bucer[15] into this more Catholic direction. And Cranmer retained in his liturgies elements of the traditional actions of the priest.

In the Communion service, arguably the centrepiece of Cranmer's operative theology, we find the priest (Cranmer's word) pronouncing absolution:

> Almighty God, our heavenly Father, who of his great mercy hath promised forgiveness of sin to all them, which with hearty repentance and true faith turn unto him; *have mercy upon you, pardon and deliver you from all your sins,*

> *confirm and strengthen you in all goodness and bring you*
> *to everlasting life:* through Jesus Christ our Lord. Amen.[16]

The language and the actions are beautifully balanced. We are
to repent faithfully if we wish to be forgiven, but the priest
tells us *all* that we are forgiven, on the authority of the
Church. Which worshipping Anglican, in their walk with God,
has not received the strongest sense of the forgiveness of God
precisely at this moment of absolution in the service, week by
week?

Cranmer went further than this. In the service for the Vis-
itation of the Sick, which is Cranmer's structural equivalent of
the Last Rites, the priest asks the sick person to confess their
sins and then says:

> Our Lord Jesus Christ, who hath left power to his Church
> to absolve all sinners, which truly repent and believe in
> him, of his great mercy forgive thee thine offences: and by
> his authority committed to me, *I absolve thee from all thy*
> *sins,* in the name of the Father, and of the Son, and of the
> Holy Ghost. Amen. *(Italics mine)*

This is a straight translation of medieval prayers of absolution, including the phrase which would have been known and
hung upon by the anxious penitent: *'ego te absolvo'* ('I absolve
thee.')[17] This was a balanced and a deeply pastoral liturgy.

So we might say that the Church of England was *never* an
exclusively Protestant church, and therefore attempts to make
it such now might be thought to be improper, even unwise.
Cranmer was a distinctive ('balanced') sort of Protestant, and
part of that distinctiveness was a self-conscious valuing of
some aspects of Catholicism which he retained in the liturgical
life of the Church of England. This is partly why I am reluctant to restrict use of the word 'Anglican' to the post-1662
situation.

One of the delights of working ecumenically and in the sort
of environment where people allow their guards to drop is that
it exposes our gut assumptions about each other. I will never

forget the surprise of a Roman Catholic ordinand when he discovered that the *Magnificat* is a regular feature of Anglican worship – or our surprise that he was surprised! Anglicans have this treasure of the Gospel canticles in their worship thanks to Cranmer.

Continuing our exploration of the Church of England as a place of balance, even in the sixteenth century: what should we make of Cranmer's ecclesiology? Why, for example, did he invest such effort in preserving the traditional structures of the Church? I think his seriousness has been underestimated. Rightly, recent historians have reminded us of Cranmer's radicalism. This was a man who was part of the destruction of a millennium of English monasticism and of the Latin Mass, and who unleashed, if not always intentionally, a thorough campaign of theological and actual vandalism – the destruction of much of the physical beauty of the medieval Church. And yet the very fact that he, along with some of his fellow bishops and the crown, drove the English Reformation through 'from above', and that it was done legally, if not justly, meant that much was preserved from the medieval Catholic Church – even archdeacons! This is not a flippant remark. Cranmer could write in the Preface to the Ordinal in 1549/50 (and it was *not* revised in the more Protestant 1552 Book) that:

> It is evident unto all men, diligently reading holy Scripture, and ancient authors, that from the Apostles' time there hath been these orders of Ministers in Christ's Church: Bishops, Priests, and Deacons...

This was of course far from evident to the Continental Reformers. The retention of much that was conservative about ministerial orders and practice left the Church of England, as we have seen, with a relatively Catholic view of its clergy. Note also how Cranmer justified this, reasonably, by an appeal to *both* Scripture *and* the Early Church. This is typical of Cranmer's way of doing theology. Without being so explicit, he too lived by the 'three-stranded cord'.

We turn now to the work of Elizabeth. She also was a woman

of balance. Elizabeth was, in some ways, as profound an architect of Anglicanism as was Cranmer. 'The only church founded by a woman' are the wonderfully provocative words of Diarmaid MacCulloch.[18] Because some of these facts have fallen out of modern Anglican consciousness, they need revisiting. As part of what is called the 'Elizabethan Settlement', as far as we can tell,[19] Elizabeth restored a form of words in Holy Communion which opened a window for belief in the 'real presence'. It was at Elizabeth's insistence that in 1559 the words for the administration of the bread and wine at Communion were altered from Cranmer's 1552 Book. She required (as many anxious curates will testify) the following mouthful to be said:

> The Body of our Lord Jesus Christ, which was given for thee, preserve thy body and soul unto everlasting life: Take and eat this in remembrance that Christ died for thee, and feed on him in thy heart by faith with thanksgiving.

The first phrase – 'The Body of Christ ... everlasting life' – is from Cranmer's first Prayer Book in 1549 and allows for a more Catholic sense of Christ's presence in and through the consecrated bread. Whereas the second half – 'Take and ... with thanksgiving' – is from 1552 and looks like a more memorialist view of the eucharist (we are encouraged to remember Christ's work on the Cross). The combination of the two was Elizabeth's genuine attempt at being inclusive.

It is also rather fun that she delighted in offending her bishops in a balanced way. So, in the first months of her reign, she walked out of services when the host was elevated during the Mass, but later insisted on keeping a cross on the altars in her chapels, much to the disgust of her Protestant bishops.

There is more. Elizabeth blocked most further ecclesiastical reforms during her reign, thereby creating space for moderate episcopal liturgical Protestantism to grow.[20] She ensured that Parker, her first Archbishop of Canterbury, was consecrated according to the Nicene Canons. She fostered a revival of liturgical church music in her own chapels and, beyond that, in the cathedrals. She heartily disliked the permission for clergy to marry, and this influenced her choice of bishops. She had Grindal, her second Archbishop of Canterbury, inhibited for refusing to control 'prophesyings' (preaching classes) and was cautious about the expansion of a preaching ministry. She intervened to block the Calvinist Lambeth Articles. She allowed for the development of a richer sacramentality in the Church and resisted for a time – even if she ultimately failed – the pressure to persecute non-Anglicans (we will return to her sense of modesty about the Church's authority in chapter 4). In terms of both ethos and specific examples, all this looks very Anglican. Anglicanism has thereafter remained deeply and sometimes uneasily balanced between Protestant and Catholic – 'reformed Catholic'?

We return now to the other question with which we began this section, which is the way of approaching the nature of Anglicanism by exploring examples of early divergences within the Church of England to which the different modern tribes can trace their ancestry. Current historians and also some modern Evangelicals rightly remind us of the Calvinism of most of the Elizabethan episcopate.[21] The word 'Puritan' did not initially mean someone outside the Church of England – far from it. This was the position of those who wanted to see the 'but halfly reformed' Church properly 'purified'.[22] Reform, the modern Puritan campaigning group, has its roots in this period of the Church of England.[23]

But on the opposite flank of the Church, in that mysterious period of the last years of Elizabeth,[24] we also find the growth of a passionate sacramental theology and spirituality, which can be found in Hooker but takes its clearest and richest expression in the life, liturgy and spirituality of Lancelot Andrewes (1555–1626). Andrewes was a court preacher and then a leading bishop under Elizabeth and James, a man increasingly at the centre of the Church of England in a key formative period. He worked in a Church alongside and against tough-minded Calvinists. But he had early on in his life acquired a deeply sacramental theology. So his private chapels were rich witnesses to his faith in the real presence of Christ in the eucharist. Whilst his ornamentation was innovative in the reformed Church of England, Andrewes' sacramental theology was rooted in the Prayer Book (see chapter 4).

Andrewes is good evidence of yet another Elizabethan theologian taking seriously the reformed Church of England's respect for the Early Church and, without any sense of contradiction to the Prayer Book, importing thoroughgoing Patristic ideas and attitudes. Indeed Andrewes, and Cranmer, would point us to the fact that the 'Protestant' Thirty-nine Articles begin (*unlike* some Reformed confessions of faith) with five articles on God and Christ taken straight from the Early Church.[25] This is why when we look at our time chart, as well as noting the Catholic tribe tracing its roots back to the sixteenth century, we must also note – following Cranmer's example – that Anglicans consciously saw themselves as being inheritors of the faith, practice and structures of the Early Church. So Anglican Catholics too have their long-standing place in Anglicanism.

The compromise that was the late sixteenth-century Church of England was sustained by James I but destabilised by the unwise Charles I.[26] However, in the buildup to and in the aftermath of the chaos and horror of the Civil War, when the Puritans and anti-Puritans inside the Church of England finally came to blows, we find the emergence of first the Great Tew Circle and then the Cambridge Platonists. These thinkers, lay and ordained, prized a combination of open rigorous argument and modest stress on fundamentals, alongside quiet contemplation, as the best method to discern the truth of God: and prized it to the extent of living and dying by these values. Remember Lord Falkland, aristocratic convenor at Great Tew, riding self-consciously to his death at the battle of Newbury in 1643 in his white shirt, in despair at the bitter divides in Church and state.[27] It would be dangerously anachronistic to describe them as 'Liberals', but the prizing of Reason as a/the key spiritual discipline is to be found here.

Above all, in so many respects Hooker is the quintessentially Anglican figure. He embodied an emphasis on the inter-relationship of the three great theological authorities cited by different groups of Anglicans – Scripture, Reason and Tradition – and in doing so reminded us that none of the tribes of Anglicanism have exclusive rights to its title deeds.

Richard Hooker and Theological Sanity in the Sixteenth Century: Scripture, Reason and Tradition as the Anglican Theological Method

Richard Hooker (1554–1600) is returning to the centre of theological controversy.[28] He would not have been surprised. His own insights were formed during a very public controversy with the Puritan lecturer, Travers, at the Temple Church in London during the 1580s, where Hooker had been placed to restore the church to conformity with the Elizabethan Settlement. Hooker preached in the morning, to be contradicted by Travers in the afternoon. Every remark had to be defensible. This may account for the sometimes slow and convoluted style of his writing as he compiled his eight books of the *Laws of Ecclesiastical Polity* (how the Church is to be ordered). But he was subsequently revered as the 'founder of Anglicanism', and for good reason, because his theological method is pre-eminently one where the different theological authorities are integrated into a system of checks and balances that limits the possibility of extremes and fosters wisdom. He can be seen as the theologian of balance *par excellence*. Lest this be thought to be too grand a claim, note the following:

> Part of the legacy of Hooker, making some of the riches of medieval thought reaccessible within a Reformation framework, was precisely that holistic worldview which insists, not that scripture should be judged at the bar of 'reason' and found wanting, but that in reading and interpreting scripture we must not do so arbitrarily, but with clear thinking and informed historical judgement.[29]

And:

> Hooker – like the Anglican tradition as a whole, it is
> tempting to add – is tantalisingly hard to pigeonhole. I
> have been trying to show that his schemas refuse to be
> classified once and for all as simply 'conservative' or
> 'radical', and that aspects of what is undeniably a local
> polemic, very much of its time and place, set off chains of
> reflection with an uncomfortable contemporary edge.[30]

... thus Tom Wright and Rowan Williams.

Hooker began from a conviction of God's orderliness and of a
structured connection between God's own ordered being and
God's creation. Hooker described this in terms of 'Laws'. We
might say principles. Just as God cannot behave out of character, neither can the angels, or nature, and nor should
humankind. This deep structure was open to human beings to
understand, including something of the nature of God and
humankind's spiritual and ethical obligations, by a process of
reasoned reflection. However, human beings have 'fallen' and
therefore are in need of rescue directly by God, and are also
damaged in their ability to perceive and relate to God. Then,
God in Christ redeems and renews humankind, but because it
is the same God who creates and who rescues therefore there
are deep continuities between the truth revealed by Reason
and the truth revealed more directly by God. Hooker suc-
ceeded in integrating the theology of the greatest theologian of
the medieval Church, Thomas Aquinas, with the insights of
the Protestant Reformation. This was quite a feat. A fuller
exposition of Hooker's theology will reveal how he did this
work of integration.

The core of Hooker's theology is buried in the middle of Book
Five of the *Laws* (chs 50–57). Here, in what is almost a
digression in the middle of a major discussion of sacramental
theology, Hooker took his readers to Christ. He argued that
God always intended human beings to share eternity with
him, but sin has left them damaged and hindered. So the
Father sends Christ to re-commence the work of uniting

humanity to the Godhead. This is primarily the redemptive work of the Cross, though very significantly Hooker retained a rounded sense of Christ's work. Christ's Incarnation is the bedrock of all his theology:

> The world's salvation was without the incarnation of the Son of God a thing impossible ... it being presupposed that the will of God was no otherwise to have it saved than by the death of his own Son. Wherefore taking to himself our flesh, and by his incarnation making it His own flesh, he had now of his own, although from us ... to offer unto God for us.[31]

This is a classic example of interweaving Reformation emphases – 'by the death of his own Son' making an 'offering' – with the richest elements of Patristic theology – we are saved by being incorporated in Christ's life, body, death and resurrection. Hooker's summary of the faith is remarkable: '... God hath deified our nature, though not by turning it into himself, yet by making it his own inseparable habitation... '[32]

How does humankind learn about Christ? Again, Hooker offered an intricately meshed system. Primarily, we come to recognise Christ because the Church leads us to him, in Scripture. We are prepared to put our trust in the Bible because the Church strikes us as trustworthy and provides clear and authoritative guidance as to the canon of Scripture and to the essence of the faith to be discerned in Scripture, summarised in the creeds.[33] We are then in a position to accept Scripture as the inspired 'word of God' overseeing the life of the Church. Reason is vitally involved in all of this work, though guided by the Spirit (see chapter 5).

Reason's role *after* revelation has been recognised as even more important theologically. As is shockingly (from some perspectives) evident in Hooker, he gave Reason a huge role in the interpretation of Scripture and Tradition, in discerning and articulating the truth of God.[34] Even key items of Christian faith – the doctrine of the Trinity or of the divinity and humanity of Christ – *require* the application of Reason to the Bible:

> For our belief in the Trinity, the co-eternity of the Son of God with his Father, the proceeding of the Spirit from the Father and the Son ... these with such other principal points, the necessity whereof is by none denied, are notwithstanding in Scripture no where to be found by express literal mention, only deduced they are out of Scripture by collection [reasoning].[35]

This is an explicit dialogue between Reason, and the Church as the custodian of the Bible, and the Bible and biblical interpretation, all held inextricably together. Within this trio Hooker does have a clearly stated hierarchy – the Bible is 'infallible'[36] – but even a statement like that is very carefully nuanced (see chapter 3).

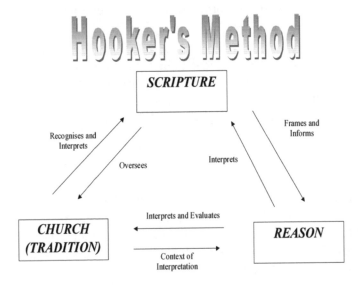

A theological example of importance for Anglicans is Hooker's understanding of how the Church develops its own structures. He started from the conviction, formed in the heat of the controversy with Calvinism, that the New Testament did not provide a blueprint for church order.[37] This in itself might be thought by some Christians to be a slightly surprising conclusion, but modern scholarship would support Hooker's views. Hooker then made the bold and honest move of suggesting that during the first century the Church had to make a decision about continuity after Christ and the Apostles and only then took the decision for episcopacy. He did not claim, as cannot be claimed, that the system of episcopacy was self-consciously set up by Christ and/or the Apostles. He was clear that this was the Church's decision, though he covered this delightfully and subtly:

> ... we may conclude that ... the Offices which Bishops execute, had been committed to them only by the Church, and that the superiority which they have over other Pastors, were not first by Christ himself given to the Apostles, and from them descended to others, but afterwards in such consideration brought in and agreed upon...

But:

> Wherefore let us not fear to be bold and peremptory, that *if* anything in the Churches Government [was given by God], surely the first institution of Bishops was from Heaven, was even of God, the Holy Spirit was the Author of it.[38]

Such weight on the little word 'if'!

This discussion is a good example of how Hooker related Tradition and Reason. The existence of episcopacy was a Tradition. For Hooker it carried the weight of having been the pattern of governance of the universal Church for about 1,500 years. The next quotation is both Hooker at his knockabout best but also shows his way of giving authority to Tradition:

> A very strange thing sure it were, that such a discipline as ye speak of [presbyterianism as opposed to episcopacy] should be taught by Christ and his Apostles in the word of God and no church ever have found it out, nor received it

till this present time; contrariwise, the government against which ye bend yourselves be observed every where throughout all generations and ages of the Christian world, no church ever perceiving the word of God to be against it.[39]

But remember that Hooker had argued that the initial decision for episcopacy was taken by the Church, using Reason guided by the Spirit.

Hooker could then argue, and this would have been contentious in his day and was more so later, that even this Spirit-inspired system of episcopacy was open to drastic reform should the episcopate become irredeemably corrupt:

[Bishops] cannot say any Commandment of the Lord doth injoyn [their status]; And therefore must acknowledge that the Church hath power by universal consent upon urgent cause to take it away, if thereunto she be constrained through the proud, tyrannical, and unreformable dealings of her Bishops ... let this consideration be a bridle unto them... [40]

Here the primacy of Scripture is indirectly indicated because if episcopacy was a 'supernatural' law of Scripture, there would be no question about changing it.

In our context, we can simply note that the 'founder of Anglicanism' is not an advocate of the view that episcopacy is of the *esse* of the Church. This is, to some Anglicans, shocking, but it should not be. Episcopacy is a good example of a practice which Anglicanism honours and is committed to but in a modest way. When we are considering Anglican church order, it might be that this combination of biblical honesty, critical faithfulness to the Tradition, along with a stress on Reason and a certain lightness of touch might be found to contain wisdom. As Rowan Williams mischievously commented, precisely after reflecting on Hooker's wisdom on this, 'episcopacy is the more desirable the less you think about it theologically... '[41]

In summary, I believe this is a beautifully balanced theological system which relies on the coherence between God's work as creator and redeemer and invests human beings with considerable dignity. (For me, Hooker is *the* theologian of human dignity.[42]) It has a strong basis in church history, in that the development of the Church in the second century exemplifies this sort of interaction. Under pressure from Gnosticism (which, with its hostility to matter, including bodies, and esoteric soteriology, was distorting the main line of development of Christianity), the Church looked to the emerging canon of Scripture for authoritative guidance about the faith. But the canon was still fluid and one of the tests which was applied to potential Scripture was of the consistency of a particular 'book' with the content of the Apostolic Faith, especially as formulated in the early rules of faith. These were themselves shaped by their derivation from Scripture as it was being recognised. Alongside this, the ministry of the Church was established and defined, using criteria of both convergence with this evolving account of the faith and also personal connection through succession back to the Apostles; so Irenaeus followed Papias who had followed John. In other words, Scripture, creed (Tradition) and Church all evolved together and were inextricably linked from this point onwards. And this was done by sustained reasonable reflection using recognised canons of argument.

The 'three-stranded cord' is not of course a simple slot machine into which we put the ingredients of Scripture, Reason and Tradition and the right answer falls out every time. Though as Bishop Montefiore commented:

> Without tradition, you'll think you're wiser than your forefathers; without Scripture, you're rudderless and if you base yourself only on reason, you waffle.[43]

Inhabiting this balanced ethos might prevent Anglicans, and others, from falling into false fundamentalisms.

In one of the most famous of his sayings, Hooker stressed

this diversity of knowing and related it directly to the will of God:

> A more beautiful and religious way for us were to admire the wisdom of God, which shineth in the beautiful variety of all things, but most in the manifold and yet harmonious dissimilitude of those ways, whereby his Church upon earth is guided from age to age... [44]

A 'harmonious dissimilitude': we might talk about a unity of knowing from a diversity of sources.[45] It sounds lovely but this had consequence in Hooker's real world. Hooker was generally eirenic, even if cunning. But occasionally his rage burst out. Hear his anger against the Puritan attempt to separate Scripture, Reason and Tradition and ponder why:

> You have already done your best to make a jarre between nature and scripture. Your next endeavour is to do the like between scripture and the Church. Your delight in conflicts doth make you dreame of them where they are not.[46]

George Herbert and the Rich Middle Way

We continue our theological interpretation of the history of Anglicanism with one of its greatest saints, George Herbert: but first, a brief linkage back to Thomas Cranmer and the *via media*.

When the Prayer Book was published in 1549, Cranmer wrote two little essays to explain and justify it: 'Concerning the Service of the Church' and 'Of Ceremonies'. These have been bound ever since into the front of the Book of Common Prayer. Cranmer was laying out his vision for what it is to be a Christian people. Central to this was daily common prayer and hearing of Scripture. When explaining the principles by which he decided on his reforms, revealingly, Cranmer noted the importance of the example of the 'ancient Fathers' as giving the pattern for how to conduct the 'Daily Office'. Then after a

little knockabout fun with the complexity of medieval lectionaries and service books, he went on to contrast those who
'think it a great matter of conscience to depart from a piece of
the least of their Ceremonies, they be so addicted to their old
customs' with those who are 'so new-fangled, that they would
innovate all things, and so despise the old, that nothing can
like them [i.e. they like nothing] but that is new...' Cranmer
then played a rhetorical trick. He wrote:

> ... it was thought expedient, not so much to have respect
> how to please and satisfy either of these parties, as how to
> please God, and profit them both.

It is the old theologian's trick of invoking God on their side.
But notice Cranmer's method: he explicitly opted for a 'middle
way' between what he saw as the extremes of traditionalism or
radicalism. This is classic Anglican *via media* methodology
and rhetoric. As a great Anglican liturgist wrote of this essay,
'[Cranmer's] defence is the first tentative statement of the
Anglican *via media*.'[47]

We might want to note the potential of this ethos for sustaining a creative conversation between Catholic and Protestant, between tradition and innovation. It cuts across any
tendency to fetishise the past or the most modern. It should
keep Anglicans both open to change but also free of contempt
for the past. And of course it was the resulting Book of Common Prayer which was the basis for George Herbert's life, faith
and spirituality.

George Herbert (1593–1633) came from a privileged background, with a career at court and at Cambridge University,
but gave it all up to become a country priest. His life and
ministry were cut tragically short at the age of 40. His
exquisite poetry and prose were all published posthumously.
There is so much that could be said, but at this point in the
book, I want to use Herbert to help us to locate Anglican
spirituality again in its formative context and then to exem-
plify another of the resulting balances.

One of Herbert's poems, which used to be widely known but

is now only read by consenting Anglican adults in private, is 'The British Church':

> I joy, deare Mother, when I view
> thy perfect lineaments, and hue
> > both sweet and bright...
>
> A fine aspect in fit array,
> neither too mean nor yet too gay,
> > shows who is best...
>
> She on the hills, which wantonly
> allureth all in hope to be
> > by her preferr'd,
>
> hath kiss'd so long her painted shrines,
> that ev'n her face by kissing shines,
> > for her reward.
>
> She in the valley is so shie
> of dressing, that her hair doth lie
> > about her eares:
>
> while she avoids her neighbour's pride,
> she wholly goes on th'other side,
> > and nothing wears.
>
> But dearest Mother (what those misse),
> the mean thy praise and glorie is,
> > and long may be... [48]

Here 'Rome' is the flashy woman on the hills whilst the Puritans are the naked woman in the valley. In our context, this is not a very ecumenical poem! But in the context of the seventeenth century, when Anglicans like Herbert felt themselves to be assailed on both flanks, it made real sense. On one side were the power of the Roman Catholic nations, the sharpness of Roman Catholic polemic, the persistence of Roman Catholic recusants, and a French Roman Catholic Queen, not to mention the Irish. On the other side were the growing belligerence of the Puritan political and religious faction, the intellectual power of Continental Protestantism, and the Scots.

Since Aristotle, holding the middle ground, the 'mean', has often been seen as holding the high ground morally and intellectually.[49] It is not the place of the dangerous unbalanced extremist. Very quickly the Church of England adopted the self-definition as a middle church. It described itself as being the *via media,* the 'golden mean' and even the 'golden mediocrity', meaning middle, not poor, quality. (Note that the *via media* was initially between Rome and the Anabaptists, as was demonstrated by the Thirty-nine Articles, but came to mean by the seventeenth century – for some Anglicans – a moderate *Protestant* middle way between Puritanism and Roman Catholicism, and by the nineteenth century, for some Anglicans, as a middle way *between* Rome and Protestantism. Even the *via media* is a moveable feast...)

As the Church of England found itself defending its theology, practices and ministry from assault on both sides, so it developed a theology designed to justify moderate ceremonial, Catholic orders, anti-papalism and an essentially Protestant soteriology. In effect, it was *forced* to develop a distinctively Anglican ethos and theology. We cannot overestimate the deep effect on Anglicanism of finding itself in the middle. It is most profoundly shaped by always having to fight on both flanks. Hence perhaps the tartness of Herbert's poem? What is clear is Herbert's pride in the Church of England, as having been given a unique gift of grace by God.

This ethos has bad and good features. As we shall see with F. D. Maurice, one of the problems is that it came to be identified with Englishness. So the Church of England was a moderate church because the English were a moderate people (unlike the Irish and the Scots and the rest of Europe). This is best left in the same *genre* as describing Englishness as warm beer and spinsters cycling to church on a summer's day! But the sense that the middle ground is almost by definition a place of truthfulness has something to commend it. Since Newman's warning, delivered perhaps with this smug English Anglican complacency in mind, that sometimes truth is to be found at one extreme, not in the compromised middle,[50] we cannot adopt it naïvely. But at the very least the 'middle way' requires attention to both sides of an argument. More and Cross describe it well when they say, comparing the Anglican *via media* to the Chalcedonian Definition, 'the middle way is not compromise, it is direction'.[51]

There is a second way of understanding being a 'middle church'. Again, it can smack of superiority but does not have to. There is a sense in which Anglicans can choose the best of both Reformed and Roman Catholic Christianity, and blend it into their own theological and spiritual system. This takes us dangerously near a cliché, but Herbert can save us with his embodied spirituality of Word and Sacrament.

One of the balances frequently talked about in Anglicanism, but often honoured rhetorically rather than in practice, is the balance of Word and Sacrament. The varying Anglican liturgies for Holy Communion embody this. For me, coming from a more Evangelical background, the discovery of the spiritual richness of a service with a meaty sermon *and* a rich celebration of the eucharist, was life-giving. Herbert exemplified this richness beautifully. In his book *The Country Parson*, which has hallowed the Church of England for over three hundred and fifty years, he described the attributes of a priest. So in chapter 7, 'The Parson Preaching', he wrote: 'The Country Parson preacheth constantly: the pulpit is his joy and his throne.'[52] He described breaking open the Word of God as being a joyful and a regal activity. It is a very high estimation both of Scripture and of the preaching office.

But then in chapter 22, 'The Parson in Sacraments', we read the following dramatic and humbling words:

> The Country Parson being to administer the Sacraments, is at a stand with himself how or what behaviour to assume for so holy things. Especially at Communion times he is in a great confusion, as being not only to receive God, but to break and administer Him.[53]

Even given Herbert's careful seventeenth-century Anglican doctrine of the eucharist, this is a shocking account of the eucharistic action – 'breaking God'. It is in modern Anglican terms, a 'high' doctrine of the real presence. And we know from elsewhere in Herbert's writing that for him the eucharist was a profound place of encounter with God.

In chapter 6 we will explore Herbert's poem 'Love bade me welcome', but we note here how effortlessly Herbert held together a high doctrine of preaching and of the eucharist, and a warm theology of Christ's welcome at the Lord's Table with a robust theology of the atonement; and how often modern Anglicans and others polarise over these same spiritual realities. Is Herbert here a wise guide to a healthy spiritual balance, a diet which contains Word and Sacrament, atonement and open arms?

F. D. Maurice and a Dynamic Sense of Balance

We need now to take a small step beyond Classic Anglicanism, though F. D. Maurice has acquired a central place for Anglicans in the last 150 years. By the nineteenth century, the Church of England found itself in a particularly messy place. The attempt to force all English people (let alone the Welsh, Irish, Scottish or Americans) into one institutional expression of Christianity had failed. It had failed badly and viciously as the Church of England had first excluded and then persecuted the seventeenth-century Dissenters, continuing Roman Catholics and the eighteenth-century Methodists. (This is why the time chart also lists those people who left or were driven out of the 'tolerant' Church of England.) By the 1830s Protestant Dissenters and Roman Catholics had gained (almost) full legal toleration. Crucially, the 'governing body' of the Church of England, the Houses of Parliament, now contained non-Anglicans.[54]

In response to this crisis, and in reaction to other changes in the political and theological world, the Church of England experienced another period of profound internal division. To aid mission, some Evangelicals wanted to restore a common identity with non-Anglican Evangelicals. So in 1844, Anglicans were very influential in the creation of the Evangelical Alliance. Other Anglicans (the Broad Church), influenced by new ideas in biblical and theological studies and also wanting to rebuild a national Church, argued for a simpler, more Liberal and inclusive theology and ecclesiology. Whilst a third group, the Oxford Movement, horrified equally by theological Liberalism and Protestant ecclesiology, and above all by the dismantling of the Anglican state, launched a movement to restore, in their mind, the true Catholic nature of the Church of England. It was a time of great bitterness, and its legacy still shapes and often disfigures modern Anglicanism. Into the midst of this spoke a man whose own life was marked by these conflicts, F. D. Maurice.

Maurice (1805–72) , born a Unitarian, a convert to Anglicanism, had been Professor of Theology at King's College, London, an Anglican foundation. As well as being a Christian Socialist, Maurice was also a progressive theologian and fell foul of the Church of England's authorities when he was thought to have cast doubt on the everlasting nature of the punishment in hell. However, Maurice also gave passionate attention to the bitter divisions within Anglicanism, and his ideas have been profoundly influential on the self-perception and actions of Anglicans thereafter. Maurice devised another way of conceiving of balance, which still has merit.[55]

Maurice tried to summarise the essence of the three great tribes in the Church. In this he was often amusing as well as wise. Thus, Liberalism was open, inclusive and expansive. In Maurice's words, 'with what sympathy do we listen to him [the Liberal] when he says that the Church is meant to comprehend and not to exclude.'[56] But he then mocked the Liberal strategy, which was to remove all the unhelpful remnants of past misguided theology – the Prayer Book, Articles etc. – so as to construct only a 'modern' statement of faith, and he warned them that this:

should bring the Church into the most flat and hopeless monotony, should so level her to the superstitions of the nineteenth century, so divorce her from the past and the future, that all expansion would for ever be impossible.[57]

The acuteness of this observation is still breathtaking.

Conversely, Evangelicals were strong on faith in the Bible, on a personal relationship between the believer and Christ, and on sharing this straightforward way of being Christian. But again Maurice exposed the spiritual corruption which can come with an assurance of righteousness, for the Evangelical response was denunciation of other Christians:

> Go forth and tell men that their baptism is *not* an admission into the privileges of God's spiritual Church; that they are *not* to take this sign as a warrant of their right to call themselves members of Christ, and to pray to God as their Father in Him. Go and tell them that they are not in a real relation with God, but only in a nominal one ... go and make these comfortable declarations to men, and mix them well with denunciations of other men for not preaching the Gospel; thus you will fulfil God's commission; thus you will reform a corrupt and sinful land.[58]

The prophetic quality of this writing is chilling in our context.

Maurice was equally acute on the virtues and vices of Anglican Catholicism. He rejoiced in its assurance about the Church:

> ... that there is indeed a Church in the world, which God Himself has established; that He has not left it to the faith and feelings and notions of men; that He has given us permanent signs of its existence; that He has not left us to find our way into it, but has Himself taken us into it ... that we belong to the Communion of Saints, and need not seek for another![59]

But he noted how this theological spirituality was lived out in practice by justifying division on the basis of an unreal Church which never existed. Maurice particularly mocked the Oxford Movement's fantasies about the Church:

> After all those splendid assurances, that the Church really exists, and that it is endowed with such mighty powers, how grievous it is to find the most strange uncertainty about the terms under which she exists; whether only as a splendid dream, whereof the record is kept only in the writings of the Fathers, and which may some day be realised; or as a potentiality, which was made a fact during the Middle Ages by the supremacy of the Pope; or, lastly, as an invisible equatorial line between Romanism and Protestantism; a line of which some dim traces, may, from time to time, be discovered, with the help of powerful glasses, in our English history... [60]

Maurice exquisitely captured that strange mixture in Anglo-Catholicism of belief in an imaginary church with the use of that belief to foment real division and sectarianism.

Maurice's response to the bitterness of these divides was to affirm the positive qualities which each of the tribes advocated, their principles. So Liberalism was properly defending the necessary role of Reason in religion, Evangelicalism was defending the Bible and personal faith and Catholicism was defending the significance of the Church. These principles were all of divine origin and therefore, ultimately, capable of harmonious coexistence, provided their adherents were not rigid in their defence of their principles by 'systematising' them.

Maurice's critique of the idea of theological 'system' is widely acknowledged to be much less clear. By it he seems to have meant a legalistic systematising of the deep theological principles which he had identified. Maurice argued that God's truth is prior to and beyond human theological formulation and that in the systems which the Church parties constructed they had, as he had so wonderfully satirised, undermined their own founding principles.[61] Quaintly, he thought systematising un-English! At its worst, the Mauricean strategy of holding together contradictory understandings of the Christian faith (partly because as systems they are not worthy of full respect and partly in the hope of future resolution) has, rightly, been criticised for allowing incoherence inside Anglicanism. Sykes unleashed his full wrath on Maurice's strategy:

> Theologically speaking, however, the effect of the proposal has been disastrous. It must be said bluntly that it has served as an open invitation to intellectual laziness and self-deception ... and the failure to be frank about the issues between the parties in the Church of England has led to an ultimately illusory self-projection as a Church without any specific doctrinal or confessional position.[62]

However, Jeremy Morris has come to Maurice's defence. He argues that the approach to comprehension in its looser form is really post-Maurice and that Maurice's own views were that, in particular, the Church of England's *structures* and *liturgy* had to be preserved if the work of comprehension was to be achieved. But Morris stresses the rich potential of Maurice's vision of conflict journeying to harmony via the affirmation of positive principles, and how this has spread now beyond Anglicanism to the wider ecumenical movement, even if its role within modern Anglicanism has become very strained.[63]

Conclusion

If we are to allow theological reflection on Anglican history to inform modern Anglicanism's values, we would have to say that there should be no monopolies in the Church of England or the wider Anglican Communion. All Anglicanism's tribes have deep roots in this always complex and messy Church. But at this point we must let out a historical 'raspberry'! *Most* of those whom we have discussed in this chapter wanted the Church of England to be a church after their own vision. They were *not* fundamentally committed to a diverse Church. But they failed. And there is a painful and pragmatic wisdom here, as Anglicans have had to come to terms with the failure of any of the tribes of Anglicanism to establish a monopoly of power, despite periods when each was dominant. Perhaps it was *hubris* to try to make the Church uniform?

More positively, as we have seen being worked out by Anglicans such as Cranmer, Elizabeth, Hooker, Herbert and Maurice, the distinctive English Reformation left the Church of England with a structure, an ethos and a theology that did not allow it to see the whole truth being located entirely on one side of the sixteenth-century debates (however much we must remember that it remained a self-consciously Protestant church until well into the nineteenth century). In that sense, the reformed Church of England was, from the outset, mindful of balance. This sensibility has become increasingly self-conscious in the last 150 years, especially because of Maurice's work.

The Church of England and subsequently Anglicanism is perhaps unusual in its degree of diversity but when we consider the universal Church as a whole, the only distinctive of Anglicanism is that so many different sorts of Christian have tried to coexist within it. Perhaps we could say that church history teaches us that Christians are *always* varied in their beliefs and practices. This could be seen as a counsel of despair but Anglicanism, as well as much failure, has also embodied moments when it has modelled how Christians might talk together across deep theological divides. It has done this in part by encouraging its members to work with the same set of tools and authorities – Scripture, Reason and Tradition – and above all to work at how to relate them. It appears to have done it, as a consequence of this theological method, with an ethos that values balance; and through the rhetoric of the *via media* has reminded itself of the need to draw on resources from across the Christian traditions. It also does it by its increasing reluctance to push out those with whom the majority might differ. If it is the case that no tribe in the Church has a monopoly on truth, it might be the case that the group whom 'we' exclude today are those who will bring wisdom to enrich tomorrow. For me this has been symbolised by the appointment to the See of Canterbury of representatives of the three tribes of Anglicanism. This is a way of embodying the wisdom of balance institutionally.

The perceptive reader will have noticed in these last paragraphs the most explicit move from describing the past to trying to articulate the wisdom that derives from reflection on that past. Obviously, there is a risk of circularity to this process. Interpreting church history is always a theologically driven activity. An alternative response, for example, to the 'mess' of Anglicanism has been be to opt instead for a 'pure' church, marked by clarity and authority of teaching and practice. However, if, as I will argue, one of the constraints of human nature and of God's relationship to human beings, even to the Church, is partial knowledge, then a mixed church is more than a possibility, it is an inevitability. It is in the light of that inescapable human reality that Anglicanism has evolved an ethos of modesty to guide church life.

2 'AN ADEQUATE SUFFICIENCY': THEOLOGICAL AND SPIRITUAL MODESTY

We start this chapter with a simple question but one which might alert us to a wise spirituality: when we come to talk of God, should we focus more on the God who reveals or on the human beings who receive revelation? I ask this because even if we believe in the gift of divinely inspired words, these words always require comprehension and almost always require interpretation; then they pass through cloudy human minds and voices. This chapter will argue that there are many pointers within Classic Anglicanism to modesty in claims for human knowing of God. Note that I am arguing for modesty, not for scepticism. Some modern Anglican apologists seem to argue that the opposite of fundamentalism is a profound lack of certainty. A better reading of the tradition is that humility, rather than uncertainty, is the hallmark of Anglican spirituality.

When I was a child growing up at home, with an Irish mum who always provided too much food, one of our polite and humorous defences against overeating was to say that we had had 'an adequate sufficiency'. It is a good metaphor for not overindulging theologically. Anglicans have traditionally believed that the knowledge they have been given is 'sufficient' for the purposes of salvation, if not for their entire satisfaction.

We will find ourselves back with Hooker. But we will also find a surprising echo in the work of John Wesley's notorious opponent, Bishop Butler, as we discuss issues of modesty, sufficiency, and probability. As part of this, we will explore the concept of *adiaphora* as another aspect of modesty. A further crucial aspect of theological modesty is the issue of language. So we will consider the different ways in which Anglicans have used words in talking of God. For some Anglicans this has led to deep caution about words, so we will touch briefly on the Anglican apophatic tradition before returning to the question of essentialism. But, as a way into discussion of theological modesty, first we look at the long-standing Anglican conviction that Anglicans believe in a simple faith.

'Mere Christianity'[1]

The Anglican claim that they believed 'only' the faith of the Early Church was a brilliant piece of polemic at the Refor-mation. In common with most of the Reformers, Anglicans claimed that they were going back to original Christianity, whereas 'Rome' had added to and corrupted the Christian faith. Apart from the most radical of the Reformers, none saw themselves as going back to the beginning and starting again – they did not rethink the doctrine of the Trinity for example – but particularly for the Reformed (that is, the Christians who looked to the Swiss churches for guidance), the emphasis was overwhelmingly on the Bible alone as the content of ancient faith. Anglicans always operated with a fuller content to Pri-mitive Christianity than this. As was most famously expressed by Andrewes:

> One canon ... two testaments, three creeds, four general councils, five centuries and the series of Fathers in that period ... determine the boundary of our faith.[2]

Classic Anglicanism was acceptance of the scriptures, creeds and orders of the Early Church.[3] This simple but rich con-ception of the content of Catholic faith had an increasing advantage, in that it enabled the Anglicans to defend them-selves against both Rome and Continental Protestantism in the succeeding centuries. At its most self-satisfied, it allowed

Anglicans to believe that they had the most authentic expression of the Christian faith.

It is striking to hear, from as recently as 1977, McAdoo stating with utter simplicity that 'there is then no distinctively Anglican faith as such but rather the explicit claim of adherence to nothing but "the faith once for all delivered"', a statement he fills out by citing another traditional expounder of Anglicanism, Bishop Wand of London:

> It is the claim of the Anglican that he holds no ... exclusive or distinctive doctrine. He claims that his faith is essentially that which was held by the early Christian Church in the days before the division.[4]

This simple self-confidence has collapsed as Anglican doctrinal uniformity fractured in the next generation, with profound consequences for the Anglican Communion (though it was already very fragile in 1977 – remember the pluralism of *Christian Believing*). But it has also been subject to a sharp critique by Sykes, who makes the basic point that the very claim to believe only the faith of the Bible and the Early Church is in itself a distinctive (and arguably presumptuous) statement.[5]

However, the point to explore now is not this claim in itself but the ethos which surrounds it. There was a profound sense of not wanting to say too much, or more than was necessary. As McAdoo rightly pointed out, Classic Anglicanism had a certain economy of theological expression,[6] in other words a sense of modesty. A key causal factor was that Cranmer and his successors had the benefit of having already seen both the noxious nature and crippling consequences of the intra-Protestant debates of the 1520s and 1530s and the deathly dispute between Roman Catholicism and Protestantism. They were already moving away from certain modes of over-extensive and exclusive religious claims. So, whilst to many modern Anglican ears the Thirty-nine Articles sound too precise, in comparison to Reformed, Lutheran or Roman Catholic confessions of faith they were eirenic, and succinct to the point of emaciation! In his still outstanding study of the Thirty-nine Articles, O'Donovan stresses this: 'Anglican *moderation* is the policy of reserving strong statement and conviction for the few things that really deserve them.'[7] Remember Hooker's famous simple definition of the visible Church, originally from Ephesians 4:5: 'one Lord, one Faith, one Baptism'.[8] As Countryman says crisply, Anglicans defined themselves against those who seemed to 'know more'.[9]

We have already spent a good deal of time reflecting on the weight Anglicans give to their history. Here we simply re-emphasise one of the implications of this. When Cranmer or Hooker argued for a retention of traditions from the ancient Church, this was in part conservatism but it was also a way of saying, 'we may not know better than our ancestors'. It was a form of modesty before the mind of the Church down the centuries. It was an appropriate modesty for the Church of a small nation on the north-western fringe of Europe. John Jewel (1522–71), Bishop of Salisbury, produced the first extended *Apology* or defence of the reformed Church of England in 1562: this was widely circulated on the Continent and for a time was to be found in many English parish churches alongside the Thirty-nine Articles. Jewel's clarity on the issue of the English Church accepting the wisdom of its ancestors is striking:

> ... we do show it plain that God's Holy Gospel, the ancient bishops, and the primitive church do make on our side ... [we] have returned to the apostles and old catholic fathers... [10]

We finish this section with a slightly florid but thought-provoking judgement on this early Anglican ethos of modesty:

> Not only in the seventeenth century but from the time of Henry VIII to the present day, if there is any outstanding note of the English temper it is a *humility of awe before the divine mysteries of faith* and a recognition of the

incompetence of language to define the ultimate paradox of experience. It is a pragmatism not of the lips only... [11]

This awe-driven modesty should be the heart of Anglican theology and spirituality.

Richard Hooker, Joseph Butler, Modesty and Probability

Hooker, early in the *Laws,* described human modesty in relationship to the knowledge of God. In the second chapter of the first book of *Laws* Hooker was describing the character of God (that God is bound to act according to the principles of God's being), and the nature of God (one-ness as well as triune), when it was as if he suddenly realised the impudence and impossibility of what he was doing and cried out:

> Dangerous it were for the feeble brain of man to wade far into the doings of the Most High; whom although to know be life, and joy to make mention of his name; yet our soundest knowledge is to know that we know him not indeed as he is, neither can know him: and our safest eloquence concerning him is our silence, when we confess without confession that his glory is inexplicable, his greatness above our capacity and reach. He is above, and we upon earth; therefore it behoveth our words to be wary and few.[12]

Here Hooker was, typically, both citing the Bible (Ecclesiastes 5:2) and weaving together Tradition (Church Fathers) and Reason (secular Classical authors).[13] The essence of God is, in some profound sense, unknowable for human beings. Human Reason is ontologically constrained. He was almost advocating a form of apophatic theology: that it is too difficult to speak of God and therefore we must simply say what we cannot say and then be silent.

Hooker went further. If Reason is constrained by the gulf between human and divine being, it is also constrained by the gulf caused by human sinfulness and limitation. A famous quotation from one of his sermons reminds us of his deep Protestant convictions about the reality of sin:

> It cannot be that any man's heart living should either be so enlightened in the knowledge, or so established in the love of that wherein his salvation standeth, as to be perfect, neither doubting nor shrinking at all.[14]

Rowan Williams glosses this:

> His [Hooker's] insistence that faith cannot be 'perfect' in the sense of self-consciously complete and exact ... is not at all a post-Enlightenment agnosticism ... but a recognition that contingent circumstances, human error and sin, and the instability of our personal passions and sensibilities all shape what we think we believe in ways that should make us very cautious at least about some of our claims ... *Theological truthfulness is not fully at our disposal because holiness is not fully at our disposal...* [15]

Classic Lutheran theology reminds us that we are *simul iustus, simul peccator* [justified and sinful at the same time] and therefore we need to be modest about our statements. As Hooker ruefully noticed, this theological conviction did not impact on all his opponents! So he made a point of stressing the distinction between the certainty which was appropriate, say for Paul, because of a unique mode of revelation, and the certainty appropriate for later Christians using their Reason.

> But consider I beseech you first as touching the Apostle, how that wherein he was so resolute and peremptory, our Lord Jesus Christ made manifest unto him even by intuitive revelation, wherein there was no possibility of error. That which you are persuaded of, ye have it not otherwise than by your own only probable collection [reasoning], and therefore such bold asseverations as in him were admirable, should in your mouths but argue rashness.[16]

'Think ye are men, deem it not impossible for you to err ... '[17] Whilst this was in part a rhetorical trick by Hooker, it seems also to be a plea from the heart, and a warning that false certainty in religion is dangerous.

Hooker coupled this with another rhetorical trick, but which also has some depth to it: he constantly contrasted the 'public reason' of the Church or the Commonwealth with the 'private reason' of individuals. Hooker was modest about the authority of the Church (see chapter 4), but he mocked the individualism of the Puritans, and their false certainty which underlay it:

> ... except our own private but probable resolutions be by the law of public determinations over-ruled, we take away all possibility of sociable life in the world ... I am persuaded, that of them with whom in this cause we strive, there are whose betters among men would be hardly found, if they did not live amongst men, but in some wilderness by themselves.[18]

Cranmer had a similarly robust attitude to those who disobeyed the visible church authorities. Behind this lies both a recognition of what is required for communal life to function, but also a sense of a hierarchy of knowing, with the communal at the top.

Hooker's sense of modesty was reinforced by his theological method. Because he believed that God's truth was encountered in rational reflection on the world, this brought human limitation into the theological task. Further, because he so carefully defined the nature of scriptural authority, the Church was left having to take many decisions. Inevitably therefore, much of our Christian understanding is 'probable'. This concept he applied mostly to private reasoning, but it of course also applied to the mind of the Church, even when guided by the Spirit.

Not that Hooker believed we were left in uncertainty. He believed in the perspicuity of Scripture, that is, its clarity about essentials. If we read the Bible honestly it will take us to Christ. This is 'sufficiency'. But even here, this belief is held by sinful human beings. Hooker stressed that faith has a moral and spiritual, as well as a cerebral element to it, and as a good Augustinian Anglican, he knew that only God knows who truly has a 'pure heart'.[19]

To sum up this section on Hooker: he would remind us that what we know of God, even through revelation and the 'supernatural law', *we* know as human beings, not as infallible holy beings outside time and space. So be modest.[20] The linkage from here to Bishop Butler is partly a verbal connection through this word 'probable', but I hope to show that there is a similarity of ethos lying behind these words.[21]

Bishop Joseph Butler (1692–1752) reminds us again of the complexity of church history. He is the man who, when as Bishop of Bristol he was confronted by John Wesley, rebuked him – 'Sir, the pretending to extraordinary revelations and gifts of the Holy Ghost is a horrid thing, a very horrid thing' – and refused to allow him to preach in his churches. But he is also the man who is known as the 'hammer of the Deists':[22] that is, he re-established the intelligibility of belief in revelation and the Incarnation as opposed to his rationalist opponents, who were arguing that all had to be universalisable and that God was at best a distant creator. Here we touch on his ideas about human religious knowing in his famous book *The Analogy of Religion*.

Butler started by reminding his readers that in almost all areas of life the knowledge on which we base our actions is 'probable'. He contrasted the certain knowledge which an 'infinite Intelligence' would have, with that of 'limited beings', and devised the aphorism: '. . . to us, Probability is the very guide to life.'[23] He applied this especially to our religious knowing, but did not make a category distinction between the ignorance we experience in religion and in other areas of life:

> Now if the natural and revealed dispensation of things are both from God, if they coincide with each other and together make up one scheme of Providence; our being incompetent judges of one, must render it credible, that we may be incompetent judges also of the other.[24]

Butler allied this gentle scepticism about the over-weening claims of Reason to a reasoned argument that started with a careful analysis of the world of nature and of humankind and suggested that 'by analogy' we could make connections to God's action which was, properly, more difficult for us to discern but which we could appreciate with a good enough degree of 'probability'.

To our ears, the word 'probable' (like 'modest') may not sound like a great rallying cry for Christian commitment, but Butler provided a powerful argument which expanded his meaning. He gave three types of situations where probable judgements would be made but with different responses.[25] Some judgements were very uncertain but because the issue did not matter, nor did the uncertainty. Other uncertain judgements which included an element of risk might provoke certain decisions. For example, as Gladstone suggested, we might avoid a road where there was a small risk of bandits, in favour of a road with none. But what if (using the example of Ian Ramsey, former Bishop of Durham) we were walking by a river, heard a splash and saw that a child had fallen in? We are not good swimmers and there is a high risk to this action – the probability of rescue is slight – but we would nonetheless attempt it from moral obligation. For Butler our religious faith has this quality of probability and moral demand. We have good reason for believing it to be 'probably' true and therefore 'prudently' we ought to act on this likelihood. And because of the nature of this particular probable issue – the demands of God upon us – we ought to act with commitment. In Ramsey's words, 'we express our belief in decisive action.'[26] As the novelist Fay Weldon has remarkably commented:

> One of the more admirable things about Anglicanism is that we are not so sure we are right, but we will still die in the name of faith.[27]

Butler's faith had deep quality. He lived it out personally, despite his bad reputation amongst Methodists, with self-discipline and compassion. With respect to our discussion, Ramsey's summary of Butler is telling:

> ... Butler never lost his nerve; he was not shaken from his *modest* theological reserve, from his sense of the ultimate 'incomprehensibility' of God. He never encouraged men to make those massive and all-embracing theological claims which, while they masquerade as genuine convictions, are in fact nothing more than proud human pretensions.[28]

Adiaphora

Adiaphora ['things indifferent'] is a crucial concept in Anglican self-understanding, and therefore worthy of attention for itself; it also indicates something about the nature of the theological task.

From the Reformation onwards, Anglicans have been explicitly committed to the concept of *adiaphora*; that there are issues which could and should not be required to be articles of faith, about which diversity was acceptable. This was not an original idea,[29] but Cranmer and the Elizabethans formalised it:

> It is not necessary that Traditions and Ceremonies be in all places one, and utterly like; for at all times they have been divers, and may be changed according to the diversities of countries, time, and men's manners, so that [i.e., provided that] nothing be ordained against God's Word. (Article 34)

We will return to this Article when we think in chapter 5 about vernacularism, but here note the straightforward recognition that the details of, for example, worship or church order have varied considerably between cultures. These are things which are not central to the faith or salvation; they are 'things indifferent'. Provided that nothing was being done which contradicted Scripture, Cranmer *et al.* warmly encouraged this diversity – at least, beyond the shores of England; at home they were fiercely committed to the new uniformity! As always, Hooker came up with a wonderful metaphor:

> But as for those things that are accessory hereunto ... as to alter them is no otherwise to change that way, than a path is changed by altering only the uppermost face thereof; which be it laid with gravel, or set with grass, or paved with stone, remaineth still the same path; in such things because discretion may teach the Church what is convenient, we hold not the Church further tied herein unto Scripture, than that against Scripture nothing be admitted in the Church, lest that path which ought always to be kept even, do thereby come to be overgrown with brambles and thorns.[30]

So we keep the path of faith clear but adorn it as we wish.

Two points are of interest: first, this concept has returned to great prominence for Anglicans. One of the issues at stake in the modern crisis is, when is something classified as *adiaphora* and when is it not? The *Windsor Report* provides some helpful detail and guidance itself in this area, not least pointing Anglicans back to the biblical roots of this in Romans 14 and 15, and reminding them of their duty of care to those with more sensitive consciences. But its summary of the Anglican practice of *adiaphora* is clear:

> This principle of 'adiaphora' was invoked and developed by the early English Reformers, particularly in their claim that, in matters of eucharistic theology, specific inter-pretations (transubstantiation was particularly in mind) were not to be insisted upon as 'necessary to be believed', and that a wider range of interpretations was to be allowed. Ever since then, the notion of 'adiaphora' has been a major feature of Anglican theology, over against the schools of thought, both Roman and Protestant, in which even the smallest details of belief and practice are sometimes regarded as essential parts of an indivisible whole.[31]

This is a good example because it is indeed the case that other churches would not allow that variation of belief about what is happening in the eucharist is acceptable.

But the second point, which is the one that really interests me, is what the concept of *adiaphora* says about our relationship with God. If it is really the case, as Anglicans believe, that that there may be some quite important things (e.g. what is happening to the bread and wine during a eucharist), to which we *do not know* the answer, there is a very strong sense of limitation here. In effect, the Church is saying 'on this we do not know for definite, therefore we live with flexibility, openness and modesty'. When we consider Anglican sacramental theology (chapter 4) we will see very clearly how this theological modesty became an attempt to undercut the bitter disputes of the Reformation era about the eucharist in particular. It also, of course, implies that God has delegated to the Church, and to individual Christians, the responsibility to take informed and reasoned decisions about many aspects of ecclesial and personal life. This is a serious theology of human maturity.

'God-talk'

One of the insights of modern philosophy and theology has been that language is not a neutral tool.[32] Here is not the place for an extended discussion of this, but we need to note the increasing sophistication with which we think about language. Succinctly, we can say that language is communal, has a flexible relationship to objects (I would assert that language can 'refer'), and is multi-layered with many functions. It is also clear that we are so immersed in language that we can no more live outside it than we could live outside air. And we might just note the strangeness of a sound being the way of communicating this complexity. As David Scott writes:

> Over and over again I find myself confronted by this mystery: how sounds strung together can be both a token

of meaning and a meaning in themselves. How saying a word brings what that word represents alive. How in saying 'God', God is given life.[33]

How then do Anglicans talk of God?

Even with something as apparently authoritative as the Nicene Creed, we move rapidly between the language of ancient religious texts (the Bible) translated from their originals – God as 'Almighty' – to the language of early Christian philosophy – 'of one being/substance' – to quite straightforward language from the everyday speech of the ancient world – 'and was crucified'. Further, the creed is full of metaphor, to much of which we become blind through over-familiarity. God as 'Father' is a *metaphor*. There is language which we easily recognise to be symbolic – Christ 'seated at the right hand' of the (incorporeal) Father – but there is a mixture of theological and linguistic dispute as to where this language becomes more than 'symbol'.[34] 'Came down from heaven'? 'Virgin' Mary?

Classic Anglicanism does not appear to have much to say about language as such, because it pre-dates these postmodern questions, but in fact it can sensitise us to this world of language in which we live. It is an old cliché that Anglicans owe their greatest debt to the fact that Cranmer was a liturgist, rather than a systematic theologian. He was also writing at time when the English language was going through a richly formative period.

> There is something about the English language of this period that has an element of the miraculous. We find this most commonly in the plays of Shakespeare and in the Authorized Version of the Bible ... Their language is not so removed from our own that we are utterly confused by it, but it is freshly coined enough to retain its life, its bite and chew. It has the power to evoke in us, physically, the moods, emotions and thoughts the words are trying to express. The words and the rhythms can make us cry and laugh and ponder with a huge intensity.[35]

Anglican theology quintessentially suggests that we need *poetry* to express our encounters with God. It is so much richer than prose. Apart from the expansive meaning of the words, the sheer sound of them is exhilarating. Cranmer's liturgies are packed with examples of his literary and poetic skill.[36] In the consecration prayer we find, 'one oblation of himself once offered'. This phrase is characterised by the alliteration which was a long tradition in Anglo-Saxon and English poetry. And, as is well known, the cadences of Cranmer's prayers were carefully refined and carry us in worship, where a lesser writer would leave us with lists. Feel the rhythm of the Collect for Purity (see also chapter 6):

> Almighty God,
> unto whom all hearts are open,
> all desires known,
> and from whom no secrets are hid...

This was an ancient clerical Latin prayer, but Cranmer placed it at the beginning of his communion service where *all* could say it.[37] For generations lay and ordained Anglicans have prayed that God will 'cleanse the thoughts of our hearts'. Literally, a heart has no thoughts, it just beats, but in English (from the Hebrew Bible), the heart is the centre of human being; it is where 'I' am most deeply.[38] Poetry is here a vehicle for divine encounter.

Anglican poetry explicitly wrestled with how to use words to speak of God. We can enjoy the way that some Anglican poets compressed and stretched language as they tried to speak of God; their confidence that language both reveals and obscures God. Herbert spoke for them when he longed to present 'a garland of deserved praise', but knew that all he had was 'this poore wreath' to give as the 'crown of praise'.[39] Words were both a great gift he can offer – 'is there in truth no beautie?'[40] – and yet so slight:

My God, a verse is not a crown...
... But it is that which while I use
I am with thee... [41]

In this poem about verbal games, Herbert used straightforward language precisely to express, with humility and a highly refined simplicity, life with God.

Conversely, some of Herbert's contemporaries revelled in the complexity of their imagery and writing. This is really a topic for a literature course but there is a theological backdrop to this complexity. John Donne (1572–1631), convert from Roman Catholicism, ex-libertine and Dean of St Paul's Cathedral, exemplifies the complexities of this metaphysical style of poetry. He wrestled in expressing God in words. From his litany:

O Blessed glorious Trinity,
bones to philosophy, but milk to faith,
which, as wise serpents, diversely
most slipperiness, yet most entanglings hath,
as you distinguished undistinct... [42]

As we might expect, language is strained by discussing the Trinity. So the Trinity is 'distinguished undistinct'; here Donne mirrored the phraseology of the Early Church. Of course this is 'bones to philosophy', i.e. hard to digest. Only 'faith' can receive it as 'milk'. But Donne plays games with us. How dare he compare the Trinity to a trio of snakes, so entangled together? And yet they are 'wise serpents', as we must be if we are to understand this. That we have to struggle to understand this poem is Donne's intention for us. These are 'bones' to make us chew, that we may come to 'love'.

Most of these poets depict a sense of their own sinfulness that threatens the value of the beauty which they were creating. Herbert seemed so often wracked by sin and by the vanity of his poetry. God brought him back to simple words:

But while I bustled, I might heare a friend
whisper, *How wide is all this long pretence!*

There is in love a sweetnesse readie penn'd:
copie out onely that, and save expense.[43]

Love is the way. We will return to the prominence of forgiveness and grace in Anglican spirituality (chapter 6), but Donne,
perhaps because of the trauma of a life involving his aban-
donment of the (persecuted) faith of his family as well as 'sins
of the flesh', clung to this love, in words that belie the Anglican
reputation for coolness before passion:

> Batter my heart, three-person'd God; for, you
> as yet but knock, breathe, shine and seek to mend;
> that I may rise, and stand, o'erthrow me, and bend
> your force, to break, blow, burn, and make me new.
> I, like an usurpt town, to another due,
> labour to admit you, but oh, to no end,
> reason your viceroy in me, me should defend,
> but is captiv'd, and proves weak or untrue,
> yet dearly I love you, and would be loved fain,
> but am betroth'd unto your enemy,
> divorce me, untie, or break that knot again,
> take me to you, imprison me, for I
> except you enthral me, never shall be free,
> nor ever chaste, except you ravish me.[44]

Donne did find the peace of knowing that God had 'ravished'
him. But perhaps it is only by the shock of such visceral language and images that we can be opened up to the extent of
God's nature and forgiveness. This is not the 'cheap grace' of
complacent Anglicanism.

David Scott, as a poet, knows that language *is* a way into
God:

> There is no simple explanation for this, but the way to
> understand it better lies in the nature of God as both
> transcendent and imminent, beyond and among. That
> paradox, which defies, or passes, all our understanding, is
> revealed through those images which can contain the
> truth of both states at once. It is the truth that the early

Church struggled over the nature of the incarnation, both Godhead and manhood, in the one Christ. Truths of this sort are best revealed in a language that helps break the conventional mould of ways of looking at things. *It is the miracle of language to reveal the miracle of God's nature.*[45]

Language does, and does not reveal God. Countryman sums up the paradox of this very well:

> What we can hope to find beyond the metaphor of the poem itself is not a pure philosophical discourse that can lay claim to a clarity of language without remainder. Quite the contrary, what lies beyond the metaphor is that which cannot finally be spoken at all.[46]

These are elements of an Anglican apophatic [negative or self-denying] theology, part of theological modesty.[47]

We can find a traditional expression of apophatic theology in Herbert's poem 'Ungratefulnesse'. He described human ingratitude for God's two great gifts to us: the Trinity and the Incarnation. The first is inaccessible, too much for human beings:

> The statelier cabinet is the *Trinitie*,
>   whose sparkling light accesse denies;
>   therefore thou dost not show
>   this fully to us, till death blow
>   the dust into our eyes:
> for by that powder thou wilt make us see.

Apart from the perverse imagery that it is with the dust of death that God will open our eyes, notice that God as Trinity is hidden from us by 'light'. Apophatic theology – God is beyond human seeing. But there is another authentic Anglican voice in the next verse:

> But all thy sweets are packt up in the other;
>   thy mercies thither flock and flow:
>   that as the first affrights,
>   this may allure us with delights;

> because this box we know;
>   for we have all of us just such another.[48]

'Because this box we know' – again we are taken back to the deep significance for Anglicanism of the Incarnation. But how playful to compare the Incarnation to a box of sweets!

Another aspect of apophatic theology is that the approach to God is through love rather than through the intellect.[49] This was characteristic of Henry Vaughan (1621–95), a Cavalier poet who lived and fought through the upheavals of the Civil War and Commonwealth and then served as a doctor in his Welsh valley. As Cluysenaar writes:

> The spiritual direction taken by Henry Vaughan combines sparkling intellectuality with preparedness to take on the limitations of human understanding and language – a willingness to accept that 'Love only can with quick accesse/unlock the way', and that it may sometimes be wise 'to carry, not search mysteries'.[50]

Love is the way to know God, but it is a particular sort of knowing: restrained, full of gaps, patient.

Anglican apophatic spirituality is inextricably linked with a sense of the 'absence' of God. In that, it was deeply fed by the use of the psalms, recited in full every month according to the Prayer Book lectionary. It also came out of the life experiences and troubled souls of these poets. Vaughan lost a brother in the Civil War, and his first wife to ill-health. Some of the barriers between God and humanity are the product of the heartache of life. Vaughan used the imagery of 'light' and darkness' to express God's strange presence in this painful world. So those whom he had loved and lost had gone into 'the world of light'. But instead of bringing hope, this 'light doth trample on my days'.[51]

Light *can* bring the touch of God. When weighed down by his own sin, Vaughan pleaded:

> But brush me with thy light, that I
>   may shine unto a perfect day... [52]

But whilst Vaughan often used this imagery of light to describe the coming of God, he also, in keeping with apophatic imagery, in one of his most famous poems described 'The Night' (reflecting on Nicodemus coming by night in John 3) as the place and mode of encounter (again notice the vivid reminders of the Incarnation):

> Gods silent, searching flight:
> when my Lords head is fill'd with dew, and all
> his locks are wet with the clear drops of night;
>   his still, soft call;
>   his knocking time; the souls dumb watch,
>   when Spirits their fair kindred catch...
>
> There is in God (some say)
> a deep, but dazzling darkness; as men here
> say it is late and dusky, because they
>   see not all clear;
>   O for that night! where I in him
>   might live invisible and dim.[53]

R. S. Thomas, the Welsh poet-priest who has given us some of the best English language poetry in our generation, wrote self-consciously in this tradition, though with that acute sense of lament and struggle with a more elusive God which has become, thankfully, a louder voice within the freedom of modern Anglicanism. In his poem *Via Negativa* he declares that '... God is that great absence/in our lives...' More: God is '... the empty silence/within, the place where we go/seeking, not in hope to/arrive or find... '[54]

A recurrent theme in Thomas is of the church building as a place of apophatic encounter. So in *The Empty Church* he asks 'Why, then, do I kneel still striking my prayers on a stone heart?' But all is not hopeless: 'Is it in hope one/of them will ignite yet and throw/on its illumined walls the shadow/of someone greater than I can understand?'[55] In the bare stones of English Anglican cathedrals, stripped of the beauty of painted walls and statues during the Long Reformation, there is almost a denial of the possibility of a visual language for God. In these cavernous buildings, the sound of the old Offices speaks of a relationship with an austere God.

However, whilst there is a sense in some, especially modern, Anglican apophatic theology that the need to renounce 'God-talk' comes from the difficulty of belief, the core of the ancient tradition was that it grew out of the conviction that God was too big to be described in words. There is an interesting echo of this in the way Anglicans talk about language in worship. Some Anglican apologists are more comfortable with the use of positive affirmations of faith in the context of liturgy rather than in, say, a textbook, precisely because the language comes with a different, and less anchored, range of meanings.[56] However, particularly in the case of the language of worship, what this reticence communicates is not a lack of faith but a faith in a God beyond normal speaking. At its best, this language of worship, and poetic language, often elusive and allusive, is still faith-filled. R. S. Thomas was held, just, by this liturgical embrace.

F. D. Maurice penned one of those purple passages whose meaning carries us further than perhaps the author intended. Describing the views of the 'English Christian', he asserted that:

> Hating all systems, he hates those most which are most perfect, because in them there are the fewest crannies and crevices through which the light and air of heaven may enter.

This is typical Maurice: evocative but imprecise. His next sentence takes us a little closer to what he meant:

> He hates the Romish system more than all Protestant systems, because the latter are inconsistent and fragmentary, the former is all-embracing and satisfactory, therefore more lifeless, inhuman, godless.[57]

This sounds more like an apologia for incoherence than for modesty, but it has a strange resonance. It speaks in a unique (and unpleasant) tone for that Anglican suspicion of elaborate and definite theological systems. It has been my experience that God is most clearly encountered in the 'cracks and crevices' of human theological systems. It has also been my experience that it is in the intermingling of principles and parties that true Catholicity is to be found. I think both experiences resonate with the Anglican ethos. No system or language has a monopoly of truth. Sometimes rich language or sometimes silence is best. But in all things, be modest. Is this an example of ecclesial evolution as revelatory?

Fundamentals and Essentials

Given this sustained argument in favour of modesty as a key characteristic of Anglican theological thinking, is it then possible to articulate what Anglicans do believe, or is it the case that the day of doctrinal statements is over? As Caroline Chartres asks, tongue in cheek, is it really the case that Anglicans can believe in anything as long as they do not believe it too strongly?[58] There are two elements to this discussion. First: is it still possible to talk about the essentials of the faith or is this too theologically complex to be viable? Second: is it possible to conceive of a Church which might be committed to the essentials but which, for a variety of reasons, also remains committed to protecting the right to ask new and sometimes difficult questions? How does a Church express and embody its commitment to generous orthodoxy?

The issue of essentials returned to prominence in the *Windsor Report*. As part of the draft Covenant, Anglican churches were asked to consider affirming that they held 'the essentials of the apostolic faith, as summed up in the Creeds'.[59] This might seem unexceptional but it is important to hear a sustained critique of this idea of essentials.

The idea that Anglicans hold to the essentials of the Christian faith has a very long pedigree. Sykes sums up, for example, Hooker's position:

Near the beginning of his third book on the *Laws of Ecclesiastical Polity* (1594) he speaks of the unity of the visible church as grounded in the outward profession of 'the essence of Christianity' (the *first occurrence of this term in English* known to me), which profession is necessary in every Christian man. Furthermore, he makes explicitly clear that by 'the essence of Christianity' he means the articles of Christian belief given as the *regula fidei* in the works of Irenaeus and Tertullian. These fundamentals are, in effect, the propositions which go to make up the Nicene and Apostles' creeds ... They constitute, Hooker asserts, the faith which Jesus taught and which has characterised the visible church from that day to this.[60]

We are back with the simple faith of the Early Church and Anglicans.

But Sykes then makes the following points. First, that modern biblical and historical study has questioned whether there is a straightforward and incontestable linkage between 'the faith of Jesus', the second-century 'rules of faith' and the fourth-century creeds. This was a period of significant internal conflict, external difficulty and, to put it at its lightest, substantial development within the Church. In our day, the *Da Vinci Code* phenomenon has brought into popular culture the debate about whether the later Church imposed a set of beliefs – particular understandings of the divinity of Christ – on to the earlier content of the faith. We will return (chapter 5) to the question of the relationship of scholarship and the formation of doctrine, but here we simply note Sykes' argument, that straightforward language about 'uncontested essentials' is problematic in the modern era.

It is problematic for a second cluster of reasons. To what extent is it proper or even possible for us to use the same words as people from the first, or the fourth, or the sixteenth centuries? In a scientific and sceptical world with bigger horizons, we must surely rethink the old statements into words and ideas which make sense in our world? Sykes reflects on one of the sharp-tongued proponents of change, Hensley Henson, Bishop of Durham from 1920 to 1939:

> There were also those who were prepared to say, as did Hensley Henson, that they believed the words of the creed *ex animo* [from the heart], meaning by that that they believed what they took to be its *essential* meaning ... With reference to the virgin birth or the resurrection this might very well be something other than the factual or physical miracle, clearly believed in by the compilers of the creeds or some of the authors of the New Testament documents.[61]

A later Bishop of Durham, David Jenkins, made exactly this point when he emphasised the theological and spiritual significance of the Resurrection, whilst being sceptical about its physicality. More recently, Don Cupitt and the Sea of Faith movement have argued that in our postmodern era, belief in God as a real personal existing being is no longer tenable, and we are better to conceive of God as the projection of the highest ideals of humankind; hence non-realism. Whilst it is important to stress the integrity of those asking these questions, we must note that all this has placed great strain on the Anglican concept of believing only the essentials.

Elsewhere, Sykes raises another question about essentialism? Whose essentials?[62] On what grounds, given that there is some acceptance of development in the Early Church, do Anglicans argue that christological or trinitarian development is acceptable but ecclesiastical development – e.g. the rise of the papacy – is unacceptable? For Roman Catholics or the Orthodox, faith in a particular expression of Church is often seen as an essential. Sykes quotes a range of theologians from Lutherans to Anglo-Catholics to Roman Catholics, all of whom argue that the issue is not identifying the essentials but rather defending the *whole* faith. Essentialism seems doomed. And with it Anglican coherence?

There are three Anglican responses to this threat to

essentialism. The first is to remind Anglicans that all their official documents commit them to a set of beliefs and practices. We have already noted documents such as the Lambeth Quadrilateral and the Declaration of Assent which commit Anglicans to Scripture, creed, sacrament and church order. The minimum way in which this is taken, for example in *Christian Believing*, is that Anglicans are committed to keeping their historic sources of faith (especially Bible and creeds), as live conversation partners in their current theological work; 'in the bloodstream so to speak'.[63] This allows for very great latitude, as it was meant to.[64] I would go further and say that, whilst almost all of these documents are capable of some latitude of interpretation, intellectual integrity requires those who subscribe to these official statements to recognise the character of the commitments they have made. The documents locate Anglicans in generous orthodoxy.

A second way of conceiving of essentialism is that the Lambeth Quadrilateral does not simply lay down theoretical beliefs, it commits Anglicans to certain practices. Again Sykes makes this point clearly:

> Here after all, is not just a list of miracles of belief, but a series of usages, the use of Scripture in the public in the vernacular, the use of creeds in worship, the celebration of the sacraments, and the practice of episcopal government.

But he takes us to the heart of the matter when he goes on:

> It is important to stress that all these *presuppose* the Church's life of active discipleship, worship and witness, *centred upon Christ*.[65]

There is a priority about what can be called the 'Christ-event' as well as convictions about the continuing activity of God in Christ, without which the actions and documents of the Christian Church make no sense. There comes a point of reinterpretation of the 'Christ-event' when there is no reason or authority, as Sykes noted in *The Integrity of Anglicanism*, for a Church to invite people to join it and trust the way of life it commends.[66] This places a boundary on reinterpretation. But I want to suggest that Anglicans can go further than this.

Third: it is tempting when engaged in discussion of the essentials to offer a snappy summary of the Christian faith. But it is not my place to do that. The deep discipline of Anglicanism is that the essence of the faith is not a matter for individual bright ideas. There *is* a given-ness about it. Rowan Williams has expressed this with some force:

> ... how we act and talk is conditioned by a history – not a history, this time, of our decisions and their consequences, but a history of attempts to bring to speech *that which* determines us. Doctrine, in other words is always a catching up with something prior to us: we do not (in both the colloquial and the technical senses of the words) 'have priority' when we try to speak doctrinally.[67]

This is why both Sykes and Williams, as we have seen, keep Anglicans fundamentally committed to the Incarnation as the foundation for faith. Buchanan uses the helpful metaphor of a charity which has trust deeds to which it must be faithful but which need to be re-worked to address a modern context.[68]

We can say further, that the crucial point is that the Church as institution is committed to the faith, in not quite a Newmanesque way.[69] This is a Church which, in McAdoo's words, 'is not so much concerned with making the troops toe the line as with establishing what the line is'.[70] Therefore, whilst the Anglican Communion is (and, I believe, should remain) committed to generous orthodoxy, the deep commitment to modesty in our language about God will make Anglicans patient with new questions and with a slow process for resolving them. As we will see (chapter 4), when we ally this theological modesty to ecclesiastical modesty, it is right and proper that Anglicanism gives much latitude to the beliefs of its members and is deeply reluctant to censure debate. The old cliché, whilst struggling in our era because of the complexity of the discussion of essentials, still has a good feel to it: 'In essentials, unity; in non-essentials, liberty; in all things, charity.' An ethos of modesty is essential for Anglicans. I am convinced that this is a good example of ecclesial evolution being revelatory.

This is a good point at which to have a little detour into overt spirituality. Much modern Christian worship is very wordy. We heap up words and emotions to describe God and use them as a mechanism for encountering God. I do want not to rubbish such an affective spirituality, far from it. It is a recurrent form of Christian spirituality and, at its best, flows from a passionate love for and encounter with God. But, as with some 'young love', there is an element of immaturity in it, and to pursue the metaphor of human love, just as a long-settled couple of old friends can just be together, wordlessly and at ease, so there is a merit in being with God without trying to generate words or feelings to give content to that being.

This can take the form of silence. And there is within the Anglican spiritual tradition, despite the carnage of the dissolution of the monasteries, much experience of and affection for silence as a strongly commended, life-giving mode of being with God. I have been struck, dipping into the spiritual writings of the Classic Anglicans, by the frequency of references to meditation, when during their private prayers they would pray or read the Scriptures as a way of being with God quietly and receptively.

> You can lead a life of heroic labour and self-denial at the external level, refuse the comforts of food and sleep; but if you have not silence – to paraphrase St Paul it will profit you nothing.[71]

So writes Rowan Williams reflecting on the Desert Fathers and Mothers. Hooker would have approved.

But a more typical Anglican mode of modesty in relating to God is the use of the Daily Office, of morning and evening prayer, of liturgy. This is a way of being with God which is not *too* closely defined; partly because the words of the services are scriptural, and so both given but also slightly alien and formal, and partly because in their very familiarity is restfulness and spaciousness. It can, at one end of the spectrum, provide an exciting vehicle for affective praise, but at the other, a solid stone floor on which to sit when life is whirling. It can provide a distraction from the 'monkey-chatter' of our conscious minds whilst our spirits commune with God, but also a stimulus for worship-shaped thought as we wrestle with God as presented in the Bible and liturgy. There is a connection between a sense of modesty in our knowledge of God and a certain formal simplicity in how we come to God.

3 'ALWAYS SCRIPTURE AND...'

I had a wise priest as a spiritual director some years ago. He told me once that he was left unable to preach from the Gospels for the first two years after theological college, because of his experience of biblical criticism. On the other hand, as a sometime parish priest, I am aware of the weak biblical knowledge in congregations.[1] And one of the amusing and worrying features of training Anglicans is that in answer to questions such as 'What authorities do Anglicans look to?', I place secret bets with myself about how long the session will run before someone says rather hesitantly, 'the Bible'. Thankfully, I have not yet led a session where the Bible has not been remembered!

As Tom Wright has succinctly summarised, Anglicans are experiencing damaging conflicts about how to hear Scripture.[2] They need to find renewed ways of hearing Scripture within the Church and also of commending its truthfulness to those outside the Church. Strikingly both the *Windsor* and *Rochester* reports include long sections on hermeneutics, which is an issue this chapter will explore. After discussing the theological place of the Bible within Anglicanism, we will go on to look at how this is lived out in practice as the Bible is heard in common worship, in preaching and through scholarship. We will finish by reflecting on how faith in the God of the Bible has been lived out liberatingly in our times.

The Primacy of Scripture but not *Sola Scriptura*

First, it is worth reminding ourselves of the prominence which the Bible holds as a source of authority for Anglicans. Article 6 says that 'Scripture contains all things necessary to salvation'.[3] Notice immediately the little word 'necessary' – not desirable or luxurious but 'necessary'. We are back with the language of what is essential or sufficient for Christians to know. If the Bible was all we had, the Reformers believed, it would lead us to Christ and salvation. Scripture is reaffirmed in the Lambeth Quadrilateral, as the first of Anglicanism's non-negotiables, and in the Declaration of Assent as the place of unique revelation. In this sense Anglicans do believe in *sola scriptura*. It is enough on its own. It is the ultimate point of reference. (But note that neither the Article nor other Anglican formularies define the nature of biblical inspiration. It is historically responsible to say that in the period of Classic Anglicanism, full inerrant inspiration was assumed, but this did not mean there was no space for careful hermeneutics, as we shall see with Hooker.) However, I would assert that Anglicans believe in the *primacy of Scripture*, but not in *sola scriptura* or the Bible *alone* as the only source of authority.[4]

What is meant by the *primacy of Scripture*? Fundamentally, whilst the classic language of Anglicanism often refers to the Bible as the 'Word of God', this always sits over against the deeper assumption that the 'Word' is Christ. As the *Windsor Report* reminds Anglicans, the phrase 'the authority of the Bible' should be understood as shorthand for 'the authority of the triune God, *exercised through* scripture'.[5] It is a relational, dynamic and transformative understanding of the nature of scriptural authority, not a fixed, restrictive and legalistic one. God 'speaks' and 'does' as the Bible is 'heard' and 'lived', in keeping with his whole mission: people and situations being brought to new life.[6] *God is primary*. That is why the Thirty-nine Articles begin with the doctrine of God, not the doctrine of Scripture.

There is a startling passage in Hooker where he tried to explain to his Puritan opponents the nature of divine authority. He contrasted Moses and Christ. Moses was a law-giver and therefore wrote many specific regulations. Christ was not a detailed law-giver and we only find his commands written in the occasional writings of the Apostles. Indeed we have no words written by Christ. But this does not lessen Christ's authority. Hooker argued that the object of Christian faith is the living Christ and this is expressed in a simpler and more concentrated set of beliefs and practices than the panoply of Old Testament law, and also in mature current discipleship.[7] It is a crucial warning for modern Anglicans.

Nor were the Classic Anglicans were not naïve in their use of the Bible. They were very aware that the canon of Scripture was an issue – the New Testament did not come with a contents page! Because of their historical understanding, they knew that Christ, the Gospel, and the community which he formed, preceded the formation of the canon, even if the embryonic Scriptures themselves were part of the Christ-event and the initial proclamation of the Gospel and have come to have primary authority. Michael Ramsey summarised this in a classically Anglican way:

> ... while the Canon of Scripture is in itself a development, it has a special authority to control and to check the whole field of development in life and doctrine.[8]

Therefore the Bible is the 'Word of God' but also requires careful introduction. Hence in 1571 Article 6 listed the Protestant, as opposed to the Roman Catholic, version of the canon. Fascinatingly, it allowed the use of the 'Apocrypha', or Protestant non-canonical books, 'for example of life and instruction of manners' following the teaching of St Jerome, though not to establish doctrine (because *Maccabees* could be used to justify the doctrine of purgatory). Indeed, books from the Apocrypha were included in Cranmer's lectionaries for the public reading of Scripture in church.

The Classic Anglican understanding of biblical authority was generously permissive – *anything can be done which is not obviously contrary to Scripture.* The opposite view was found in some Reformed perspectives which were strictly limiting – only that can be done which is explicitly commanded or allowed in the Bible. This latter view is sometimes described as 'biblicist' or 'scripturalist'.[9] A simple example, still alive today, was the Reformed discipline of singing only unaccompanied psalms, because that was described in the Bible, as opposed to singing hymns or anthems accompanied by organs or other non-biblical musical instruments, which was not. But in Article 20 and again in Article 34 it was clearly stated that the Church has authority in controversies of faith, order and worship.[10] It was allowed to develop practices and disciplines which could not be found explicitly in Scripture, provided they were not directly forbidden by Scripture. This implied that the Bible did not have 'literal' answers to all the questions facing the Church, either because such issues were not discussed in the Bible or its answers could not be unequivocally discerned. (This was all too painfully evident even in the mid sixteenth century and is still true today.)

Further, Cranmer was not blind to the complexities and risks of reading the Bible. He was adamant that interpretation of the Bible was not an individualistic activity but should be done by properly trained and authorised teachers in the Church. So if people were troubled by the 'high mountains' of Scripture, [the hard to understand passages], God would send learned help:

> ... it cannot be, saith St John Chrysostom, that he [the puzzled reader] should be left without help. For either God Almighty will send him a goodly Doctor to teach him ... or else, if we lack a learned man to instruct and teach us, yet God himself from above will give light to our minds... [11]

Despite this intriguing suggestion of direct illumination by the Holy Spirit, Cranmer was not naïve about the more 'difficult' parts of the Bible. So, notwithstanding the lengthy passages which he required to be read at each service so that the Bible could be heard in a year (the Old Testament, not completely, once and the New Testament, not completely, twice), he edited out what he considered to be the least edifying books and chapters from the lectionary, for example most of the Book of

Revelation.[12] Clearly Cranmer's pastoral and hermeneutical (and archiepiscopal) sense was sharply at work.

Always Hermeneutics

For the Classic Anglicans, a key word was 'perspicuity'. The essentials of the Bible were clear enough that they could be understood by an ordinary reader with an open mind. As Cranmer wrote with some beauty and passion:

> For the Holy Ghost hath so ordered and attempered [styled] the Scriptures, that in them as well publicans, fishers and shepherds may find their edification, as great doctors their erudition: for the books were not made to vainglory, like as were the writings of the Gentile philosophers and rhetoricians ... whereof nothing can be understand [*sic*] without a master or an expositor. But the apostles and prophets wrote their books so that their special intent and purpose might be understanded and perceived of every reader... [13]

Hooker wrote more simply:

> Some things are so familiar and plain, that truth from falsehood, good from evil, is most easily discerned in them, even by men of no deep capacity. And of that nature, for the most part, are things absolutely unto all men's salvation necessary ... they are not only set down, but *also plainly set down in Scripture; so that he which heareth or readeth may without any great difficulty understand.*[14]

This remains the mainstream Anglican view.[15] However, Hooker glossed this carefully. The most important sentence in Hooker about Scripture is:

> The main drift of the whole New Testament is that which St John setteth down as the purpose of his own history: 'These things are written, that ye might believe that Jesus

is Christ the Son of God, and that in believing ye might have life through his name' (John 20:31).[16]

Hooker believed that God in Christ comes to bring life and so he always interpreted the Bible from this hermeneutical perspective.

Hermeneutics is the discipline of interpretation. To use a powerful metaphor, it requires of us that we grasp the horizon of the biblical text – the history and meaning of the words, their background, their relationship to the wider canon – so as to do our very best to understand the words as they were originally used. Then we must understand our own horizon – our convictions and also our context – so that we come to the Bible as self-aware as possible. We are then in a position to bring these two horizons together to enable honest dialogue. There is obviously much more that could be said,[17] but in case this sounds like a new-fangled modern game, the question of how to interpret the Bible was pressing for Classic Anglicans.

Anglicans had to consider their strategy for interpreting the Bible. Is it all of the same importance? The Articles warned Anglicans against interpreting Scripture so that one passage was made to contradict another (Article 20), but they were also heirs to the Christian tradition which had interpreted the ceremonial law of the Old Testament as being part of the old covenant. The issue of disentangling this from the moral law of the Old Testament was sharp during the Reformation and this dispute has left its mark on the Articles. In 1553 in the Forty-two Articles, the forerunner of the Thirty-nine Articles, Cranmer included the following in Article 19 [later Article 7]:

> ... no man (be he never so perfect a Christian) is exempt and loosed from those commandments, which are called moral.

This is a good early example of hermeneutics because it was distinguishing which parts of Scripture were still relevant and which were not.

Hooker took this issue head on. He noticed that these ceremonial laws which his Church was telling him to ignore had
been given as 'the Word of the Lord'. How could they then no
longer be the Word of the Lord?

> ... the whole law of rites and ceremonies, *although
> delivered with so great solemnity*, is notwithstanding
> clean *abrogated*, inasmuch as it had but *temporary* cause
> of God ordaining it.[18]

The Word of the Lord here is 'temporary'.

Underlying this was Hooker's sophisticated hermeneutic.
He said we must learn to distinguish between different genres
in Scripture. Is a particular passage a law for all time –
'supernatural' law? Or is it a detailed worked example, for a
specific period in the life of the People of God, of how to embody
a principle, but which is no longer to be taken literally –
'positive' (or changeable) law? The task of discernment
requires careful attention to the overall narrative and purpose
of the Bible and also to any specific passage if we are to
accurately understand its genre. It also requires attention to
the current context because it may be that we had previously
understood a particular passage to have one permanent
meaning, which is now open to reinterpretation because of our
changed perception of reality. In Hooker's language, something we once took to be a supernatural law is later seen as a
positive law. A humorous example is Hooker' discussion of the
oscula sancta, the holy kisses.[19] It was clearly an apostolic
command (1 *Thess.* 4:26), but Hooker believed it was no longer
to be taken literally. It could be seen as having the form of a
supernatural law, but closer examination revealed it to be a
contextualised command. Therefore, Hooker argued – perhaps
with some relief! – it was no longer required. But the underlying principle, which was love for fellow church members,
would now need to be expressed in a suitable cultural form.

All this is brilliantly explained by Stephen Sykes.[20] He
notes, for example, that the biblical witness about women in
ministry is not mono-vocal and therefore we need to pay

attention to the genre of the passages which forbid public ministry by women. But the crucial move is to recognise that what Hooker in the sixteenth century took to be an immutable law of nature – that women are inferior – is now no longer seen in this light. Therefore the biblical laws must be revisited to understand their genre. If it becomes apparent that the restrictive laws are temporary – designed to produce good order in the first-century church – but that the deeper supernatural law is about the implications of the Gospel for equality in Christ, then it is right that the Church revises its traditional understanding.

Further, as we explored specifically in chapter 1, whilst the Thirty-nine Articles talk of the creeds being 'proved by most certain warrants of Holy Scripture' (Article 8), Hooker reminded his readers of the complex process of discernment by the Church which produced the creeds. In other words, the sufficiency of the Bible was in some ways quite constrained. Hence Hooker argued that *Reason is crucial for the reception and interpretation of the Bible.*

This is part of a wider understanding that Christians read the Bible from within a community of interpretation – 'I' read it in a certain way *because* 'I' am a disciple of Christ. This view is becoming more widely accepted again as, in a postmodern world, the realisation that everyone speaks from somewhere has made the idea of reading the Bible from a specific perspective intelligible again. As Christians we always read the Bible in the context of Tradition. The very fact that we come to it as believers in Christ shows that we are already interpreting it in a Tradition-Christian way.

This insight was most provocatively expressed by Newman. He summed up the difference between the Bible and the creeds:

> Surely the sacred volume was never intended, and is not adapted to teach us our creed; however certain it is that we can prove our creed from it ... From the very first ... [the rule has been] ... for the Church to teach the truth,

and then appeal to Scripture in vindication of its own teaching.[21]

This caused great offence at the time because it was thought to undermine the doctrine of the perspicuity of Scripture and to elevate the authority of the Church. I might wish to argue that too great a divide between Scripture and creed – which Hooker would never have countenanced – can communicate a contempt for the biblical authors which is unwarranted. On literary and intellectual grounds, let alone theological, *John's Gospel* takes us deeply into the Incarnation and its essential meaning. But, having said that, these statements of Newman resonate strongly with Hooker. The *precision* with which the Council of Nicea defined the relationship of the Father and the Son or the Council of Chalcedon defined the relationship of humanity and divinity in Christ went far beyond the conceptual world and the language of Scripture. But it is with such doctrines in mind that the Church now looks back to the text of Scripture. 'We' interpret Christ in the light of these doctrinal statements.

This is not to say that Anglicans never try to read Scripture with fresh eyes. This is a difficult but necessary discipline to help Christians check that they are hearing Scripture as it was originally written. Of course, it *can* be highly problematic if these supposedly fresh eyes deconstruct Christian faith and distract the Church. As the *Windsor Report* cautions:

> Where a fresh wave of scholarship generates ideas which are perceived as a threat to something which the Church has always held dear, it is up to the scholars concerned ... to explain how what is now proposed not only accords with but actually enhances the central core of the Church's faith.[22]

The Anglican way is that Bible and Tradition and Reason are inseparable. Greer sums up the Classic Anglican attitude to the Bible with perfect balance:

> What we have is God's divine law for salvation revealed in

scripture and interpreted by our fallible reason. The Church of England [stood] in the middle ground between Rome's belief in the insufficiency of scripture and the Puritan view of its omnicompetence. Hooker has no wish to supplant an ecclesiastical infallibility with a biblicism that would make our interpretations of scripture infallible.[23]

The problem with phrases such as the 'authority of Scripture' is that the issue is often one of the interpretation or evaluation of a specific text, rather than a blanket question of authority. The *Rochester Report* offers four tests to help Anglicans with good interpretation:[24]

1 Simple hermeneutics: careful work on the original texts to help us to understand them as fully as possible in their original context followed by 'asking how we translate what is said in them ... to our historical situation ... *that was never envisaged by the human author...* ' *(Italics mine.)*

2 Note if there is a range of voices within Scripture. We must not make the Bible tidier than it is in itself. But we also ask, is there an over-arching biblical narrative or development which helps us to make sense of some of this diversity?

3 Do not bypass difficult texts. Who would have thought 20 years ago that an obscure law in *Leviticus* about releasing slaves – Jubilee – would become the theological motif for global debt relief? Conversely, as I note below, sometimes honesty will require us to speak out our horror at some of the 'texts of terror'.[25]

4 Ask 'whether applying the trajectory of the biblical narrative seriously leads us to go beyond the explicit teaching of the Bible itself in order to follow through that trajectory in our own historical situation'. For example, the Bible does not condemn slavery but, in time, Christians came to believe that slavery was utterly contrary to the dignity of

human beings as made in the image of God. They went beyond the Bible faithfully.

A little example: we had a gifted Nigerian Anglican priest in college writing a thesis on the household codes at the end of the Pauline Epistles. He was especially looking at the teaching about the roles of men and women in marriage and family. He finished his study by telling us that, in his context, if this teaching was adopted it would radically *improve* the treatment of women. But he then asked a wider question about how we were to understand the purpose of these texts? Were they intended to provide a law for all time (one of Hooker's supernatural laws) or were they, especially in the light of the life and teaching of Jesus, to be seen as contextual and instrumental pieces of teaching by Paul? Their purpose was precisely to improve the treatment of women by men in these Christian communities *at that time*, but hermeneutically this teaching sat on top of a much bigger biblical trajectory, which was about the flourishing of women (and men) in God; and *that* trajectory had a much more radical and open-ended agenda. Indeed it has, arguably, only come to fruition with the (ongoing) liberation of women in the last 150 years. To amend the little bracelet slogan, good Anglican hermeneutics are: 'WWJDN – what would Jesus do *now?*'

The Bible and Honesty

I had just finished (so I thought) leading an ordination retreat and was enjoying our last lunch before the service, when a young Evangelical Anglican ordinand asked for a quiet word. My alarm bells went off. This man was about to be ordained. Standing in a corridor, he asked me if he was required to believe that the ethnic cleansing in Joshua was really ordered by God and was right? In the few minutes that we had, I tried to lay out a variety of possible strategies for handling these texts of terror. I could see that my words were not having much impact, so I said simply from the guts, 'No, you are not.'

And writing here very personally as someone nurtured by Evangelicalism, for whom time with Scripture is like a drink of cool sparkling spring water on a hot summer's day, I have to say that requiring the consciences of Christians to mangle themselves as they try to force themselves to believe that such stories are right (and they can be presented in Scripture as the will of God), is cruel as well as wrong. As Hooker taught over 400 years ago, the standard and plumb-line of Scripture is Christ and Christ has already shown the way when he said, 'It was written, but I say to you. . . ', as he revolutionised over half a millennium of Scripture. If a particular story in Scripture seems to the Church to fall short of the standards of Christ, then Anglicans have been trained by Christ's example to be honest about this. Anglicans are not required to describe as good what is bad in the name of the authority of the Bible.[26] Here, I have touched on the ethical difficulties of Scripture. I could equally have looked at the textual or theological problems. The Bible *just is* an untidy sourcebook for faith. We will not commend faith in the God of the Bible by dishonesty.

To sum up: Anglicans believe that the Bible gives us enough to be saved, but not everything that we might wish for, and it provides a springboard for dynamic forward motion – sufficiency without being suffocating. It is clear in its essentials but is also a text in need of interpretation. Above all it is a book which answers back. It is both formative and transformative for Christians.

All this has very important consequences for the ways in which Anglicans hear the Bible. If Scripture is primary then it will require their best attention. It will function as the bedrock of spiritual life. But attention to Scripture will always be in an ecclesial context and may often be a communal activity. Further, attention to Scripture will be done in the context of prayer and worship and belief, as well as reasonable study. Hearing the Bible is a holistic task. Perhaps it is for this reason that at the heart of Anglican Scriptural spirituality is the Daily Office. In Cranmer's own words about the words of Scripture, in one of his most beautiful collects (Advent Two), we are to 'hear them, read, mark, learn, and inwardly digest them'. The purpose of this is to comfort us and help us to live patiently (grounded on faith despite life's troubles) so that we will 'embrace' the hope of life with Christ for ever. It is a compassionate and pastoral vision of the purpose of the Bible, entirely in keeping with Cranmer's own experience.

Hearing God in the Bible in Worship

The Bible is heard so that God can be heard, and this is done primarily in worship. The first place many sixteenth-century English people heard or read the Bible in English was in their parish church. It remains one of the most moving features of the English Reformation to hear the 'humble' expressing their delight at being able to access the Bible. Cranmer was ada-mant that the Bible was to be available in a language which all could understand:

> And moreover, whereas St Paul would have such language spoken to the people in the Church, as they might understand, and have profit by reading the same: The service in this Church of England these many years hath been read in Latin to the people, which they understand not; so that they have heard with their ears only, and their heart, spirit, and mind, have not been edified thereby.[27]

We should remember that amidst the murk of the 1530s, when Cranmer was complicit in some unsavoury actions and the progress of Protestant theology was hesitant, arguably the most positive achievement of Cranmer, and indeed Thomas Cromwell, was to require that the new English Bible be placed in every parish church.

Cranmer also tried to ensure access to the Bible by having a simple lectionary, so that there was disciplined attention to the breadth of Scripture, not just the parts approved by the local clergy. (That is why Anglicans have lectionaries ... it is to protect local churches from idiosyncratic clergy.)

To catch a flavour of Cranmer's passion for the Bible, dip

into his 'Preface to the Great Bible'. For him the 'Word' was 'light', 'food' and 'fire' – three of the essentials for life. Because his Daily Office was based around the old monastic offices, there is more than an echo in Cranmer of the old monastic way of reading the Scriptures, the *lectio divina* (divine reading), which was a meditative chewing rather than an intellectual analysis. This was profoundly formational for the Classic Anglicans. For the poet-priests we are encountering – Donne, Herbert, Traherne – who lived this discipline of the Daily Office, they were so drenched in Scripture that it is almost impossible to count the references and allusions to it in their poems. In the Daily Office Anglicans 'inwardly digest' the Word in the Bible.

I could not write this section without pausing at the King James translation. It has, of course, as a scholarly translation, been superseded as textual knowledge of the Bible and translation skills have advanced. But by a blessed synchronicity, the King James version was being produced when the English language was in an immensely rich period of development. More even than the Book of Common Prayer, it provided the spiritual heart of English-speaking Christians for at least 300 years and many of its cadences live in the memory long after more correct or more accessible translations have faded. Hear the words of *Genesis* 1:1:

> In the beginning God created the Heaven, and the Earth. And the earth was without form, and void, and darkness was upon the face of the deep: and the Spirit of God moved upon the face of the waters.

A recent book has detailed the precise changes made to earlier versions by King James translators when they worked on this verse: from the insertion of commas and colons to produce the memorable rhythms, to the use of the word 'face' to translate the original Hebrew 'surface' ('surface' was a new and technical word in the early seventeenth century. whereas 'face' was old and English and tangible). And who was most clearly responsible for this beautiful, powerful and meticulous translation? Lancelot Andrewes, harrier of the Puritans, sacramentalist, brilliant scholar of fifteen languages, lover of the Bible. The translating group he directed – which translated *Genesis* to 2 *Kings* – included both conformists and leading Puritans. Uneasy compromise rather than balance perhaps, but out of that extraordinary milieu came the Authorised Version. As Nicolson writes:

> ... Andrewes introduces two new qualities to add to Tyndale's: an aural fluency and the sense of ease which comes from that; and, allied to that ease, a pace of deliberate and magisterial slowness, no hurry here, pausing in its hugeness, those bass colours in the vocabulary matched by a heavy, soft drumming of the rhythm. It is as solemn and orderly as the beginning of a steady and majestic march.[28]

If the only thing the Church of England had done was to organise this translation, it would have been enough to justify its existence.

The point of listening to the Bible is to hear God speaking. Whilst there are theological problems with the modern English Anglican liturgical response to the reading of the Bible ('This is the word of the Lord'), it reminds the congregation every time that they listen to the Bible that they are in a place where they can hear God speak. It is consistent that for most Anglicans the place where they hear God speaking through the Bible will still be in corporate worship. As the *Windsor Report* says:

> This is why, from very early in the Church, the apostolic writings were read during worship, as part of both the Church's praise to God for his mighty acts and of the Church's drawing fresh strength from God for mission and holiness. This, rather than a quasi-legal process of 'appeal', is the primary and dynamic context within which the shorthand phrase 'authority of scripture' finds its deepest meaning.[29]

As an English Anglican priest I am required by the canons to say Morning and Evening Prayer daily, 'being at home and not being otherwise reasonably hindered'[30] and except 'not being let by sickness or some other urgent cause'.[31] This canon is honoured more in the breach than the observance by many of us. However, the discipline of listening with the whole Church (even if I am sitting alone in my cold parish church) to the same passages of Scripture on a daily basis is profound. In his essay 'Concerning the Service of the Church' Cranmer imagined that

> ... the curate shall cause a bell to be tolled ... a convenient time before he begin [the Daily Office], that the people may come *to hear God's word*, and to pray with him. *(Italics mine.)*

The English people gathered daily in prayer around the Bible – this was part of Cranmer's beautiful vision of a Christian commonwealth. It did not happen. But as a curate I was trained to ring the bell and read the Scriptures in church (almost) every day. In a modest way, it can preserve us from the risks of too individualistic a hearing of the Bible. One of the huge encouragements in the last two decades in England has been the rediscovery of the use of a Daily Office, a simple pattern of daily prayers and Bible readings, which can be done in church, at home or when travelling. This has often been a lay phenomenon. Cranmer would approve! By reading the Bible primarily in the context of liturgy, prayer and worship, it reminds us that we are wrestling with Scripture within the life of the whole Church down the ages and in times of conscious relationship to God.

This commitment to hearing the Bible in the Daily Office was exemplified liturgically by Hooker and visually by Herbert. The Elizabethan Church, even by the 1590s, was still not fully staffed by clergy who had a licence to preach. Therefore many services were taken by clergy who would simply read the liturgy and a homily either from the Books of Homilies or one issued for a special occasion. Hooker felt compelled to defend

this practice against the Puritan insistence on the necessity
for a sermon every time Scripture was read. Indignantly he
argued: 'Reading doth convey to the mind that truth *without
addition or diminution*, which Scripture hath derived from the
Holy Ghost.'[32] This is the doctrine of the perspicuity of Scripture lived out. Hooker mocked the Puritan insistence upon
preaching as *the* instrument of salvation by asking if God had
given the Bible only to provide preachers with texts? In
keeping with his doctrines of Scripture and human fallibility,
Hooker reminded the Puritans that the 'Word' was the Bible,
not the human sermon:

> For touching our sermons, that which giveth them their
> very being is the wit of man, and therefore they oftentimes
> accordingly taste too much of that over corrupt fountain
> from which they come.[33]

Herbert expressed this faith in the simple reading of the Bible,
in a visible feature of the church at Leighton Bromswold, when
he made the lectern and the pulpit identical and placed one on
the north and the other on the south side of the church. Perhaps he should have made the lectern more imposing?

We had a visiting student one term, a bright Hungarian
Reformed pastor. He relished the Daily Office. Slightly puz-
zled, we asked why. 'Because I can just listen to the Bible
without someone always trying to "explain" it', was his reply.
Hooker would have understood.

All of this is not without its problematic features. If Sunday
worship were the only time of encounter with the Bible, then
Anglicans would be on a minimum diet. Whilst the Evangelical
'quiet time' can tend towards an individualistic sense of relationship with God, it is at least that. Certainly, a weekly
hearing in a church service of a passage of the Bible, often
poorly read, is not enough to sustain this hearing of the Word
of God. One of the tragic ironies of the modern Western
Church is that we have never had such a plethora of Bibles in
accessible formats, and yet I wonder if the Bible has been
generally as unread in any generation since Cranmer? To go

back to F. D. Maurice: perhaps the Evangelical model of the believer with the open Bible and a personal faith is indeed a divine principle for Anglicans to receive again? But there are other ways in which Anglicans have traditionally heard God in Scripture.

Hearing God in the Bible in Preaching

Given our use of Hooker and Herbert to justify the reading only of the Bible, it may seem strange to begin a section on the need for preaching with them. But Hooker composed another of his purple passages on preaching as:

> ... the blessed ordinance of God, sermons as key to the kingdom of heaven, as wings to the soul, as spurs to the good affections of man, unto the sound and healthy as food, as physic unto diseased minds.[34]

We noted earlier Herbert's love of the pulpit as his 'joy and his throne'. *The Country Parson* can make us smile with its quaint excesses. Herbert advised not preaching for more than an hour and trying to interest 'thick and heavy' country folk by, amongst other things, audible exclamations to God during the sermon, 'Oh Lord, bless my people and teach them this point'! But his intense seriousness that the Word of God needed to be lived and spoken by the priest for his people, and was transformative, is still moving:

> He often tells them that sermons are dangerous things, that none goes out of the church as he came in, but either better or worse; that none is careless before his Judge, and that the Word of God shall judge us ... but the character of his sermon is holiness: he is not witty, or learned, or eloquent, but holy... [35]

Charles Simeon took this very seriously too.

Contrary to some prejudices, it is not always the case that Evangelical Anglicans make the best (or worst) preachers, but they have taken preaching seriously and none more so than

Simeon (1759–1836). He wrote or delivered 2,536 sermons. When published, a diligent reader could have read one a day for seven years... [36] Simeon's family background was typical restrained mid eighteenth-century English prosperity, with a cool religion. His conversion soon after arrival at Cambridge appears to have been out of the blue, though it was triggered by the requirement to receive Holy Communion. Simeon became an extraordinary preacher and leader, and alongside 54 years preaching as Vicar of Holy Trinity, Cambridge, he was at the heart of the spiritual and institutional work of the Evangelical Revival.

We note here two words used to describe his values: 'balance' and 'Anglican'. Pollard points to Simeon's careful balance between Arminianism and Calvinism – a *via media* which believed in both extremes at once, as Simeon teased his zealous contemporaries.[37] And, in an amusing foretaste of Maurice, remember Simeon's delightful epigram: 'Be Bible Christians and not system Christians.'[38] With regard to his Anglicanism, Moule and Smyth devoted whole books to Simeon's respect for the order and treasures of the Church of England.[39]

Simeon was truly a classic Evangelical; preaching Christ, sin, forgiveness and the need for personal conversion, from the Bible, in season and out. (He was hugely unpopular in his early ministry, being locked out of his own church.)

> He [Simeon] would wish his work to be brought to this test: Does it uniformly tend TO HUMBLE THE SINNER? TO EXALT THE SAVIOUR? TO PROMOTE HOLINESS?[40]

Simeon held to the Classic Anglican view on the perspicuity of Scripture:

> I love the simplicity of the Scriptures; and I wish to receive and inculcate every truth precisely in the way, and to the extent, that it is set forth in the inspired Volume.[41]

Simeon tried to make the biblical passage the absolute

template for his preaching. In his own writing on the craft of preaching, he provided the following rules:

1   understand the passage thoroughly so as to come to a view as to what 'you believe' is 'the mind of God in the passage';

2   note the '*character* of the passage' (e.g. declaration, precept, promise etc.);

3   note the '*spirit* of the passage' (tender, passionate etc.) and preach in that spirit.

'Seize the *sense*, the *character*, and the *spirit* of his text.'[42] The Bible, for Simeon, shaped the sermon completely.

But why preach? Why not simply let the Bible speak for itself? Simeon's first answer was that he did just preach the Bible. Part of his commitment to Bible 'not system' was a 'modesty' (a Simeon word),[43] about his capacity to harmonise all the texts. One commentator described Simeon's method:

> He did not consider it his duty to attempt to reconcile all the apparent difficulties in St Paul, but to preach every part of that great apostle's doctrine in its place and bearing, and for the end for which each part was evidently employed by its inspired author.[44]

This reveals a high doctrine of biblical inspiration but modest beliefs about the relationship between Scripture and systematic theology; though Simeon did use the Church of England's formularies as the test of orthodoxy. Above all, Simeon believed that God had condescended to use humble 'means', i.e. human preachers, to spread 'divine knowledge'.[45]

Implicit in the duty of preaching was the assumption that the Bible needed explaining: in other words. preachers must use the gifts of Reason and speech to make clearer the Word of God. Simeon might not have put it this way, but Scripture benefited from the preacher's applying to it a clarifying simplicity and an emotionally intelligent connection to the congregation. At the heart of Simeon's vision of expounding Scripture was an appeal to the hearer's spiritual sense, emotion and conscience. Simeon also stressed the necessity of coherence between the preacher and the sermon in that word beloved of eighteenth-century Evangelicals, 'earnestness'. He himself preached with extraordinary moral and spiritual authority. In other words, Simeon incarnated the scriptural message he preached.

This takes us to the final point of this brief section. Simeon the preacher takes the ancient words of the Bible and makes them relevant to the hearers now. Whilst he disowned artifice, clearly Simeon was a dramatic preacher. Pollard provides an eye-witness example:

> Standing up, he [Simeon] announced his text ('Will a man rob God?' *Malachi* 3.8). With much deliberation repeating his text, he then looked round on the assembled multitude, and said in tones as only Simeon [could], 'You have all robbed Him': and pointing with his finger in various directions, said, 'You! and You!! and You!!!.'[46]

The point of this anecdote is not that we might approve of Simeon's exegesis but that we note the process: the hearers of the Word are being brought deeply into an existential encounter with themselves, the preacher, Scripture, and God. Put simply, they were challenged.

One of the weaknesses of the Anglican spiritual life is the relative absence of moments of crisis or choice, when an individual or community can find themselves confronted by the call to deeper commitment. Without this experience of crisis, which is a natural feature in human life, people look elsewhere for their moments of intensity, and the life of the local Anglican church remains bland. There are a variety of ways of enabling challenge to be part of Anglican life – missions, retreats – but preaching as an instrument of God's Word speaking to individuals and communities *now* is one consistently found in Anglican spirituality.

One last reflection on Simeon, Evangelicals, the Bible and Anglicanism. The classic Evangelical question is, 'but is it biblical?' I hope that this book will have indicated that this is a much more complex question than it first appears. But when pressed to justify Anglicanism biblically, I find myself talking about two sayings of Jesus. The first is from *Mark* 9:40, 'Whoever is not against us is for us.' The second is *Matthew* 12:30, 'Whoever is not with me is against me.' The context of the first saying is the angry desire by some of the disciples to punish an exorcist working in Jesus' name but who was not part of their group. The context of the second is where the Pharisees have accused Jesus of being a servant of Beelzebul. I wonder if the first story lies behind Hooker's ideas. Here Jesus protects another servant of God, but from a different group, because the other is doing the work of God. The work is done in the name of the Lord and for human well-being. 'One Lord, one Faith, one Baptism': so even a Roman Catholic in the sixteenth century can be a Christian. Whereas the accusation by the Pharisees seems to me to be a good example of calling bad that which is good. Indeed, *Matthew* goes on to include Jesus' saying about the sin of blasphemy against the Holy Spirit and another saying that people are most truly revealed by the 'fruit' of their actions. Good trees by definition produce good fruit. Again, this could be the basis for a warning against the spiritual tendency which has often surfaced in the life of the Church, calling bad that which is really good. When we put these two passages together there is a strong pressure to recognise the spiritual worth of others who do not follow in the same visible group and a strong warning against condemning good things in the name of religion. Sounds like Anglicanism.[47]

Hearing God in the Bible in Study

Classic Anglicans were committed to providing a body of clergy who were trained to study the Bible and to preach. Whilst Herbert taught that the key requirements for Bible study and teaching were a holy life and prayer, he also recommended that clergy had a commentary on every book of the Bible, many works of the Fathers, the Schoolmen and even 'the later writers', so that they should be open to learning from others; 'that there may be a traffic in knowledge between the servants of God for the planting both of love and humility'.[48]

In the early nineteenth century some Anglicans received from Germany the discipline of biblical criticism. That is the study of the text of the Bible using all the tools of literary and historical analysis, without giving the Bible the privilege of a sacred text before the analysis. The slogan was, treating the Bible 'like any other book'.[49] Its earliest manifestations were to raise questions about the nature of the Old Testament.[50] It caused an immediate reaction. Pusey (1800–82), Professor of Hebrew at Oxford and the initial leader of the Oxford Movement, hated it and the trigger for the rise of Anglo-Catholicism was initially a rejection of this sort of Liberalism. Evangelicals reacted by re-emphasising the verbal inspiration of the Bible. Thus the focus of the argument came to be on the nature of biblical inspiration and authority. In what sense and how is the Bible God's Word? Partly for sociological reasons (English Anglicanism was deeply inter-meshed with the university system) and partly for theological reasons (the valuing of the place of Reason in the elucidation of the faith) biblical criticism had an earlier and deeper impact on Anglicanism than on most other denominations. We will explore its wider impact on the life and doctrine of the Church of England generally in chapter 5 but here we need to note three features about Anglicans and the Bible as part of this process.

First, the key books which epitomised this sort of biblical study came right from the heart of the English Anglican establishment, and these disputes had ecclesiastical as well as theological aspects. *Essays and Reviews* (1860) numbered amongst its authors Frederick Temple (later Archbishop of Canterbury). It was condemned by the bishops and convocations of the Church of England for undermining the doctrine of biblical inspiration. Temple's later appointment as Bishop of Exeter occasioned a bitter crisis in the Church. Bishop Colenso's mathematical calculations with the Pentateuch in the 1860s provoked a crisis in the Church of England overseas and were a trigger for the calling of the first Lambeth Conference in 1867. *Lux Mundi* (1889) [the Light of the World] tore Anglo-Catholicism apart by accepting the new critical views of the Old Testament and beginning the Anglican journey into *kenotic* Christology. It was edited by Charles Gore, later Bishop of Oxford.

Second, a recurrent issue was the character of the criticism to which the Bible was subjected. Rowan Williams has categorised the attitudes of the 'Liberal' critics into two types. First, there are the Enlightenment sceptics who, in Williams' phrase, 'target the formulae' of the faith as in need of questioning. Second, there are those who express scepticism about human language about God because of the limitations of humankind.[51] He suggests that the Church needs both sorts of scepticism. But when he categorises the former as those who believe that Christian language 'says less than it claims to say', whereas the latter believe that 'Christian language always says more than it initially seems to say', the implication is clear: the latter approach is more life-giving. Williams expands this with a brief case study of Westcott, which we will explore even more briefly, alongside a look at the ideas of Colenso.

Colenso (1814–83) was a Cambridge Fellow, Norfolk Vicar and first Bishop of Natal in South Africa (1853). With hindsight, we can see in him that mixture of prophetic radicalism (allowing converted polygamists to keep their wives rather than dump them) and destructive belligerence (he caused a schism in his diocese) which is so typical of a certain sort of Anglican Liberal. However, we note him here as an example of the knockabout form of biblical criticism which acts both as a cleansing purge but also as a hammer hitting a thumb. He was one of the first Anglicans to apply mockery to the Pentateuch. In his book *The Pentateuch and the Book of Joshua Critically Examined* (first published 1862–79) he set out to demonstrate the unhistorical character of the books, the late origin of the books and their compound authorship: i.e. they were not written by Moses, which was the long-standing traditional belief. Now is not the time to examine these points; rather note the *tone*. Commenting on *Numbers* 3:10 and the workload of Aaron and his two priest sons, he wrote:

> The single work, of offering the double sacrifice for women after childbirth, must have utterly overpowered three Priests, though engaged without cessation from morning to night. As we have seen ... the births among two millions of people may be reckoned as, at least, 250 a day, for which, consequently, 500 sacrifices (250 burnt-offerings and 250 sin-offerings) would have been offered daily. Looking at the directions in *Leviticus* i, ix, we can scarcely allow less than *five minutes* for each sacrifice; so that these sacrifices alone, if offered separately, would have taken 2,500 minutes or nearly 42 hours, and could not have been offered in a single day of twelve hours, though each of the three Priests had been employed in the one sole incessant labour of offering them, without a moment's rest or intermission.[52]

He then went on to suggest that Aaron and sons would have had to eat 80 pigeons a day to keep up!

The contrast to this tone about Scripture in the work of B. F. Westcott (1825–1901), Cambridge professor and Bishop of Durham, is immense. Westcott was regarded by some as a dangerous Liberal, not least because of his involvement with the Revised Version of the Bible in the 1880s, the first new translation into English for 270 years. He was a Liberal in that he was opposed to the prevailing literalism and he was a progressive in his social and political views. But Williams writes of Westcott's 'near-sacramentality' regarding Scripture and describes Westcott's method of study beautifully:

> The Bible is given us by our creator not first as a set of clear narratives and instructions but as something more like a massive canvas depicting the nature of the giver. You need to stand back again and again to see the whole; but you have to crawl over its surface inch by inch, not stopping to abstract and frame one section of that surface, but tracing the connections that, detail by detail, make up the whole.

Interpretation for the believer is thus a shuttling between the closest possible reading of the text, with all the resources available, and the repeated attempt to find words to articulate the complex unity that is being uncovered.[53]

I cannot imagine Westcott mocking even the least acceptable passages in the Pentateuch. Williams categorises Westcott as a Liberal in the tradition of modesty, that humankind ought to be careful not to say too much about God. In this he sees Westcott as striving for a new model of biblical authority that is neither the rigidity of inerrancy nor the scepticism of self-assured Liberalism.

Third, there is no going back. Anglicans must and do re-evaluate the work of biblical criticism, but they cannot un-think the new insights into the nature of the Bible as a human document which have emerged in the last two hundred years. At its best, this has set the Bible free. Anglicans have moved from treating the Bible as a textbook of timeless systematic theology to a thoroughly human, developing, but also given, reflection of God's interaction with humankind. We might regard this as another of those developments where we can describe ecclesial evolution as revelatory.

As we noted at the beginning of this chapter, we are living through another age of transition in terms of how the Church understands Scripture. In particular, questions about how the Bible has been used have come to the fore. And it is not just a question of whether the Bible has been used to oppress people (it has), it is even more profoundly a question of whether parts of the Bible are oppressive.

If Anglicans cannot deny the flawed humanity of the Bible, but also wish to retain their faith that this book is one of God's historic and living gifts, then the answer might be to meet the Bible 'as it is', *expectant* that even in its strangeness it is *still* God's gift and God will speak through it. As Anglicans have confidence to take their questions to the Bible, to spend time expectantly with the Bible, and to act creatively in keeping with its deepest trajectories, then they can believe that God will speak through it again. In Tom Wright's hugely helpful model, we are now in the fifth act of a play.[54] The first four acts comprise Scripture but we are now beyond the world of the Bible. We have to improvise. But we do this in keeping with what has gone before, or else we put ourselves in a different play. And it is in our doing, based on our faith in the Bible, that we may hear God best. Hence this chapter finishes with a reflection on hearing God in the Bible in action.

Hearing God in the Bible in Action

This last example of how Anglicans can hear God's Word is when the Bible is liberated to speak by and into specific contexts. Liberation Theology is not an Anglican invention but some Anglicans have heard God speak words of liberation which have galvanised them into action.[55] To return to the beginning of this chapter, the purpose of the Bible is to enable us to be transformed by God. There is a pattern in history of the Bible breaking out of the shackles within which the Church has imprisoned it and of working with revolutionary power. We have already seen in this chapter how much the Bible came to mean to Cranmer and his contemporaries and how it set them free for a new life. We could look at the way *now*, all across the churches, the Bible is being experienced as a text of justice and liberation. This deep development of 'social Christianity' is the great reformation of our modern era and we might well want to define it as another example of ecclesial evolution as revelatory. But I want to focus briefly here on the work of just one Anglican, Archbishop Tutu.

The Archbishop's life story is well-known. He was nurtured as a Christian and found a home in Anglicanism. His was a pragmatic journey into ordained ministry, though deeply marked by the unusual sight of a white priest doffing his hat to Tutu's mother. Blessed with a good intellect and supportive colleagues, he had the privilege of theological study in the West, on the basis of which he returned to teach the Old Testament in South Africa. One of his students remembers:

He taught us the Old Testament prophets. He was very strong on the role of Amos, on the role of justice, but that was all academic. We never associated it with real life.[56]

Tutu himself was then radicalised by brutal experiences of apartheid but also by the realisation that the academic study of the Bible which he had undertaken did not listen to or speak to the situation of black South Africans. He became a Black theologian and an African theologian, arguing that the only true theology was contextual theology which spoke God's words into specific, not universal situations. Tutu wrote of Black theology:

It is a clarion call for man to align himself with the God who is the God of the Exodus, God the liberator, who leads his people, all his people, out of all kinds of bondage, of sin and disease, into the glorious liberty of the sons of God.[57]

This is a different way of reading the Bible. It catches that sense of the Bible being a vehicle for God's clear words in a particular time and place; words that are a mandate for action.

It is crucial to stress that this is not a political as opposed to a spiritual reading of the Bible. Tutu's discipline in the organisations where he served was clear:

The Church exists first and foremost to praise and glorify God ... So for us prayer, meditations, Bible reading are not peripheral to our operations. These things are at the centre of our lives. We are not embarrassed that we put God first.[58]

But, most famously, he replied when questioned about his overtly political actions: 'When people say the Bible and politics don't mix, I don't know which Bible they are referring to. It's not the one I've been reading.' Hence his prominent involvement both in the anti-apartheid campaign and also in the Truth and Reconciliation Commission. His work can stand as an example of when God, the Bible and hard real-life situations come together, and the Bible speaks, empowers and is liberated itself.

4 'IT WORKS BUT DON'T ASK ME HOW': ANGLICAN TRADITION

One of my abiding memories of being a young Evangelical ordinand is attending a 'Blessing of the Oils and Renewal of Vows Service' in Durham Cathedral. David Jenkins was our bishop and I vividly remember the mischievous grin on his face as he processed in and the black-shirted Anglo-Catholic clergy bowed their heads in symbolic obedience to this 'arch-heretic'! He seemed to spend much of his sermon gently teasing them about sacramental preciousness, but I owe him my pass in Systematic Theology Paper Two (Church, Ministry and Sacraments). 'God doing something for people, with things, to faith' was, as I remember it, his summary of sacramental theology. It was good Anglican sacramental theology: confident in what it believes and experiences, but reticent about God's detailed ways of working.

In this chapter, we will first outline some key Anglican beliefs about the Church (because beliefs about sacraments are inseparable from beliefs about the nature of the Church), before proceeding to think about Anglican sacramental theology. This will take us out beyond the Church to reflect on ways in which Anglicans have described the sacramentality of the world. But the first thing to attend to is what we mean by the word Tradition, the second of the strands in the Anglican cord.

Tradition or Traditions?

First, a reminder of what we established earlier; in Classic

Anglicanism as a source of authority, Tradition came a definite second compared to the Bible. This is still the case in modern Anglican formularies. However, note that the Lambeth Quadrilateral gives high status to two of the creeds, which are in effect part of Tradition, and also to the sacraments of baptism and the eucharist, which are best located on the cusp of Bible and Tradition. Further, we have given theological weight to the argument that some of the institutions of the Church, the canon of Scripture and the creeds all evolved together in an inextricable way in the Early Church. We have also argued that Anglicans do not now exist in some Olympian place but that we read the Bible through the lens of 'traditional' Christian beliefs. Thus, as Hooker reminded us, Bible and Church (Tradition) are inseparable. But we need to define this word Tradition more carefully.

The medieval Catholic Church was not uniform. After the splintering of the Reformation, different national and local churches rapidly developed even more varied traditions of practice and church government. Some of these were sufficiently important that these churches had to make settled rulings on them (as had the Early Church). Cranmer gave much weight to such judgements. Article 34 warned that:

> Whosoever through his private judgement, willingly and purposely, doth openly break the traditions and ceremonies of the Church, which be not repugnant to the Word of God, and be ordained and approved by common authority, ought to be rebuked openly, (that others may fear to do the like,) as he that offendeth against the common order of the Church, and hurteth the authority of the Magistrate, and woundeth the consciences of the weak brethren.

Notice that disobedience to publicly agreed 'traditions and ceremonies' is explicitly condemned here. (For Anglicans this has often been a cause of difficulty. For example, the wearing of certain vestments has been a source of conflict in many decades. The least we might say is that contempt for public agreed common traditions does not have a good pedigree in Anglicanism.)

However there is a second meaning of the word Tradition which is more problematic. This is the idea that alongside Scripture there is a separate stream of authoritative teaching which flows from the Early Church onwards, and which requires a universal obedience. Again, the Anglican Newman is eloquent:

> Whatever doctrine the primitive ages unanimously attest, whether by consent of the Fathers, or by Councils, or by the events of history, or by controversies, or in whatever way, may fairly and reasonably be considered to be the *universal* belief of those ages, *is to be received as coming from the Apostles* ... Infant baptism, for instance, must have been appointed by the Apostles, or we should not find it received so early, so generally, with such a silence concerning its introduction ... The Sabbatical rest is changed from the Sabbath to the Lord's day, because it has never been otherwise since Christianity was a religion.[1]

John Keble (1792–1866), the third of the Oxford Movement leaders and for a time Professor of Poetry at Oxford, defended what was then a very dangerous viewpoint, for an Anglican:

> Because it is affirmed that the full tradition of Christianity existed before the Christian Scriptures, and so far independent of them, we are charged with alleging two distinct systems or words of God, the one written, the other unwritten, running as it were parallel to each other quite down to our own time ... Tradition and Scripture were at first two streams flowing down from the mountain of God, but their waters presently became blended, and it were but a vain and unpractical enquiry, to call upon every one who drinks of them to say, how much of the healing draught came from one source, and how much from the other.[2]

This was a hugely contentious argument for the contemporaries of the Oxford Movement, not least because it had been at the centre of Reformation conflict. The Council of Trent had, reactively, stressed the authority of the Church and of Tradition alongside that of the Bible to counter the doctrine of *sola scriptura*. To contradict this, Article 20 specifically denied that the Church had authority to *require* certain beliefs unless they were to be found in Scripture. Later Anglicans, even those with a high view of Tradition,[3] had preserved the primacy of Scripture. The challenge to this by the Oxford Movement was genuine innovation.[4]

It is now an acceptable historical perspective that there were traditions in the Early Church which shaped the evolution of doctrine and practice and which did have a separate life, for a considerable time, from that of Scripture. Indeed, when looking at the examples Newman cites, it is striking that Christian worship changed to Sunday from the Jewish Sabbath without clear teaching on this being recorded in the New Testament. This practice, as certainly as anything, does go back to the Resurrection and the Apostles. However, the idea that we can claim that other practices were *universal* in the Early Church, for example infant baptism, and *certainly* went back to the Apostles carries much less weight now with historians, and so with Anglicans. Therefore, overall, the idea of Tradition as a separate source of authority is less contentious now, except in certain selected areas.[5] Nonetheless Tradition still carries weight for Anglicans. Hooker would remind them that even post-Apostolic Tradition is the collected wisdom of the Church and not to be lightly dismissed.

A Fallen Church and Therefore a Modest Church

It may seem odd to begin an account of Anglican sacramental theology and spirituality with bad news, but the conviction that the Church is fallen – still inherently sinful, therefore prone to sinful behaviour and in need of structures which manage the consequences of sin – is a profound Anglican insight and ultimately conducive to good spiritual health.[6]

The conviction that the Church is fallen is embedded in the Anglican formularies. Article 19 includes the famous section:

> As the Church of *Jerusalem, Alexandria,* and *Antioch,* have erred; so also the Church of *Rome* hath erred, not only in their living and manner of Ceremonies, but also in matters of Faith.

This was not an unusual statement in the sixteenth century, when the churches were busy anathematising one another, and nor is it without humour – I suspect Cranmer's knowledge of the contemporary Orthodox and Oriental Churches was sketchy – but it is theologically significant. The reformed Church of England was asserting that the four great ancient patriarchates had all fallen, not just into temporary sin but into serious errors of belief. This is all the more startling because the Early Church was a foundation to which Cranmer appealed elsewhere for authority. In other words, Cranmer was convinced that even the most important centres of the ancient Church had not been preserved by God from falling into sin and error.

Three brief points about Cranmer are important background as we consider Anglican convictions about the fallibility of the Church. First: it is a moot point how far Cranmer worked his convictions about a fallible Church into his own understanding of the Church. He was of course convinced that the English Church had previously fallen into sin and was still in need of huge reformation, but he was also a person of his era, and retained a very strong sense of authority within and for the Church which he led.

Second: more widely, the Reformers faced serious theological questions. How could an otherwise sovereign God not preserve the Church from sin and error? Or where had the Church (that is the true and holy Church – the Body of Christ), gone during those long periods of sinfulness during the Middle Ages? Cranmer's response was Augustinian, believing that in the visible Church 'the evil mingles with the good' (Article 26), and that 'the decrees of predestination are unknown to us' (Article 17, deleted in 1563), so we cannot certainly distinguish between the wheat and the tares in this life. He was also a good Augustinian in stating clearly that the sacraments were Christ's and were *not* invalidated by unworthy ministers. (See Article 26. Have Anglicans forgotten this?) In practice, all this resulted in a certain pastoral gentleness and inclusivity.

Third: Cranmer's language about the Church was not entirely coherent.[7] For example, it is clear that Cranmer did not exercise sufficient terminological rigour in his use of the word 'Church'. So earlier in Article 19 (20 in 1553) he used a Lutheran formula to describe the Church – 'a congregation of faithful men, in the which the Word of God is preached, and the Sacraments be duly administered' – which implies a sort of congregationalism, but in Article 21 (20 in 1553) he declared, 'The Church hath power to decree Rites and Ceremonies', by which he can only be referring to, at least, a national Church structure.[8]

Returning now to our main argument: all this controversy and lack of clarity has left Anglicans with a very mixed theology of the Church. One of the deep consequences of the conviction that even the greatest of the churches had fallen was that therefore no ecclesiastical institution could be invested with infallible authority. This may, in part, lie behind some of the persistent anticlericalism of the Tudor, and subsequent, governments and wider society. The clergy are not to be let free to run the Church on their own, because their track record is very bad! This was compounded by the grisly and corrupt history of the English Reformation. One of the old standard pieces of anti-Church of England polemic was to point to the disreputable behaviour not just of the greedy and lustful Henry VIII but also of the cowardly Cranmer. There was of course enough sordid reality to justify such criticism. (Cranmer is criticised for not standing up more robustly for Anne Boleyn or later Thomas Cromwell; for dishonestly accepting the office as Archbishop; for dissembling under

Henry; for arrogance under Edward; and for his cowardly capitulation under Mary. Perhaps the most sickening of Cranmer's actions was burning sacramentarians [those opposed to transubstantiation] at a time when he himself was also opposed to it.[9]) No Christian community with all this as part of its history can imagine for a moment that it has an unchallengeable claim to spiritual authority.

Anglicans have paid serious theological attention to this reality. Convictions about the fallibility of the Church lie behind the determined commitment to dispersed authority.[10] No one organ of church authority can be allowed to have a monopoly on power because all organs of church authority are prone to falling, and a monopolistic fallen authority would be very dangerous. And the laity *must* have a role in church government. It is in effect a system of checks and balances. In Bishop Selwyn's words to his synod in nineteenth-century New Zealand: 'neither will I act without you, nor can you act without me.'[11] It may be that this wisdom is one of the insights Anglicanism needs to embody more effectively itself and to share quietly with the wider Church. But its spiritual consequence is an instinctive modesty about the institution of the Church, a caution about claiming too much for it.

One of the most extraordinary examples of this is to be found in Hooker. He argued that even when the Church had excommunicated a person – as the Church of England could still do in the sixteenth century, despite the emasculation of its church courts – this was not a certain guide as to their eternal fate:

> As for the act of excommunication, it neither shutteth out from the mystical, nor clean from the visible, but only from fellowship with the visible in holy duties.[12]

This was because the visible Church was never to be equated with the invisible Church:

> For lack of diligent observing the difference, first between the Church of God mystical and visible, then between the

> visible sound and corrupted ... the oversights are neither
> few nor light that have been committed.[13]

Therefore the visible Church's judgements will always be modest.

Hooker took this much further and at some risk to himself. Because of his simple definition of a Christian ('one Lord, one Faith, one Baptism'), as long as someone or some community had testified to this and, in however minimalistic a way, kept to it, they were still to be counted as Christian, as Church, even if a diseased or corrupt part:

> If by external profession they be Christians, then are they
> of the visible Church of Christ; and Christians by external
> profession they are all, whose mark of recognizance hath
> in it those things which we have mentioned, yea, although
> they be impious idolaters, wicked heretics, persons
> excommunicable, yea, and cast out for notorious
> improbity.[14]

Note, that Hooker is *not* saying that such people are members of the mystical Church. But in this world, they are to be treated as Christians. The Church must be modest in its judgements. Therefore – and he spoke out for this around the time of the Spanish Armada, which was a papal crusade against Protestant England – it was right to say that Roman Catholics as individuals could be Christian and the Roman Catholic Church was still Christian.

Nonetheless, Hooker did not denigrate the visible Church. Because faith is a communal activity and being Christian is about continuity with those who have gone before, the visible Church is not an irrelevance. In one of his most famous passages, Hooker wrote:

> For preservation of Christianity there is not anything
> more needful, than that such as are of the visible Church
> have mutual fellowship and society one with another. In
> which consideration, as the main body of the sea being
> one, yet within divers precincts hath divers names; so the

Catholic Church is in like sort divided into a number of distinct Societies, every of which is termed a Church within itself. In this sense, the Church is always a visible society of men; not an assembly but a Society.[15]

By this Hooker was arguing both for national churches and for the importance of the continuous visible structures and life of these churches, as part of the whole Church. Bradshaw sums it up perfectly:

This is distinctively Anglican, refusing to deify the Church while holding the visible Church and its historic structures in high regard as belonging to the *bene esse* [well-being] of the Church.[16]

It is within this framework that we consider an Anglican understanding of the sacramentality of the Church. (I am using 'sacrament' here as a metaphor.) Remembering Hooker's warning, we can never simply equate the Church with the Body of Christ, but, as the Prayer Book Ordinal puts it: 'The church and congregation whom you must serve, is his spouse and his body.' It is striking that Cranmer used his stylistic trick of repetition and elaboration here. Is this phrasing indicating that the whole Church as well as a specific local congregation is to be taken as Christ's body? Whilst 'sacrament' has become an increasingly popular image of the Church, it is not straightforward to use in an Anglican context, partly because of the complex history of the word within Anglicanism. Nonetheless, because for Cranmer and Hooker the Church is so clearly an instrument of grace, especially in its ministry of word and sacrament, and because of the rich language of the identification of Christ and the Church, Anglicans can legitimately describe the Church sacramentally.

The Anglican theologian who has done most to evoke a rich sacramental theology of the Church, but without losing touch with this ethos of modesty, is Michael Ramsey (1904–88), Bishop of Durham and Archbishop of Canterbury. In his beautiful and lucid book, *The Gospel and the Catholic Church,*

Ramsey argued that the ongoing visible life of the Church was inextricable from the Incarnation. He delighted in organic imagery:

> The Catholicism, therefore, which sprang from the Gospel of God is a faith wherein the visible and ordered Church fills an important space. But this Church is understood less as an *institution* founded upon the rules laid down by Christ and the Apostles than as an *organism* which grew inevitably through Christ's death and resurrection. The Church, therefore, is defined not in terms of itself, but in terms of Christ, whose Gospel created it and whose life is its indwelling life.[17]

Which he summarised:

> ... the impact of the Gospel moulds the form of the Church, and its order itself proclaims that the Christ has come in the flesh and that His people are one family.[18]

This high doctrine of the Church reached a sharp point as Ramsey went on to assert that episcopacy is of the *esse* of the Church.[19] This begins to sound 'unAnglican'. But Ramsey brilliantly, and 'Anglicanly', subverted this potential ecclesiastical imperialism when he reminded his readers that the universal Church was primary and that no one denomination corresponded to the Church. All were corrupted and maimed by schism:

> This view insists that valid orders *depend upon the Church's life*, and that authorization by *the whole Church* is an integral part of their validity. And a corollary of this view is that, while the orders of the Protestant bodies are gravely deficient [note here Ramsey's later passion for reunion with Methodism], the *meaning of the historic orders themselves is maimed* by the divisions in historic Christendom, and that the restoration of outward unity is needed in order that the full meaning of orders may be seen.[20]

Therefore, whilst Ramsey believed that episcopacy was of the *esse* of the Church, it was not Anglican episcopacy that was essential. This led on to one of his most famous passages, which encapsulates his Anglican ecclesial modesty:

> For while the Anglican church is vindicated by its place in history, with a strikingly balanced witness to Gospel and Church and sound learning, its greater vindication lies in its pointing through its own history to something of which it is a fragment. Its credentials are its incompleteness, with the tension and the travail in its soul. It is clumsy and untidy, it baffles neatness and logic. For it is sent not to commend itself as 'the best type of Christianity,' but by its very brokenness to point to the universal Church wherein all have died.[21]

Here is the deep paradox of the sacramentality of the Church. It is, and is not, at the same time, the Body of Christ. We might note in passing that if Ramsey was right, then Anglicanism as an institution is open to very considerable change, including its own death and incorporation into a reunited Church, provided that the values in which it believes are preserved.

We can say more. Anglicans believe they are in continuity with the essentials of the faith of the Early Church. Anglicans also believe that they are only ever part of the whole Body of Christ. Most fundamentally, they believe that the Church is both God-given and a fallible human creation. Therefore, on the one hand, Anglicans believe their role is not so much to make the Church's unity as to preserve the unity it has by virtue of who made it. As Williams argues, reflecting on Hooker: 'The Church exists and is sustained by God's action not human consensus.'[22] But on the other hand, Anglicans also believe that the Church is fully human and fallible. When gathered together, these different strands lead Anglicans to the combination of a *Catholic ethos* (unity and fellowship in Christ must be the primary values) with as *simple a structure* as is needed to sustain that ethos (concise core beliefs and only such ecclesiastical order as is necessary). This is why 'communion' has become the key Anglican word to describe the nature of Church.[23]

Communion, from the Greek word *koinonia*, captures the organic and relational meaning of the Church. It does not disallow the need for structures but, as with Ramsey, they must be organic structures before they are made into institutions. The roots of the recent flowering of this concept lie partly in Scripture (1 Cor. 1:9); partly in systematic theology – the recovery of the understanding of the Trinity as a 'social' entity into which the Church is drawn; partly in the recovery of baptism as the fundamental of Christian identity; and partly in the work of the Ecumenical Movement, where this organic metaphor of how Christians are together both describes the reality of Christian fellowship and provides a way of subverting the institutional barriers between Christians. As the *Windsor Report* reminds Anglicans, communion is both 'gift' and 'challenge'.[24]

This organic sense of the Church also has benefits for Anglican understandings of church life. If we put together the argument from chapter 2 about the essentials of the faith to which Anglicans are committed with the current argument about the necessity for modesty about the authority of the Church, then we produce a commitment to essentials but without the self-assurance which would exclude those who disagree. If we then translate this into an organic model, we will find ourselves talking about a Church where there is a core, but the boundaries may be blurred. Bradshaw uses the metaphor of a 'centre-circumference' model.[25] The Church will be like this for positive reasons, not just by default. In the phrase associated with Archbishop Runcie, Anglicans will be a church with 'a warm heart and soft edges'.

Because this is a dynamic model, this means that there will be tensions and even strains. A spirituality and an ecclesiology of generous orthodoxy will allow for robust debate. It will allow for movement. But it is also likely to produce a sense amongst *some* of those advocating or resisting change that they are on the edge, that they are eccentric! To speak plainly, they are.

But Hooker's warnings against neat and tidy divisions between the healthy and the unhealthy and Luther's teaching that *all* are fallen will undermine the self-righteousness of those 'at the centre'; so Anglicans will remain in communion with Christ and each other, even as they fight together.

Given that the accusation that 'anything goes' is the one that stings the most for Anglicans, it is helpful to summarise the Anglican theological justification for keeping the Church as comprehensive as possible (see diagram on p.131). Comprehension is driven by a consistent modesty about both the Church's authority and the Church's doctrines. There is also a suspicion that the Church's divisions of one age may be resolvable in the next, but that schisms are easier to cause than to heal. To this, we might add the very pragmatic point, which has been present in the debates in the Church of England on this topic, that 'heresy trials' are almost always counter-productive both for the Church and for the individual. As Rowan Williams advocates, 'passionate patience' is the way forwards.[26]

All of this has important pastoral consequences. Again I have to express this carefully because Anglican churches do exercise, properly, pastoral discipline. But if Anglicans have a fundamentally modest view of the authority of the Church, and of the clergy within it, and therefore are cautious about a legal or indeed an inquisitorial role for the Church, then this will affect how they handle pastoral encounters. In England, this applies especially to the occasional offices – baptisms, weddings and funerals – hence its relevance in this chapter.

A young mother comes asking for her child to be baptised. She is in a non-married relationship with the baby's father. She is hazy about Christian faith. But she wants her child to receive (my words) God's blessing. In the parishes where I have served, we would share our faith with such a person and also give them options, for example a service of thanksgiving. But if, when asked if they would still like baptism (or 'christening' more likely), they answered 'yes', then the Church's answer was 'yes', because of the 'charitable assumption'.[27]

Simply put, if someone tells an Anglican that they believe, the Anglican response is to take this statement at face value. 'Judge not... ' It is a modest pastoral theology of humility about the Church and of trusting in the grace of God.

Before we go on to look at sacramental theology proper, we need to note here why ordination matters in this Anglican ecclesiology. It is not that the Church exists primarily in the clergy. The *Porvoo Common Statement* has made explicit what has, I think, long been Anglicanism's operative theology, which is that *apostolicity* is carried by the whole people of God, not just the ordained. But a combination of biblical discernment, deep faithfulness to traditional patterns in the Church, and the wisdom that comes from generations of settled pastoral care and mission, means that Anglicans know they need 'ordering'. There is no such thing as a structureless human community, or Church, and therefore the issue is about appropriate structure. Whilst honouring the Reformation recovery of the vocation of all Christians to be Christlike in their daily lives, the Church of England preserved in its Ordinal the special calling of the ordained. We have already studied Cranmer's Ordinal, so we finish this section with more reflections from Hooker.

Hooker stated that the purpose of ministry was to apply to humankind 'the sovereign medicines of grace'.[28] He expounded in the *Laws* his high doctrine of the Church when he contrasted the indirect appointment of 'princes' by God with the 'direct commission' by Christ of his 'ambassadors' [the clergy]; this was radical in the era of the 'godly prince'. In a striking summary of ministry, Hooker wrote:

> What angel in Heaven could have said to man as our Lord did unto Peter, 'Feed my sheep: Preach: Baptize: Do this in remembrance of me: Whose sins ye retain they are retained: and their offences pardoned whose faults you shall on earth forgive'?

In a passage which takes us into our discussion of an Anglican theology of sacraments, Hooker went on:

> The power of the ministry of God raiseth men from the earth and bringeth God himself down from heaven, by blessing visible elements it maketh them invisible grace, it giveth daily the Holy Ghost, it hath power to dispose of that flesh which was given for the life of the world and that blood which was poured out to redeem souls... [29]

Hooker's passion for ordered sacramental ministry is evident.

'It Works But Don't Ask Me How'

Anglican sacramental theology and spirituality was formed at
a time of bitter controversy, especially about the eucharist. It
is worth pausing to remind ourselves again of the horror of
Christians killing each other because of what they believed
happened to the bread and the wine during a communion
service. There were real issues at stake – real in the sense that
they were often to do with the power of the Church and its
clergy. Therefore, I think it is no surprise that the settled
approach of Classic Anglicanism was a form of the *via negativa*.[30] We will listen in a moment to Hooker and Andrewes and
hear them speaking with one voice: 'we are grateful for the
grace we receive in the sacraments but are not over-precise as
to how God gives this grace.'

First, a brief comment about Cranmer. It ought to be easier
to describe Cranmer's views about sacraments, and especially
the eucharist, than most other aspects of his theology because
his published writing was on this topic.[31] Indeed, some have
thought that they had a clear understanding of Cranmer's
views. Dix famously described Cranmer's 1552 Communion
service as 'the only effective attempt ever made to give liturgical expression to the doctrine of "justification by faith"'.[32] If
there is one area of Cranmer's ministry that has given most
offence to later Anglican Catholics it is his eucharistic liturgy
and rubrics. It is the case that in 1552 the prayer of consecration is minimalist and the words of administration are
memorialist. The congregation do not offer anything to God,
except themselves and their praises, and that mostly after
reception. There is almost no reverence for the consecrated
elements; indeed, the curate was encouraged to bring home
the bread and wine after the service (though there is some
ambiguity as to whether these were the consecrated elements
or not). The stone altars were (supposed to be) destroyed and
communion was celebrated with the congregation kneeling
around a portable wooden table in the chancel.

And yet Cranmer's liturgical expertise and conservatism

meant that some key ingredients of the ancient and medieval services were retained. Another deeply Anglican prayer, the Prayer of Humble Access, is a Cranmerian composition,[33] but is a mixture of a translation from the Eastern Liturgy of St Basil, biblical verses and Aquinas. It is strongly realist in its language. We are to 'eat the flesh of thy dear Son' and to 'drink his blood'. Even the clearly Protestant prayer of consecration contains more of this realist language. (How could it not, given Cranmer's Patristic scholarship?) Most significantly, the fact that the words of institution are set as a prayer, not as a reading, as was the Reformed tradition, was the strongest act of continuity with ancient and even medieval eucharistic spirituality. It is no surprise that the most sensitive scholars are reduced to describing Cranmer's eucharistic theology simply as 'Cranmerian'.[34] And MacCulloch offers the very helpful phrase 'spiritual presence' to describe Cranmer's understanding of the presence of Christ in the eucharist.[35]

In other words, Cranmer had a richer theology and spirituality of sacramental grace than that for which he is sometimes credited. This is confirmed by the Articles. Article 25 (slightly amended from 26 in 1553) states:

> Sacraments ordained of Christ be not only badges or tokens of Christian men's profession; but rather they be *certain sure witnesses* and *effectual signs of grace* towards us, by the which *he doth work invisibly in us*, and doth not only quicken, but also confirm our faith in him. *(Italics mine.)*

Notice the certainty of the language: these are 'effectual signs'. That is they achieve their effect. We might say, 'God does things to people through sacraments.' Though carefully hedged around with Protestant qualifications, this left a rich sense of sacramental grace at the heart of Anglicanism.

This was precisely picked up and amplified by Hooker:

> For we take not baptism nor the eucharist for bare resemblances or memorials of things absent, neither for

naked signs and testimonies assuring us of grace received, but (as they are indeed and in verity) for means effectual whereby God when we take the sacraments delivereth into our hands that grace available unto eternal life, which grace the sacraments represent or signify.[36]

And because his soteriology was strongly orientated to union with Christ, for Hooker the eucharist was crucial. The following quotation gives a flavour of this passion (he is citing an older text which is written as if from Christ):[37]

> ... *this hallowed food, through concurrence of divine power, is in verity and truth, unto faithful receivers, instrumentally a cause of that mystical participation, whereby as I make myself wholly theirs, so I give them in hand an actual possession of all such saving grace as my sacrificed body can yield, and as their souls do presently need, this is* to them and in them *my body...* [38]

In other words, in the eucharist we are made participants in Christ's life, as he gives us his grace in 'his body'. But this is to those who are faithful. Hooker exemplified what I think is the Classic Anglican ethos about the sacraments, which is that the focus is on Christ as giver and on the human recipient of grace, not so much on the instruments of grace: 'The real presence of Christ's most blessed body and blood is not therefore to be sought in the sacrament, but in the worthy receiver of the sacrament.'[39]

The Anglican rejection of transubstantiation, which was sustained with great vehemence throughout the period of Classic Anglicanism, was driven by a rejection of the importing of alien philosophical (Aristotelian) categories into Christian theology. Trying to believe in 'substances' and 'accidents' obscured the mystery of Christ's presence. In the face of that mystery, Hooker believed, the only proper response was silence and gratitude:

> All things considered and compared with that success which truth hath hitherto had by so bitter conflicts with

errors in this point, shall I wish that men would give themselves to meditate with silence what we have by the sacrament and less to dispute of the manner how.[40]

But the gratitude was intense. It provoked one of those outbursts of spontaneous praise in Hooker:

> ... what these elements are themselves it skilleth not, it is enough that to me which take them they are the body and blood of Christ, his promise in witness hereof sufficeth, his word he knoweth which way to accomplish; why should any cognition possess the mind of a faithful communicant but this, O my God thou art true, O my soul thou art happy![41]

There is one other feature of Hooker's sacramental theology which we must not overlook. In direct contradiction of Calvin, Hooker argued that in normal life, actions were often more effective than words:

> We must not think but that there is some ground of reason even in nature, whereby it cometh to pass that no nation under heaven either doth or ever did suffer public actions which are of weight, whether they be civil and temporal or else spiritual and sacred, to pass without some visible solemnity: the very strangeness whereof and difference from that which is common, doth cause popular eyes to observe and mark the same. Words, both because they are common, and do not so strongly move the fancy of man, are for the most part but slightly heard: and therefore with singular wisdom it hath been provided, that the deeds of men which are made in the presence of witnesses should pass not only with words, but also with certain sensible [felt with the senses] actions, the memory of whereof is far more easy and durable than the memory of speech can be.[42]

This is a fascinating example of Hooker's method. Here he is, in effect, using Reason and experience to inform a theological judgement. Behind this lies a wider conception of what it is to be human, which is about embodiment as opposed to being a mind or a spirit uneasily inhabiting a body. This is a first taste of a wider sacramentalism which we will explore shortly.

We have already encountered Lancelot Andrewes in a variety of roles. We can explore his passionate sacramental theology and spirituality by taking one example, his 1617 Easter Day sermon in Durham Cathedral. Andrewes contrasted the limited nature of the sign of Jonah being released from the belly of the great fish, a traditional symbol of the resurrection, with the efficacy of Christ's sacraments:

> For some other [Christ's sacraments as opposed to Jonah's work] there be that *shew and work both* – work what they show, present us with what they represent, what they set before us, set or graft in us.[43]

Note these words: the sacrament 'works' what it 'shews'. In other words, it achieves in the believer that which it outwardly contains. (Here Andrewes is showing his deep dependence on the Cranmerian settlement, not least Article 25.) In baptism, we are washed clean as the water washes; in the eucharist we are united with Christ as we eat the consecrated bread and wine. Therefore, for Anglicans to neglect these means of grace is to ignore this spirituality. Remember Cranmer begging in his exhortations in the communion service:

> ... according to mine office, I bid you in the name of God, I call you in Christ's behalf, I exhort you, as you love your own salvation, that ye will be partakers of this holy Communion.

This is not the voice of a man indifferent to sacramental spirituality.

In his sermon, Andrewes demonstrated his facility with the technical language of sacramental theology, handling lightly the language of matter and substance, form and circumstances. This was not a trivialised sacramental theology. Andrewes then proceeded to expound the nature of sacraments, demonstrating his primary concern for the action of the sacraments on the faithful believer but without losing a sense of reverence for what they are in themselves. As Bishop Kenneth Stevenson pointed out, this is sacramental theology 'that is strong without being impersonal, and humanward without becoming entirely subjective'.[44] It is quintessential Anglican sacramental theology.

Andrewes elsewhere did of course did go far beyond Cranmer in his theology of the real presence and eucharistic sacrifice. Cranmer could not have preached, as Andrewes did:

> For look how we [in the eucharist] do give back that He gave us [His Body], even so doth He give back to us [His Body in the form of bread] that which we gave Him, that which He had of us.[45]

As Stevenson makes clear, in his careful language about the eucharist as a re-presentation of the sacrifice of Calvary but not a repeat of Calvary, Andrewes is 'strangely prophetic' of the modern ecumenical convergence.[46] This has found its way, cautiously, into modern English Anglican eucharistic rites, though the focus remains – with Cranmer – on the eucharist as a gift to us, to which we respond with a grateful sacrifice of thanks and praise. Stevenson provides an exquisite quotation from Andrewes' 1610 *Responsio* [reply] to the Roman Catholic polemicist, Cardinal Bellarmine:

> And that sacrifice [i.e., Christ's] but once actually performed at His death, but ever before represented in figure, from the beginning; and ever since repeated in memory, to the world's end. That only is absolute, all else relative to it, representative of it, operative by it.[47]

Whilst it would be foolish to deny the gulf between this (and also Andrewes' own liturgical practices) and Cranmer, the focus on the essence of the sacraments and on modesty above all else *is* in keeping with the ethos of Cranmer and Hooker. In the most famous of Andrewes' sayings on the eucharist, we hear this modesty loudly:

Christ said, 'This is My Body.' He did not say, 'This is My Body in this way'. We are in agreement with you as to the end; the whole controversy is as to the method. As to the 'This is,' we hold with firm faith that it is. As to the 'This is in this way' (namely, by the Transubstantiation of the bread into the Body), as to the method whereby it happens that it is, by means of In or With or Under or By transition, there is no word expressed. And because there is no word, we rightly make it not of faith ... We believe no less than you that the presence is real. Concerning the method of the presence, we define nothing rashly... [48]

It was partly to this rich sacramental tradition, though not always to its moderation, that the nineteenth-century Anglo-Catholics looked back.

Active Earthy Sacraments

In this next section the focus is not so much on the theorists of the Oxford Movement – Keble, Newman and Pusey – but on the second and third generations of 'do-ers', the 'slum priests', who took the reconstruction of Anglican Catholicism, gave it an earthy content, and silenced their opponents by the sheer quality of their lives.[49] Not that the theory was unimportant – we will return to that briefly – but it is in the reality of their lives that this sacramental theology has power.

We could look at many examples but one will suffice: Robert Dolling (1851–1902). He was an Irish Protestant who was caught up in the radical exhilaration of late nineteenth-century urban Anglo-Catholicism. He had an unhappy time during training, when he announced that the Oxford Movement was 'made up out of books', but thrived when given charge of St Agatha's, Portsmouth in 1885. It was a difficult, poor parish with many of the disadvantages of a naval port: drunkenness, violence, prostitution, crime, family breakdown. His achievement there in 10 years was staggering: he built up a vibrant church life and also engaged effectively in social action.[50] He resigned after one quarrel too many with his bishops – the third altar in his church to pray specifically for the dead pushed the Church of England too far – but he eventually found another post in Poplar, in East London, where he served till an early death from overwork.

Apart from this remarkable record, what is striking is the centrality of the sacramental presence of Christ to his spirituality and ministry. His normal working pattern was to celebrate 'mass' at least daily. He was not liturgically precious about the minutiae of ritual, though he was committed to the full panoply of nineteenth-century Anglo-Catholic practices, not least because they were alive and attractive. Palmer quotes him:

> I believe you want two kinds of worship – one very dignified and ornate, which enables them [the people] to realize that they are making an offering to the Lord of Heaven and Earth; the other very simple and familiar, that they are talking to a loving Father who knows all their needs and wants to help them. If you had the ornate worship alone, there would be a danger of mere ritualism. If you had the familiar worship alone, there might be a danger of what some people seem to be so unnaturally afraid of – too much familiarity. At any rate, saying Evensong every night, you would certainly have neither of the dangers, but, on the other hand, you would have none of the educational or heart-touching power.[51]

Dolling had a broad conception of Christ's work. This was salvation of bodies as well as souls. Dolling was an active Christian Socialist and in the last great conflict of his life, he challenged the Water Board in Poplar about their inadequate service, declaring that Christ was as concerned with the drains of Poplar as he was with people's souls. 'I speak out and fight about the drains because I believe in the Incarnation.' The sense I have from studying his life, and those of his colleagues, was that it was precisely the sacramental presence of Christ in the bread and the wine at the altar which gave them the conviction and the energy to believe and live so passionately that Christ was truly present in the midst of their battered communities. 'As God the Father wills to be known in the Incarnation, so the Son of God wills to reveal himself in the breaking of bread... '[52]

A Sacramental World

This was all part of a wider sacramental sensibility, which believed that this world is still fundamentally God's world; that it speaks of God and that God's qualities permeate it:

> There is a book, who runs may read,
> which heavenly truth imparts,
> and all the lore its scholars need,
> pure eyes and Christian hearts.
>
> The works of God above, below,
> within us and around,
> are pages in that book, to show
> how God himself is found.
>
> Two worlds are ours: 'tis only sin
> forbids us to descry
> the mystic heaven and earth within,
> plain as the sea and sky.[53]

So had written Keble in his best-seller, *The Christian Year*, first published in 1827, as the poem for Septuagesima Sunday. This poetry was part of the Romantic Movement which had re-sacralised Nature, but it was also a life-giving traditional Christian insight.

If this world is sacred and sacramental, then it follows that human beings are sacramental and that human spirituality has tangible, not just spiritual, form. As the Anglican Newman wrote:

> Religion must be realised in particular acts in order to its continuing alive ... There is no such thing as abstract

religion ... Scripture gives the *spirit*, and the Church the *body,* to our worship; and we may as well expect the spirits of men might be seen by us without the intervention of their bodies, as suppose that the Object of faith can be realised in a world of sense and excitement, without the instrumentality of an outward form... [54]

This was in part why the Oxford Movement led to a richer ritual in worship. They argued that this appealed to the whole of a human being, not just the mind, which was their allegation against the other traditions.

The core of this theology was the doctrine of the Incarnation, because here God in Christ both united 'human being' in its fullness to himself and demonstrated that he was using human and tangible means to work out his purposes on earth. As Manning, another Anglican to become a Roman Catholic Cardinal, wrote in his Anglican days:

The Incarnation is the channel of His influence, of His Presence. He dwells in man as He never dwelt before ... He took our manhood and made it new in Himself, that we might be made new in Him... [55]

We can hear the echo of Hooker. But as with Hooker, it is very important not to allow our modern flavouring of the word 'incarnation' to obscure the wholeness of this older conception. This was not, as in modern polemics, incarnation as opposed to atonement. Both were held inextricably together. In our jargon, we would have to talk of the significance for humankind of the whole 'Christ event'.

This took sacramental shape, of course, in the eucharist itself. As Keble wrote:

Fresh from th'atoning sacrifice
the world's Creator bleeding lies,
that man, His foe, by whom He bled,
may take Him for his daily bread.

O agony of wavering thought
when sinners first so near are brought!
'It is my Maker – dare I stay?
My Saviour, dare I turn away?'[56]

But we must stress the growing impact of this sacramental
theology on how Anglo-Catholics, such as Dolling, conceived of
God's mission, and the long-term effect this has had upon
modern Anglicanism. To return to the work of Ramsey, he put
it very simply:

> First, let us agree that the priority is to preach the gospel
> to men and women so that they may be converted to our
> Lord. But if a person is to be truly converted the conver-
> sion must embrace all his personal and social relation-
> ships ... Convert him you say. So be it, but the Christ to
> whom you convert him wants the whole of him.[57]

The 'whole of him'. It is this conviction that God loves the
whole of human beings, not just their spirits, that has been one
of the theological driving forces behind the revolution of social
Christianity in the last 150 years. It has a sharp relevance.
Whilst he is critical of the sometimes vague sacramental
principle beloved of generations of Anglican theologians,
Rowan Williams reminds us that the sacraments teach and
embody the love of God, even in the most extreme of human
situations:

> We may find it odd that sixteenth-century Spanish theo-
> logians had to argue about whether the native peoples of
> the Americas were human (and so able to be converted to
> the Catholic faith), but, as they and their compatriots well
> knew, there was an immediate political linkage between
> being capable of receiving baptism and the capacity to be a
> 'citizen'. To be even potentially the object of affirming
> regard and adoption [in baptism] makes certain policies
> such as systematic enslavement of one group by another a
> good deal more problematic ... we need to remember that
> the appropriateness of baptizing slaves was still being

questioned in *British colonies* in the eighteenth century...[58]

Personal Postscript

As an Evangelical curate, I had not expected that presiding at the eucharist would be such an intense experience or that it would become a focus of my own spirituality. I found it to be simply true that in the eucharist, the most significant people and events of the day or the week came with us to our Lord's Table, and that Christ's presence was never so close as when we broke bread together. There are many reasons why the eucharist has become so central to some modern Anglicans, in a way quite unlike many of our Anglican spiritual ancestors, who would have existed on communion as little as three times a year. The Bible, preaching and the Daily Office sustained them. But it is not a choice of one or the other. In keeping with a theology and spirituality of balance, Anglicans can have both. It is true and frightening that Ramsey's words apply especially to priests, but the sense of the tangibility, the close-ness, the holiness and the love of Christ present at the eucharist is for all Anglicans:

> As teacher and interpreter of the Eucharist, and as the one who leads the people in their sacramental worship, the priest has an immense role. But for him, in his own life, the Eucharist is more than that. As Christ's own minister in the words and the acts of the consecration he is drawn closer to Christ's own priesthood than words can ever tell. You will find yourself, as celebrant at the Eucharist, privileged with a unique intensity to 'be with God with the people on your heart'.[59]

Anglicans have a rich, wide and deep sacramental spiritual Tradition, which at its best, is not marred by preciousness or rigidity. It is kept open by healthy doses of, especially, Reason.

5 'GOD-GIVEN REASON'

I remember running a seminar on Anglican Liberalism. The group included three bright committed Evangelical Anglican ordinands. Instead of starting with history and theology, we started with a flip-chart exercise, 'Why might someone want to be a Liberal?' We filled several sheets with largely positive comments. I paraphrase: 'freedom to think, freedom to ask questions, freedom to get it wrong without fear'. There was a little silence in the room when we finished and looked back at what we had written. I couldn't help saying, 'What have we done as Evangelicals that these values of freedom and openness, of lack of fear, of confidence in God's grace and human Reason, have been squashed amongst us?' It was a little epiphany for me. Liberalism has, at least in part, brought life.[1]

In this chapter, we explore the third of the Anglican trio, Reason (and also theological Liberalism, though the two are not to be equated). We can notice again where some tensions arise within the three-strand system, because Reason is both a method and a source of authority.[2] (In reality there is not an absolute distinction between these definitions of Reason.) It is therefore the slipperiest of the three Anglican theological authorities.

Discussion of the potential of the human mind will also take us into another crucial Anglican word: the 'vernacular'. Reason does not exist in a cultural vacuum. What does Reason mean in the context of postmodern Britain in contrast to postcolonial Africa? What is revealed as Christianity is indigenised into a local culture?

As we reflect on this wider definition of Reason, so we will find ourselves drawn into considering the place of experience. Some Christian traditions explicitly give weight to experience as the fourth leg of the theological chair.[3] Because experience, when considered in a theological context, is always handled reflectively, I prefer to keep it broadly under the heading of Reason, but this significantly expands Reason as a category. This means we also have to think about how we justify paying attention to experience theologically. Is this just about having to cope with the messes of human living, or is there a deeper principle here, of discerning God's wisdom?

If we define wisdom as the navigation of the interface between real life and our principles, then it is a close cousin to Reason. But the language of wisdom may help us to subvert purely cerebral accounts of how human beings make sense of this world and God. Further, this wisdom is about communal lived experience. But we are getting far ahead of ourselves. We must first define this word Reason.

So What Is Reason?

In the most basic sense, Reason is about how human beings think and discuss. We 'reason' together. We could offer sophisticated accounts of how an argument is to be conducted, of rules of logic and evidence. But already this is taking us into a second meaning of Reason, because what counts as good evidence is not fixed. Once upon a time it was enough to cite an authority for an argument to have weight, whether it was the Bible or the Fathers. Later, only that which was scientifically verifiable could be counted as weighty evidence. Neither of these viewpoints might strike a postmodern person as reasonable. A little historical perspective here may help.

First, it is worth reminding ourselves of the view put forward in chapter 1, that the Liberal tradition of how to live christianly has a long pedigree within Anglicanism. Hooker was a self-conscious advocate of the valuable role of Reason. He stood in the tradition of Thomist Christianity, where Reason is received as a gift from God within a God-shaped universe.

However, in terms of intellectual history, Hooker was not an Enlightenment advocate of Reason, where Reason stands separate from and increasingly disallows the world of faith.

That was more like the Enlightenment world within which Butler lived. For these Enlightenment Christian rationalists, Reason and faith were truly allies. They believed that clear thinking about theology and about human life showed that they cohered; though increasingly the emphasis came to be that what was believable was what was reasonable. Hence the title of Locke's famous book, *The Reasonableness of Christianity as Delivered in the Scriptures* (1695). In Greer's phrase, Reason was coming to sit in judgement over Scripture;[4] though given my argument that Reason was *always* used in the interpretation of Scripture, perhaps it is more accurate to say that Scripture was being evaluated by what was credible in certain Enlightenment academic circles. This was not always a precursor to disbelief. Quite the opposite; for men like Locke, Christianity could indeed be proved rationally.

This initially mid and late seventeenth-century movement was also a self-conscious reaction against the dogmatism, intolerance and horrors of the wars of religion: the experience of the failure of strict advocacy of the authority of the Bible or of Tradition to build the Church. The name given to some members of this movement in England, the Latitudinarians, or 'Latitude Men', shows its essence. They tried to be as inclusive as they could be, according to their insights at the time.[5] The Enlightenment, which can be portrayed as an entirely negative assault on Christianity, was in part a reaction by *Christians* as they tried to discern a way of being Christian that set up fewer boundaries with other Christians and that had stronger connections to the world around them.[6] It was, of course, also an increasingly fierce assault on Christianity itself and its place in public life, and this has left a legacy of unreflective secularism.

The Enlightenment was the stepping-stone to the nineteenth-century explosion of learning, as intellectual study became professionalised and increasingly divorced from the

Church. Theology went from being the 'Queen of Sciences' to having to fight for a hearing in dialogue with new disciplines, such as economics and later sociology or psychology, which claimed to give better understandings of the human condition. All this was set alongside the shift to a dominantly scientific paradigm of what counted as truth. Reason, in these new modernist forms, was now often a powerful rival to faith, and Christian theologians struggled to keep the debate open. This was part of the backdrop to the nineteenth-century 'Broad Church' movement which tried to engage with these developments and also to keep the Church of England open, as they saw it, to as broad a cross-section of English society as possible. Thereby they hoped to engage in the renewal of national, not just Church, life.[7]

But now, in the postmodern West, where society is emerging from the modernist world view, belief in the objectivity of the human mind has been severely criticised and confidence in science has been battered. We can add to this the swamping of human minds by a tidal wave of information and complexity, and also a recovery of the sense of people as whole beings, shaped by body and emotion and psyche as well as 'pure' thought. In this context, the meaning and status of Reason is much more slippery.[8]

To sum up with a couple of metaphors. Reason is the air that we breathe. We cannot talk of God without using our minds and thought-processes. It is spiritually essential. But the idea of Reason as a separate, and most reliable, way of accessing truth is gone. It is now a fragile strand of the cord.

Nonetheless, if I am right in suggesting that we conceive of the Enlightenment, at least in part, as a healthy reaction against authoritarian versions of Christianity in Early Modern Europe, then we might regard the modern Church's fundamental commitment to reasonable dialogue as a piece of ecclesial evolutionary wisdom. The Church has had to learn that coercing people into faith is wrong. There is an enforced modesty here; even if the old rhetoric about the clear-cut authority of Reason has now been exposed.

We must now explore Reason further, with some sharper theological questions. First, what is the relationship between Reason and human sinfulness and limitation and secondly, what is the relationship between Reason and the direct work of the Spirit? Here, we go back to Hooker again.

The Limits of Reason?

A major plank of Calvinist theology was the doctrine of the 'total depravity' of humankind. That is, human beings were completely sinful and all parts of human beings were corrupted by sin. As was stated in the Westminster Confession, the most important English language statement of the Reformed faith:

> By this sin they [human beings] fell from their original righteousness and communion with God and so became dead in sin, and *wholly* defiled in all the parts and faculties of soul and body.[9]

Therefore Reason was deeply suspect.

Hooker reacted against Calvinism. He too believed in the deep and pervasive effects of sin but he also believed that Reason was one of God's greatest gifts to humankind, and still had a crucial place in accessing the truth of God. But we have to define this very carefully. Voak has established that, in common with the previous Christian Tradition, Hooker thought there was a sharp distinction between what could be known by non-Christians or Christians.[10] Voak describes these different categories as 'mere natural reason' and 'divinely enhanced reason'.[11] This feels deeply uncomfortable to us, partly because it smacks of Christian superiority and partly because it does not appear to be self-evidently true that Christians know more and more clearly than non-Christians. It feels like a circular power game: Christians believe what they believe because they have been born again and those who disagree are incorrect because they are unspiritual ... We may need to acknowledge that on this specific issue of Reason and sin, we do think differently to many of our Christian ancestors. Wrestling with this issue will take us to important insights.

Austin Farrer (1904–68), a distinguished Oxford Anglican theologian whose work is returning to prominence, was intriguing, and humorous, on this point:

> We believe in God (it was said) by force of reason ... As a positive account of the matter, it is utterly useless ... because it involves us in accusing all well-informed atheists either of mental imbecility or of intellectual dishonesty, or of both. As though their disinclination to believe in God were on all fours with the bias I feel against the tax inspector's estimate of my liability.[12]

But concepts which we have already identified help us in this discussion.

First, we might want to give weight to the insight that Christian minds remain subject to sin and fallibility, and so neat and tidy distinctions between good Christian minds and bad non-Christian minds are highly problematic. This would be in keeping with earlier arguments in favour of an Anglican sense of fallibility.

We might, secondly, want to transpose this into a discussion about the insight that comes from inhabiting a way of life: that there are clear insights which come when a person lives within a particular pattern, which are not available in the same way to those who do not. We will revisit this when we discuss prayer and study. Farrer put it provocatively:

> There is no short cut to understanding God's promises. You cannot do it by the wisdom of this world, or by logical sleight of hand. You can do it by active faith alone, by believing in God who has promised, by persevering in purity of life, in constant prayer, in Christ's sacraments, in obedience to every showing of God's will.[13]

In other words, Reason is shaped by the *practice* of the faith, by holiness.

Thirdly, we can simply recognise, without engaging in moral

and spiritual judgements about superiority, that Christians and non-Christians just do see and understand the world very differently. This is still true, even if we take seriously the insights of apophatic theology. Farrer put it simply and beautifully:

> If God might be comprehended, he would not be God. An over-confident dogmatism is as fatal to theistic belief as scepticism itself: it pretends to prove and to define, only to discover that what it has defined and proved is not its Lord and God ... You can no more catch God's infinity in a net of words, than ... you can fish out of the sea the glories of the dying day.[14]

In other words there is, in part, distinctive Christian Reason.

What then might be the relationship between the Spirit and Reason? Hooker strongly defended the role of (Spirit-led) Reason in the life of the Church but the question remains: in practice, how do we decide what is good? He argued:

> The rule to discern when the actions of men are good, when they are such as they ought to be, *is more ample and large than the law which God hath set down in his holy Word, the Scripture is but a part of that rule...*[15]

As we have discovered before, Hooker says that God's guidance about goodness is broader than in Scripture alone. Proving that God approves of something requires of us the application of Reason to Scripture and the world.

> Sufficient it is for the proof of lawfulness in any thing done, if we can show that God approveth it. And of his approbation, the evidence is sufficient if either himself by revelation in his word warranted it, *or we by some discourse of reason*, find it good of it self, and unrepugnant unto any of his revealed laws and ordinances.

Note that phrase, 'by some discourse of reason'. Hooker is here saying that if Reason leads us to conclude that something is good (and it is not evidently contrary to Scripture), then it is good and pleasing to God. This is a very high affirmation of Reason and indeed of natural human decision-making, which we might call wisdom. Simply put: *'Of all good things God himself is Author* and consequently an approver of them.' Here Hooker is affirming the gift of Reason from God to humankind, and the maturity that goes with its use, but he is also affirming the goodness of much natural human living, all those myriads of things about which we make ordinary decisions and which are part of God's good world.

Voak emphasises this aspect of Hooker strongly and opens up the discussion of the relationship of the Spirit and Reason. He argues that Hooker believed that the Holy Spirit worked in human beings with most certainty through their Reason, rather than through, for example, their emotions or their inner sensations. Thus:

> By making reason the prime instrument of the Holy Spirit, Hooker creates a kind of barrier or filter, between the Spirit and the believer. This is most clearly seen in his statement that the work of the Spirit should be discerned from 'the qualitie of things beleeved or done', as opposed to basing one's beliefs upon the supposed direct work of the Spirit. The believer is inevitably distanced from the Spirit in this process, no longer expecting to detect his [the Spirit's] operations in moments of intense feeling or emotion.[16]

At first sight this may not be a very attractive notion. It seems cold and cerebral. Voak denies this by pointing both to Hooker's passionate joy in the gift of grace by the Spirit and to Hooker's holistic account of worship.[17] And it has one other great merit. It requires Anglicans to use common human tools and criteria for conversation and disallows the appeal to 'special revelation' which can bedevil church life.

Voak confirms our overall reading of Hooker. Citing *Laws* 1.xiv.15, he writes:

> Holy Scripture and reason 'both jointly and not severallye'

serve to give humans knowledge of all that is necessary for salvation, and this is of the very essence of which Hooker's *magnum opus*, the *Lawes*, is built.[18]

Given this very high status for Reason, Hooker finishes this discussion powerfully, with an echo of Jesus' warning about calling bad that which God declares to be good:

We offer contumely, even unto him, when we scornfully reject what we list without any other exception than this, *the brain of man hath devised it.*[19]

In effect it is a form of blasphemy to deny the authority of Reason when properly used.

This is why the favoured slogan of the seventeenth-century Cambridge Platonists, forerunners of the Latitudinarians, and first used by Whichcote, was that Reason was 'the candle of the Lord'.[20] Reason is a means of God's guidance. In a striking piece of continuity, we find exactly the same language being used by Butler in the eighteenth century. After he had argued effectively for Reason's limitations, he stated: '... but it is urged with great caution of not vilifying the faculty of reason, which is *the candle of the Lord within us'.*[21] Elsewhere he reminded his readers that despite his criticism of the capacities of Reason, it was 'indeed the only faculty we have wherewith to judge concerning anything, even revelation itself... '[22]

To conclude this section, one last delightful piece of continuity. During his time at Cambridge, Westcott discovered Whichcote, and (in Patrick's paraphrase) echoed much that we have discovered about this tradition:

Man's ability to know God has not been obliterated by the Fall. Sin is unnatural, and in Christ God re-establishes his loving purpose. There is no sharp division between reason and revelation. In the life of faith, our reason is not to be laid aside, but rather is awakened and stimulated. Reason and faith are not to be separated.[23]

These are some of the deep theological reasons for Anglican respect for Reason and learning.

The Weight of Learning

This respect for learning has positive and negative characteristics. English and North American Anglicanism has been socially embedded in academia and the professional classes and this has shaped how beliefs and values can be conceived. At a trivial level this is the acceptability of the common room or the suburban dinner party. But, as we have seen already, Anglicanism faced a serious intellectual and structural crisis in the nineteenth and twentieth centuries because of the 'weight of learning'.

Whatever the deep divides between Protestant and Catholic and Latitudinarian Anglicans, the common conviction that the Church of England believed in Primitive Christianity – Bible and Early Church – was widely accepted. But the nineteenth century saw this settled assumption fundamentally challenged. As Owen Chadwick summarises:

> Three forces were driving Christianity to restate doctrine: natural science, historical scepticism, moral feeling. Natural science shattered assumptions about Genesis and about miracles. Criticism questioned whether all history in the Bible was true. Moral feeling found the love of God hard to reconcile with hellfire or scapegoat-atonement.[24]

We might add to this the impact of historical criticism on the account of the unanimity of the Early Church. (Note how much of this learning was in non-theological disciplines and conducted by non-Christians – proof positive of the weight Anglicans have given to learning, broadly conceived.) In other words, the authorities that Anglicans had relied upon to provide them with the basis for the faith 'once for all delivered to the saints' were undermined by learning.

A new word has begun to have weight in contemporary Anglicanism, 'reception'. When theological or practical change is suggested for the Church, how is this evaluated? Here, we touch briefly on the phrase *consensus fidelium*, the united mind, practice and sense of the wide body of Christians in a place and, in theory, universally, and 'reception'.

In his detailed essay, 'Reception', Henry Chadwick spelt out with care the mechanisms by which important doctrinal developments in the Early Church were 'received', that is tested, by local churches.[25] This included even the Nicene Creed itself. This is, in part, a simple fact of human institutions. Each group has to be able to make sense of and approve, or not, ideas coming in to it from elsewhere. But it has a wider theological meaning: part of the Body of Christ, discerning if developments elsewhere are healthy. The *Windsor Report* provides a neat definition:

> The *consensus fidelium* ('common mind of the believers') constituted the ultimate check that a new declaration was in harmony with the faith as it had been received. More recently, the doctrine has been used in Anglicanism as a way of testing whether a controversial development, not yet approved by a universal Council of the Church but nevertheless arising within a province by legitimate process, might gradually, over time, come to be accepted as an authentic development of the faith.[26]

Two points are of particular relevance at this point. First, the process: in keeping with the stress on the dispersed authority of the Church, the *consensus fidelium* requires an important role for lay people. Therefore, for example, whilst the House of Bishops within the General Synod of the Church of England has special powers in respect of issues to do with the faith and order of the Church, lay people take a full part in and vote in the relevant debates. Sykes makes the point well that one implication of this process, which has a long pedigree, is that the Church therefore has a responsibility to facilitate serious study by all its members: 'The Christian life was such that an uninstructed or passive laity was unthinkable.'[27]

Second, the mechanism by which such reception is done and

the nature of the outworking of the decisions: Anglicans have to reason together, to study and pray together. Again, Sykes puts this unapologetically:

> Unless I am very much mistaken, this is the only kind of authority justifiable in the universal Church of Christ, and is one which we as Anglicans have every reason to explore, to expound and to defend ... The distribution of God's gifts to the whole Church means that there are *voices* of authority, not one unambiguous, unequivocal *voice* of authority.[28]

He sums this up very simply: '*Any* authority without consent is tyranny.'[29]

One of the deep characteristics of the 'death of Christendom' is that the churches as institutions are now best understood as voluntary societies, not scaled-down versions of sovereign states. This is not an argument in favour of chaos – procedural, moral and even doctrinal discipline is not incompatible with a voluntary organisation (clubs have rules) – but it does mean that the Church's fundamental mode of operation is *discussion before decision-making*. And the greatest penalty that can be exercised in the Church is 'walking apart'. (Of course, the One who is most harmed by schism is Christ. As the *Windsor Report* says: '"to turn from one another would be to turn away from the Cross", and indeed from serving the world which God loves and for which Jesus Christ died.'[30])

For the purposes of this chapter, this question of 'development/reception' is focused in a specific question. Is doctrine open to change on the basis of the new insights of scholars – theologians and non-theologians? The life-story of Bishop Charles Gore (1853–1932), Bishop of Oxford and arguably a founder of 'Liberal Catholicism', reveals the pain and difficulty of resolving this question. He had been at the forefront of theological change with *Lux Mundi* but by the 1920s was fiercely resisting what he saw as the deconstruction of the doctrine of the Incarnation. The question had arisen: once biblical and historical criticism have been allowed to have weight in moulding doctrine, at what stage is their influence restricted? Gore's response was to *require* all clergy to come to the same historical conclusions. But this was seen to be inconsistent and the issue did not go away. Sykes quotes Archbishop Ramsey:

> If criticism is allowed to modify thus far the presentation of the faith, what if criticism questions the substance of the faith as the creeds affirm it?[31]

Can the Church change its doctrine because of the weight of learning?

The Anglican answer to this question is both 'yes' and 'no'. And this paradox will be the springboard which will take us on into the rest of the chapter. The 'yes' is both simple and also complex. It is simple precisely because as Christianity is a historical faith, the possibility of it being proved to be historically fraudulent or misconceived must exist, even though our best reasoned judgement and, I am tempted to say even more, our current reasonable experience of God in Christ, convince us that it is true. It is complex in that we need to ask which *parts* of doctrine can be modified. Is belief in Limbo compulsory for Anglicans? Clearly not.[32] Is belief in the Virgin Birth required? If we remember Henson's words, then it depends on what is meant here by all the words involved – and what is at stake in the belief or non-belief of this clause in the creed? But surely belief in 'Nicene Christianity' is required (i.e. that Jesus Christ is 'God from God')?

This is an appropriate point to note Newman's insight that the idea of a fixed inheritance of faith was not only wrong historically but also tied the Church to a fixity of expression which was unwise; hence his idea of 'development'. For both Evangelical and Catholic Anglicans this has been a very threatening idea. The idea that the faith could develop was deeply alien. Also suspicion-inducing was the consequence that, for Newman, this became a reason for looking to the Church as the arbiter of development. Thus he became a Roman Catholic committed to papal authority. I would not wish to go as far as Newman in commending the idea of development. But it seems to me to be an accurate reading of Anglican history to note at least variation in the way doctrines are expressed or in the emphasis that is put on different aspects of the faith, and indeed the generation of new insights. There is development in Anglicanism.

But now we come to the 'no'. Anglican belief is, however varied in details, part of a broad continuity: Scripture reveals to us God in Christ and this is confirmed by the creeds and the ongoing Tradition, the *consensus fidelium* and, not least, our current experience of God in Christ.

So, to answer Ramsey's question: it is possible for Anglicans to believe that scholarship changes doctrine. To think otherwise is to be self-deceiving. Taking seriously the reality of the partial fluidity of Christian doctrine strikes me as another example of ecclesial evolutionary wisdom. *But partial is not the same as essential change.* Here the answer is that Anglicans might be open to essential change, but that nothing has yet convinced them that it is required. And one of the reasons why Anglicans are held within generous orthodoxy is, as we have mentioned several times, that the question of faith is not just an issue of Reason but is inextricably one of practice. In the famous aphorism of Evagrius (346–99): 'the one who prays is a theologian.'

This was part of Ramsey's answer to himself. He wrote of 'the Anglican sensitivity to the significance of spirituality, the life of prayer, for theology'.[33] We have already heard Farrer stress the same thing; that faith is understood from within spiritual practice, which is itself shaped by study. The deep instinct of Anglicans that prayer and study are not to be divorced – and that the Enlightenment fantasy of disembodied neutrality was just that, a fantasy – means that Anglicans believe in the institutional embodiment of prayer and study. Rowan Williams, reflecting on Ramsey, tries to summarise this core of belief and practice which is Anglican essentialism:

> [Ramsey] did, however, take it for granted that there was a focus to Christian belief and practice which, precisely because it was not a matter of conceptual structures, but a multiple and elusive sense of the divine action in Jesus and the worshipping community, was simply not vulnerable to intellectual or cultural fashion... [34]

One of the insights of postmodernity is exactly that Reason is *never* disembodied. With its location of Reason always within a holistic sense of human being and stressing modesty and a certain fluidity, Anglicanism is well placed to flourish within a genuinely pluralist postmodern world.[35]

In this chapter I have mocked the English Anglican Establishment's over-close relationship with the academic professional classes. But as I look out of my window at Durham Cathedral and the (secular) Durham University Department of Theology and Religion, side by side and institutionally and personally inter-mixed. I think that this way of learning, which celebrates people's faith identities without wishing either to emaciate these or to use those faith commitments as a way of suppressing conversation, is a model whose time is coming again.

There is another aspect to these Anglican perspectives on the relationship of Reason and faith. Whilst there are common disciplines of argument, as we noted right at the beginning of this chapter, what is reasonable in one culture may not count as reasonable in another. Hence, the long-standing Anglican commitment to taking local culture seriously. Anglicans believe in living with Christ in the vernacular.

Living in the Vernacular

We have already had cause to discuss Article 34 a couple of times under the headings of *adiaphora* and of the authority of the Church. Here we focus on the issue of vernacular or national churches. The relevant section reads:

> Every particular or national Church hath authority to ordain, change, and abolish, ceremonies or rites of the

> Church ordained only by man's authority, so that all
> things be done to edifying.

This was of course in part directed against Rome and argued
that the Church of England had the authority to reform itself.
However, when we put this alongside other words in this
Article (see chapter 2) about proper national variation, then
we have the beginnings of a theology of inculturation.

Again we have to describe this *very* carefully. The Acts of
Uniformity meant what they said. Unlike the pre-Reformation
Catholic Church, Cranmer – and his contemporaries in Rome
and in other Protestant churches – did want uniformity. This
was connected to the fear of internal disorder and to the
growing self-consciousness of political states. For the first
time, ever, in England, there was one service book for everyone
to use. This does not feel like inculturation. And it did not feel
like inculturation to the Cornish, who revolted against Cranmer's English and his theology!

But there was another side to this. Looking from England to
overseas, it was not the case that people had been oblivious to
national differences before, but these differences were
becoming more clearly defined in the sixteenth century.
Cranmer, as a Protestant politician, was compensating for the
considerable variation which had already developed amongst
Protestants in barely 30 years. But it was also a genuine
expression of respect for national differences. One small sign
of this was Cranmer and Elizabeth's determination to have the
Bible and Prayer Book translated into Welsh, so that the
Welsh could hear Scripture and worship in language 'under-
standed of the people'. Alongside this was a growing sense in
the Church of England that it was *the* church for the English
people. It had grown in English soil. It was suited to their
needs and temperament. This was an incipient theology of
inculturating the Gospel.

For centuries this remained an incipient theology, because
in fact what happened was that the English culture of the
Church of England was simply exported to America or the

West Indies, embodied in the Prayer Book and the Authorised Version of the Bible. However, in the nineteenth and especially the twentieth centuries, we see the emergence of a full-grown theology and practice of vernacularism. We might look to the individuals involved in this – the early indigenous bishops such as Crowther, the first black African Anglican bishop (1864) in Nigeria[36] – but the key theorist was Henry Venn (1796–1873), General Secretary of the Church Missionary Society. The word 'prophet' can be glibly used but it is surely right to apply it to Venn. In the mid nineteenth century, in a series of policy papers he laid down the principles for the establishment of new churches. These principles were submerged in late nineteenth-century resurgent imperialism, but came back to shape mission thinking in the twentieth century. Venn argued that, following the example of Paul, new churches ought to be 'self-supporting, self-governing and self-extending'. The external missionaries were the scaffolding which would be withdrawn once the local church could meet these criteria. This was both a missionary policy – the missionaries were supposed to be free to move to other unchurched areas – and an ecclesiological policy. Venn's vision was of new national churches.[37]

Another demonstration of vernacularism was the structure of the Anglican Communion. For a variety of reasons, not least English-American rivalry, apart from a few extra-provincial churches or some very new provinces, final legal authority has been kept at provincial level. So the Lambeth Conference, from 1867 onwards, is formally a consultative, not a legal, body.[38] In recent generations this autonomy has become highly problematic, as tensions between the provinces have threatened to break the Communion. Hence the increasingly anguished (and in my view legitimate) criticisms of simplistic autonomy by Runcie, Carey and now the *Windsor Report*. Nonetheless, whilst the old language of vernacular may be problematic in a global village, the careful restraint of centralising authority, precisely so that it does not cramp the culturally sensitive mission of local churches, remains a prime Anglican value.

A structural anxiety and a positive anecdote conclude this section. Until after the Second World War, as well as the Lambeth Conference, the Anglican Communion was held together by common worship. Even where the Prayer Book(s) had been translated into local languages, it was the Prayer Book(s) which had been translated. Despite the exporting of English church party differences to the new churches, this common liturgical pattern was a strong practical mechanism for sustaining Anglican identity. For good missiological and pastoral reasons this uniformity has been deconstructed. (I vividly remember attending a Book of Common Prayer marriage in Nigeria and inwardly shrivelling at the language, the theology, the dreary music and the hopelessly inappropriate vestments, in comparison with the vibrancy of the Nigerian local choir.) But can Anglicans retain a common identity without keeping identical services? New vernacular liturgies have been developed that are suitable for the cultural contexts in which Anglicans find themselves, and their beauty and dynamism are proof of the value of this. But as with the issue of structural autonomy, so with liturgical autonomy. If there is not a *conscious* effort to maintain connections to older common Anglican liturgical traditions, then Anglicans will drift apart. If we do not worship together, we will indeed not believe or even be together.[39]

One year we were blessed with the presence of a very gifted Tanzanian Anglican priest in College. When I have the chance, I invite a 'recipient' of Western Christianity to talk about this experience. Our overseas visitors are invariably gracious about the cultural insensitivity with which the Gospel was brought to them. But this alert young priest decided to tease our English students. He started to explain the policy about converts who were polygamists. This is not a hypothetical issue. I have met a polygamous witch doctor in rural Nigeria, and such people are still being converted. Polygamous converts are allowed in some provinces to keep their wives, though they are barred from certain church offices and are disciplined if they marry again.[40] It was fun to notice who was more shocked by his words, our feminists or our Conservative

Evangelicals. But the Tanzanian patiently explained what happens to polygamous wives if they are divorced when their husband converts. There was silence. This was the sort of wisdom which only comes from indigenising the faith.

Get Wisdom

Anglican views about the nature of this world provide further justification for making positive use of Reason. Remembering one of the disciplines we established in chapter 1, we must note straightaway that there are two main Anglican views about this world. The first is negative. Shaped by Reformation understandings of the fallenness of the world and the sinfulness of human beings, the world was seen as a bad place from which Christians were to be rescued. Remember the words from the Ordinal on the duties of priests. They were to:

> ... seek for Christ's sheep that be dispersed abroad, and for his children, which be in the midst of this naughty world, to be saved through Christ for ever.

We could find many examples of such views from Cranmer to the twenty-first century, and as we will explore in chapter 6, taking seriously the reality of sin and holiness remains an Anglican priority.

The other view of the world is less negative. Earlier in the book, we noted the developing view within Anglicanism that this is *still* God's world. This might take the form of Hooker's natural laws, or the sacramental principle or the more recent view of the English Doctrine Commission that we are not to make rigid divides between God's work as creator and redeemer. There is deep within Anglicanism a fascinating witness to this perspective from Cranmer's own hand, the Collect for Ash Wednesday (from the 1549 Prayer Book).

> Almighty and everlasting God,
> which hatest nothing that thou hast made,
> and dost forgive the sins of all them that be penitent;
> create and make in us new and contrite hearts,

that we worthily lamenting our sins,
and acknowledging our wretchedness,
may obtain of thee, the God of all mercy,
perfect remission and forgiveness;
through Jesus Christ.

There is much in this collect worthy of reflection, but here I want to stress the second line. In Cranmer's mind, God did *not* hate anything that he had made. Therefore, there is much in this world which is to be enjoyed, and learning about it is good.

If there is one Anglican who has helped us to enjoy God's world more, it is the vibrant poet-priest Thomas Traherne (c.1636–74). Beginning life as a Puritan, he chose Anglicanism positively in 1660, being re-ordained, and was deeply influenced by the Cambridge Platonist movement. He served most of his life as a country priest outside Hereford. With many of his works only recently being discovered and published, we hear him freshly.

I have spent much of this book stressing the modesty of Anglican knowledge, and it is the case that, for example, Anglicans have been cautious about too sharp a divide between supernatural and natural knowledge of God; because both forms of knowledge exist in the same fallible human beings and come from the same God. But Traherne's modesty, whilst real, is infused with delight. Indeed, he is almost the opposite of much of the sense of modesty, because he was so enthusiastic about the presence of God in the world around him. The most famous example is his meditation on a country scene when the gap between earth and heaven seems to disappear:

> The Corn was Orient and Immortal Wheat, which never could be reaped, nor was ever sown. I thought it had stood from Everlasting to Everlasting ... Eternity was Manifest in the Light of the Day, and som thing infinit Behind evry thing appeared... [41]

But my favourite is his meditation on 'The Fly':

Had but one of those curious and High stomachd Flies, been created whose Burnisht, & Resplendent Bodies are like Orient Gold, or Polisht Steel; whose Wings are so strong, & whose Head so crowned with an Imperial Tuff, which we often see Enthroned upon a Leaf, having a pavement of living Emrauld beneath its feet, there contemplating all the World, That very flie being made alone the spectator & enjoyer of the Universe had been a little, but sensible, King of Heaven & Earth. Had some Angel or pure intelligence, been created to consider him, doubtless he would hav been amazed at the Height of his estate. For all the labours of the Heavens terminate in him... [42]

Apart from the glorious richness of the language, there is humour here and the atmosphere of scientific curiosity which marked the Restoration period. Clearly Traherne had looked carefully at flies! As Denise Inge explains:

What strikes me again and again as I consider Traherne's vast array of sources and influences is his voracious appetite for learning and a conviction that every discovery could lead one further into truth. There is in him no fear of knowledge, or science or of exploration ... All point to a person of unshakable faith and intellectual honesty. [43]

Traherne's vision of the wise man is passionately joyful and communicates a sense of the 'unimaginable divine generosity woven into the very fabric of the universe' [44]:

He feels, he sees, he tastes, he knows,
he like his Maker grows.

He loves, & prizes all his Works
even as his God doth doe,

and Ponders oft what Glory lurks
in all things he doth view.

While evry thing enflames his soul with love;
and evry thing his Joy, his Bliss, doth prove. [45]

Westcott put all this beautifully:

> Those who are 'in Christ' are bound to serve God with
> their whole being, with their intellect no less than their
> heart and their strength and their substance ... For them
> all that falls within human observation is a potential
> parable of spiritual realities, through which fresh vision
> may be gained of the glory of God. They will be the keenest
> of men to watch for the dawn of new ideas. For them there
> can be no despondency and no indifference. They bring to
> the Lord the firstfruits of all that He has lent them and
> commit their gains to his keeping.[46]

Therefore the search for understanding and wisdom about how
to live in this mixed world, especially when Anglicans believe
that God has delegated to humankind much responsibility for
discernment, must be a high Anglican priority. A Church of
England Doctrine Commission report summed it up clearly:

> Wisdom is not the same as information or knowledge,
> though it includes both. Wisdom is about how we live well
> before God alongside other people in our world. How can
> we arrive at an understanding that helps to shape good
> living? What are the best resources for insight into basic
> features of human existence today? Those are wisdom
> questions.

And:

> Wisdom is not a destination where we or our Church can
> arrive at some time. It is classically described as a way, a
> path, or a journey. There is always more wisdom to be
> found, and the desire to learn it is a core dynamic in good
> living.[47]

A word often used to describe Anglicanism is 'pragmatic'.[48]
Again, like many of the words used in this book, it may not set
the heart racing or even sound especially Christian, but it is
another word for wisdom. This word sums up a great deal of
what I am trying to say in this book. First, the language of

wisdom assumes that whilst there are principles, their relationship to the realities of life is *not* straightforward. As
Hooker has taught us, discerning what to do requires our full
mature engagement. There is a deep modesty about the conclusions which such discernment will reach. Second is the
conviction that this is still God's world, and God's purposes are
for the well-being of the whole of the created order, not simply
the rescuing of individual souls. Therefore, Anglican Christians must try to understand the wider world and discern
God's actions within it. Again, this will be a modest venture:
an 'is it?' rather than an 'it is' discipline. Third, wisdom has
clear goals, the renewal of the whole of creation, but the means
by which this is to be achieved may be experimental, in that
we may not be sure of the outcome. They may properly be
temporary and provisional: 'This is what is needed in this
place, at this time and will only get us to the next step.' So, to
use an old cliché, wisdom learns from experience. If we are not
entirely clear what we must do but we have a general idea,
then as we act and then reflect on our experiences, so we will
learn how to do it better. To use the modern jargon, there is an
element of *praxis* here; that is purpose-driven activity which is
self-consciously reflective. All of this is pragmatic wisdom.

The ethos which we have just been describing has real and
sometimes unexpected consequences for how Anglicans relate
to the world around them. When a Church of England ordinand is applying for a post as a curate, she will be confronted
with a form which asks her to state what style and type of
church she prefers. There are a growing number of categories
– social, churchmanship etc. – but one that might catch the eye
of an outside observer is 'civic'. This is the sort of church which
has strong structural relationships to the institutions of local
government and business, educational establishments, perhaps the Armed Forces. It is the sort of church which may find
itself hosting large civic services. In my experience it is not a
form of ministry which is attractive to those just beginning
ordained ministry, *unless* they have a well-thought out theology of the mission of God, especially in the world. Simply put,

this form of Christian ministry brings a Christian spiritual presence and framework to what may seem quite secular activities. This happens at both a local and at a national level.

The Church of England is *unique* amongst Anglican churches in terms of its formal relationship with a state, being an established Church. So it finds itself supervising many civic occasions, including the coronation of the sovereign. But other Anglican churches, including minority Anglican churches, find themselves fulfilling this role of chaplain and 'sacred canopy' to secular affairs. We might think of the Episcopalian National Cathedral in Washington; a minority church offering a national ministry. Again, we must say this is not unique to Anglicanism, but it is characteristic of Anglicans. This ministry flows from Anglican theological convictions about the mission of God in this world, and about wisdom.[49]

In a fascinating study of and argument with the Anglican Church in Australia, entitled insightfully *A Church Without Walls*, Bruce Kaye explores the roots and implications of Anglican civic theology in his context. He writes:

> Of all these contexts in which Anglican theology is practised ... it seems to me that the most important fundamental is that of Christian life in society. I have already drawn attention to the fact that the Reformation Settlement presents us with a Christian society which was at once political and religious; that the church and state were not separate entities but aspects of one single identity.[50]

Here he is of course taking us back to Hooker and that sense of God's relationship being with a whole community, not just its ecclesiastical manifestation. Kaye then takes us to the post-Christendom situation of contemporary Australian Anglicanism, but without relinquishing this sense of a big perspective of God's mission. He urges his fellow Australian Anglicans to 'be an engaged church, to be a statement about the compassion and activity of God'[51] and goes on to discuss Christian perspectives on issues to do with society, politics and economics. This is absolutely in keeping with the mainstream Anglican tradition, which has not allowed for tidy divides between what is 'of Caesar' and what is not. In one sense, all is God's. And it takes deep wisdom to navigate this world.

We can allow Rowan Williams to summarise the theology which lies behind this language of wisdom. When reflecting on Hooker he writes, '. . . God's reality is *not* encountered simply as will and command'. Rather 'it is encountered in the law of things'. Further: 'Our encounter with the nature of God as law or wisdom cannot be separated from [our] *interpretation* of this.'[52] This takes us back to human responsibility and pragmatism. *We* have to work at these understandings.

But, and this is where this chapter must finish, to use another cliché, this is not 'unprincipled pragmatism', or we might say, it is not 'unspiritual pragmatism'. Hence the discernment of wisdom will come in dialogue with Scripture and Tradition. It will come indeed through prayer and worship. In Rowan Williams' phrase, it will be a 'contemplative pragmatism';[53] that is a wisdom which grows out of spirituality. This is not a piece of remote theologising. If Anglicans are serious about God and about the state of the world, *both wisdoms must coalesce*:

> If we are not somehow bound by what God is and what we are, however stumblingly and inadequately we can speak of these things, what possibility is there of sustaining a belief in the common good of human creatures. . . ?[54]

To borrow the words of one of Anglicanism's wisest theologians, when we try to put together all that we have discussed so far, we might define Anglicanism thus:

> *Anglicanism ideally follows a distinctive pattern in which the gift of God in Jesus Christ is embodied in worship, wisdom and service in a historical continuity of contextually sensitive mission.*[55]

It is this dynamic of worship and holiness that we will explore in our last chapter.

6 THE 'BEAUTY OF HOLINESS': WORSHIP AS THE HEART OF ANGLICANISM

If we were to ask a representative group of English Anglicans what is meant by 'the beauty of holiness', I guess that we would hear replies which stressed order, good taste and restraint; bare stone walls and chanted psalms! But this phrase has a far richer meaning.

In this chapter, we have reached the *heart* of Anglicanism, which is worship; the *purpose* of Anglicanism, which is to foster Christlike holiness, individually and socially; and the *essence* of Anglicanism, which is that the two cannot be separated. If there is one activity which dominates the spiritual lives of Anglicans it has been, and often still is, *common public worship*. In a crucial and deeply Anglican statement, Ford and Hardy write:

> Renewal has always come through people whose first interest in life has been adoring and realistic attention to God. Any experience of Christianity that does not participate in this has missed the point.[1]

Worship as the Heart

It is rightly said, that if you want to know what makes an Anglican tick, don't ask her about her doctrine, worship with her. Worship is the quintessential Anglican activity. Another of the clichés about Anglicanism is that it is 'two-legged':

Scripture and sacrament. But in dialogue with my Charismatic colleagues, and reflecting on the content of Anglican prayer books, I have realised that in fact Anglicans sit on a three-legged stool: Scripture, sacrament *and worship*. Again, this is not distinctively Anglican, but it is classically Anglican. The worship of God is the first thing an Anglican does when she opens her service books: 'O Lord, open our lips. And our mouths shall proclaim your praise' (the introductory versicle and response for Morning Prayer in *Common Worship*). Or revisit the Collect for Purity: Anglicans pray for the Spirit to cleanse them, so that they may 'worthily magnify' God. Anglicans believe that to worship is what it is to be human, when in relationship with the Creator and Redeemer. It is the response which we have found in Cranmer, Hooker, Donne, Herbert, Traherne and Vaughan. Even when Anglicans cannot fully name God, they are still drawn to worship.

We have noted other key features from the history of Anglicanism, which have shaped its current character and put worship at its heart. The fact that Cranmer was more gifted as a liturgist than as a theologian meant that, in effect, he gave priority to the worship of the Church. His legacy was forms and habits of worship rather than treatises of systematic theology. This means that Anglicans do not define themselves in relationship to a particular body of theological writing but in relationship to the living use of liturgical texts.

There is a deeper Anglican conviction here, that theology is fundamentally worship. So people are most truly with God and language about God is most authentic in praise and prayer. This is a two-way relationship. Whilst *lex orandi, lex credendi* ('as one worships, so one believes') is often cited as a key slogan about Anglicanism, to soften its theological core, the essence of worship is that it is responsive. We are here taken back to the priority of God and grace.

The most prominent feature of Anglican worshipping life is that it is 'common worship'. From 1549 Anglican prayer books have been entitled 'Common'.[2] They are for the whole people of God to use together. They are vernacular in the fullest sense of the word. That everybody – in theory – had access to all the liturgy meant that there was no private clerical *gnosis* ('secret knowledge') which made the laity into second-class Christians. The Daily Office was to be said together. Said and sung responses were hardly new in Christian worship, but the extent to which Cranmer's services were collaborative, and became more so as liturgical practice developed, is striking and has fostered deep expectations about participative worship amongst Anglicans.

There is more to recollect about this Anglican ethos of common worship. There is the realisation that language is not an individual but a communal property. To prioritise worship in common is to acknowledge that all our talk of God is communal. There is the practice of attending to Scripture communally. There is the strong theology of participation in Christ together, sacramentally. There is the insight that faith is expressed best in common religious practice rather than in carefully formulated theological statements. There is the instinct that regular, holistic, communal worship takes our common humanity seriously, including our frailty. Hooker expressed this in a way which feels utterly contrary to our own privatised culture:

> ... the good which we do by public prayer is more than in private can be done, for that besides the benefit which here is no less procured to ourselves, the whole Church is much bettered by our good example... [3]

Anglicans believe that all benefit from communal participation. There is even benefit in communal repetition and familiarity:

> To its hotter Protestant critics, the familiarity of the Prayer Book was its fatal flaw, turning it into an 'idol'. To the liturgy's adherents, its familiarity was its greatest aid to devotion. [4]

Familiar words and actions allow for relaxation in worship.

This embodies a sort of trust: a sense that God does not have to be conjured up by human effort.

Anglican worship, broadly conceived, takes seriously our embodiedness. That is very significant, given the theological value that has been placed (including by Anglicans) on human embodiedness by emphasising Christ's participation in full humanity. If all of this can be achieved, at least in part, by common worship, then it should be sustained. In the era of *Mission-Shaped Church*, the beneficial spiritual effects of common worship need to be received once again. Hence my repeated suggestion that alongside the eucharist, a form of the Daily Office to be said individually in common or communally should also be the bedrock of Anglican spirituality. In a post-modern context there can be freedom about how and when, but in the *doing* of this worship, prayer and Bible reading together, forms of unity and community can be created which may enable Anglicans to navigate the floodwaters of very fluid social patterns.

However, in England, we are living through an era when attendance at all sorts of public gatherings, and membership of organisations which require attendance, is waning. This poses particular problems for Anglicans because of the centrality of public worship in Anglican spirituality. One response can be that we try harder to make our public worship attractive, but it may also be that Anglicans need, in a missionary situation, to discover the vernacular mode of worship, which may not be on a Sunday morning. For Victorian working-class Londoners, Sunday was the only morning in the week when they could have a lie-in. But many clergy persisted for decades in refusing to provide evening Communion services, and even treated with contempt those who just came in the evening. That was not vernacular, and may have contributed to the grave problems of the Victorian Anglican Church in working-class districts. 'Do it in the vernacular' means more than just speaking in English! 'Fresh expressions' is another phrase for 'vernacular'.

A little zig-zag: at the beginning of this chapter I mocked

English Anglican snobbery about worship. But part of this can be a desire to do worship well. As the presence of God is honoured in worship, so excellence – 'beauty' – becomes a dominant value. Partly because of the legacy of Cranmer and the Authorised Version, with their self-consciously exquisite English, as well as the flourishing tradition of choral music preserved by Elizabeth I, there is a long-standing ethos of aesthetic excellence in Anglican worship. If public worship is truly the shop-window of Anglican spirituality, then excellence in worship – *but now in all styles* – is an appropriate value. If we add to this the insights derived from our discussion about the 'rich *via media*', then it is possible for Anglicans to include in contemporary worship ingredients which in the recent past they have held apart. It is possible to have services with a rich visual liturgy *and* good preaching.

There is serious theology under-pinning this ethos. It has two aspects. First, if many of the Anglican poets are right and 'putting God into words' is an art rather than a science, then beauty is essential. It is not a luxury. (There is an unexplored area here of an 'Anglican aesthetic': do Anglicans believe God is 'beautiful' and therefore that God is *best* communicated in beauty?) Second, if God is to be encountered in 'beauty' then this takes our relationship with God far beyond simple intellectual assent into a more holistic account of human spirituality. All our senses will be involved, and our imagination, and our affections. Again this is a justification for enriched public worship. And if it is the case that we are living in an era dominated by the visual sense, then Anglicans can draw much from their Tradition which will enrich sensory worship in a theologically alert way.

Now, however, we must allow for another historical raspberry. The scale of destruction of religious sculpture during the Reformation in England was second only to that in Scotland. Much that we might consider beautiful was self-consciously destroyed by Anglican Protestants for theological reasons. Visual beauty was an irrelevant criterion. The vandalising (at worst), or neglect (at best), of the Church's buildings was a scandal in the sixteenth century. Whilst Archbishop Laud may have had a range of motives for order-ing the beautifying of church buildings in the 1630s, including the theological one of making them visible symbols of the Church as 'the greatest place of residence of God upon earth', he was at least in part motivated by disgust at the condition of the church buildings after the depredations from the greed of the Tudor gentry and state.

The story of the revival of this instinct for visual beauty is intriguing. In a fascinating essay, Croft has shown how Robert Cecil (the son of William, Elizabeth's Secretary of State and himself holding the same offices under Elizabeth and James), moved from a position of moderate Elizabethan Calvinism to a renewed (proto-Laudian) delight in visual beauty for God by the early seventeenth century. Croft describes his chapel in the newly built Hatfield House:

> The chapel's brilliant stained glass is the first with reli-gious imagery to be commissioned since the iconoclasm of Edward's reign. Around the walls are richly coloured mannerist paintings of the life of Christ, and around the dazzling east window, figures of the prophets appear surrounded by gilded borders and scrolls. Even in winter, the morning sun coming through the glass still creates staggering colours.[5]

Cecil was Andrewes' patron and often heard Andrewes preach. It was as if visual beauty could not be suppressed any more. Anglican balance here has almost the character of a self-righting boat.

In England, alongside Christians in much of Western Eur-ope, Anglicans are now dealing with the legacy of an excessive number of church buildings which can absorb huge amounts of time and energy. These buildings are not 'the Church'. More ridiculously, from every town in England to the suburbs of Detroit, to Kaduna in Nigeria and even to Bangkok, Victorian fake gothic has exerted a mind-numbing hold over Anglican church architecture. And yet, if the rediscovery of the

theological instinct which lay behind these buildings is right –
and we must set it alongside English Victorian imperialism as
a motivating force – then both a sense of place and also physical beauty are crucial to Anglican spirituality.[6] Remember
Hooker and Newman: for Anglicans there is no such thing as
disembodied Christianity.

One *distinctive* feature of Anglican worship is its musical
tradition. Choral Prayer Book Evensong, with its combination
of beauty and spaciousness for the participant, remains deeply
attractive. I was struck by how many of the 'great and the
good' who wrote in Chartres' book, *Why I Am Still An Anglican,* said that Prayer Book Evensong is their spiritual home. If
English Anglicans are serious about sustaining a church with
soft edges, then the revival of Cathedral life and worship is of
great significance.[7] As MacCulloch writes:

> At a deeper level he [Cranmer] would have been appalled
> at the spirituality which may be represented by the love of
> evensong. This is the exploration of religion by those who
> have decided to remain on the fringe of the Church, gen-
> uinely concerned to pursue their encounter with God, yet
> not prepared to demonstrate the degree of commitment
> demanded by the eucharist. For them, the encounter with
> the Anglican offices, however infrequent, can provide a
> spiritual home: a place where they can show that they still
> wish to look beyond the surface of events and say that
> there is more to human life and creation than the obvious,
> the everyday. That home has been bequeathed to them by
> Archbishop Cranmer.[8]

In an age in the West when people are suspicious of institutions, worshipping communities which offer space and do not
rush at newcomers with demands are potentially very
valuable.

There is a wonderful diversity of music beyond Choral
Evensong which also feeds Anglican spirits. Some of the most
lyrical writing in Hooker is to be found precisely on the topic of
music. In chapter 38 of Book 5 of the *Laws* he provided a

wonderfully balanced defence of the place of music in the life of the Church, moving seamlessly between Scripture, Tradition and Reason. Hooker thought that the power of music to touch the affections of human beings reflected a deep principle of harmony in humankind, nature, and even God:

> ... such ... is the force thereof, and so pleasing effects it hath in that very part of man which is most divine, that some have been thereby induced to think that the soul itself by nature is or hath in it harmony.[9]

Hooker went on to describe a transition from a physical process (the making of musical sounds and the hearing of them), through to a spiritual process (the care for and teaching of a human soul):

> ... the very harmony of sounds being framed in due sort and carried from the ear to the spiritual faculties of our souls, is by a native puissance and efficacy greatly available to bring to a perfect temper whatsoever is there troubled, apt as well to quicken the spirits as to allay that which is too eager, sovereign against melancholy and despair...

This is a profound description of a sacramental process; physical and spiritual elements inextricably combined, giving grace and generating wholeness. And Hooker delightfully turned on its head the Puritan objection that the use of music pandered to human sinfulness in not just accepting God's words when, quoting Basil, he wrote:

> O the wise conceit of that heavenly Teacher, which hath by his skill, found a way, that doing those things wherein we delight, we may also learn that whereby we profit.[10]

This is a very strong example of Hooker's appreciation of the humility of God in using ordinary means for holy purposes. It is, of course, an example of the principle of Incarnation. If God can be humble and accessible as well as unknowable, what might that imply for Anglican worship? Ford and Hardy provide good guidance:

> There is a knowledge of God that can only come in praising God ... All our faculties play a part in knowing God, and any one can take the lead – the imagination by entering into the symbolism of worship, the voice by singing and expanding one's conception by its soaring, the arms by lifting up and freeing one's whole self for something larger than it, the feet by dancing, taste by eating, and so on.[11]

This is another argument in favour of the broadest and richest conception of 'beauty' in worship.

Rowan Williams expands his reflections on Hooker on music to a wider description of the nature of worship:

> We are to be concerned about something more than ideas in worship because the act of God in Christ is more than the conveying of information to us; it is the renewal from within of what is possible for human experience.[12]

This takes us back to the key point of this chapter, which is that worship is more than an end in itself; it has wider purposes. As Anglicans worship in common together, it is with the intention of building good communities under God. Ultimately, the 'beauty of holiness' is a living Christian community. We can let Ford and Hardy express this theologically again:

> The supreme social benefit of praising God is, however, that it helps in discovering the strongest of objective bonds with others ... Praise actualises the true relationship between people as well as with God, and it is no accident that in the symbols of heavenly bliss the leading pictures are of feasting and praising.[13]

Holiness as the Purpose

Characteristic of Anglicanism – though *not* of course distinctive to Anglicanism – is the quest for Christlike personal and social holiness.[14] Worship was key to this. As we have seen, Cranmer's vision was to grow a Christian nation, not just a gathered church. Cranmer imagined his people gathered daily around the Bible and prayer – and to a surprisingly regular degree, also the eucharist – living lives of Christian neighbourliness. It was in worship that Cranmer saw the people being instructed in the faith as Scripture was read (and preached), cleansed from their sins, restored to communal living and, without stretching the point too far, both made and reminded that they were 'very members incorporate in thy mystical body' (second post-Communion collect).

A further aspect of the linkage of worship and holiness was Cranmer's deep concern to foster good Christian behaviour. This was in part out of a concern for social order, but more deeply it was a serious conviction that faith did have to produce fruit in good works, if it was real faith. As Collinson argues:

> ... it is certain that Cranmer placed a distinctive premium on those good works done [after justification], the works and fruit of faith, and that he even defined salvation as perseverance in those faithful works, amounting to personal union with Christ ... This is especially true of the Prayer Book collects ... In these supplications, the Prayer Book serves as a manual for a Christian life which must persist in faith and the good works which spring from faith if it is to come safely to its end and attain salvation.[15]

This produced the strong 'so that' ethos in his liturgy, which Cranmer bequeathed to later Anglicans. Modern Anglicans are heirs to a Tradition that expects encounters with God to generate tangible changes in people's lives, while patiently respecting the speed at which real people change.

Crucially, the character of Prayer Book worship was well-adapted for a gradualist approach to the Christian life; partly because of its deep historical roots in the Western liturgical tradition, and partly because of the unique nature of Cranmer's and Elizabeth's personalities and also of mid sixteenth-century England. As Collinson has lucidly written of Cranmer himself:

> [His] was a hand which, for all that it was guided by an essentially Protestant mind, could compose out of a time-worn original such a prayer as the second collect at Evensong, redolent of a cradle-to-grave, static and institutional religious structure, as timeless as the parish church where for generations it would be read... [16]

With its pattern of occasional offices for the key moments of life – birth, marriage and death – and prayers according to the seasons, and for the needs of an agricultural and seafaring society, it was indeed a prayer book for a settled Christian life. It took the ordinary natural rhythms and events of life seriously as God-given, and as occasions where grace should be active. It is a form of spirituality for the long haul, the steady walk in unexciting places when life is, as it often is, routine.

Cranmer was always conscious that he was the Archbishop for the English nation and this moderated his private theology (for example, his views on predestination), when he wrote his public liturgy. Cranmer produced public liturgies which were experienced as inclusive.[17] Apart from people who had been (unusually) disciplined, all could come and participate in worship; all could receive the Christian sacraments and a Christian burial. If we doubt the weight of this, both in theory but even more in practice, we are not taking seriously the depth of Puritan dissatisfaction with the Prayer Book: 'an unperfect book, culled and picked out of that popish dunghill, the mass book, full of abominations'.[18] Puritans knew why they objected to Cranmer's more inclusive Church.

As a parish priest in West Newcastle faced with raising a considerable diocesan share, I experienced the spiritual tensions which this vision of an inclusive Church can cause. After yet another Sunday morning service dominated by the baptism of children of those who had tenuous links with the local congregation, and as we counted the small change dumped into the collection bags, it was tempting to slip into angry disdain. It requires a very great deal from a congregation by way of a spirituality of hospitality to put up with disruptions to its worship and demands on their giving when they appear to be taken for granted. But it is the Anglican way. Sustaining a Church with a 'warm heart and soft edges' requires much grace. Anglicans still do much of their mission as they keep open doors into their worship.

It is time for a final historical raspberry, at least in part. In the Introduction we noted the 'Five Marks of Mission of the Anglican Communion', and the way they express the Anglican sense of the breadth of the mission of God. In Cranmer's mind, the mission of God was primarily about the salvation of individuals and the management of a fallen creation. I do not detect that social justice was a prominent feature of Cranmer's operative theology. And, truth to tell, the vision of social as well as personal holiness has waxed and waned in Anglicanism. But it has never been eradicated, despite the alliance between the Church of England and the English state and political élite. Indeed, we can put this more positively. In the work of Latimer, Cranmer's fellow martyr; the martyr Laud; the Wesleys (good Anglicans!); the Evangelical Reformers like Wilberforce; the Anglo-Catholic slum priests like Dolling; the Broad Church social reformers and their fellow-travellers like Maurice and Westcott; overseas missionaries like the martyr John Patteson of Melanesia; *extraordinary* women like Josephine Butler with her campaigns for the rights of women, including prostitutes; and the descendants of all of these in the twentieth century, not least the Ugandan martyrs; there is the fiercely held conviction that God is a God of justice, who desires to see the 'poor' treated justly.

We have noted all too briefly in this book the flourishing of a fully fledged 'social Christianity' in the last 150 years – with of course many antecedents – and we have also noticed the work of William Temple in the field of Anglican doctrine. Here, we bring these together in a quotation from his immensely significant best-selling book *Christianity and Social Order* (1942), which was the product of a lifetime's research on social and economic issue. It was one of the key motivating forces behind the establishment of the British welfare state after World War II. Temple wrote very simply:

> The primary principle of Christian Ethics and Christian Politics must be respect for every person simply as a person. If each man and woman is a child of God, whom God loves and for whom Christ died, then there is in each a worth absolutely independent of all usefulness to society.[19]

If this is the fruit of Anglican ecclesial evolution by the mid twentieth century, then we may feel ourselves confident in identifying it as the genuine work of the Spirit. This idealism, translated into hard-headed social policies – good housing, free education, health care, compulsory paid holidays, free school dinners and milk, proper support for the unemployed, and more controversially workers' councils and even the nationalisation of the land – looks like 'social holiness'. But fascinatingly, Temple finished his book with the following paragraph:

> This book is about Christianity and the Social Order, not about Evangelism. But I should give a false impression of my own convictions if I did not here add that there is no hope of establishing a more Christian social order except through the labour and sacrifice of those in whom the Spirit of Christ is active, and that the first necessity for progress is more and better Christians... [20]

Arguably Western Anglicanism's greatest social prophet is here stressing the need to convert and nurture more Christians as a precursor to social holiness. If we wanted proof positive of the Anglican sense that worship and holiness are inextricable, we have it here. Grace is essential.

'We Can Do No Good Thing Without Thee'

Whilst I have had cause in this book to query some of Ashley Null's interpretations of Cranmer, he has nonetheless in a most engaging way got right to the heart of Cranmer's own spirituality; which is love for God, won from human hearts, by God's forgiving grace. As Null sums it up:

> As Cranmer read the Scriptures afresh ... he realized that the Protestants were right, that only knowing the unconditional love of God made known in free salvation – only that promise of unmerited forgiveness and grace – could ever enable the heart to begin to love God more than sin.[21]

For Cranmer, repentance was the channel whereby God's grace re-ordered the will and the affections so that human beings could love. There is a little sign of this in the distinctive way in which Cranmer translated the Latin version of the 'Collect for Purity' into English. A straightforward translation of the Latin would read:

> God, to whom every heart is open and every wish speaks, and from whom no secret lies hid; purify by the inpouring of the Holy Spirit the thoughts of our heart; that we may deserve to perfectly love and worthily praise thee. Through Jesus Christ our Lord. Amen.[22]

Apart from the sheer beauty of Cranmer's translation in comparison, notice that Cranmer has removed any sense that we might 'deserve' to love God. Instead, we simply pray 'that we may perfectly love thee'. This is of course sound Protestant theology, denying that we could ever merit loving God of ourselves. But it also takes us to the heart of Cranmer's vision, which was that human beings would be enabled, by grace, to be in a relationship of love with God.

Two comments on Cranmer himself and then I want to place this theology in a different theological framework. First, Cranmer lived this spirituality of repentance and forgiveness. As Null poignantly points out, Cranmer had a forgiving nature and this was a self-conscious strategy of winning over those whom he believed were estranged from Christ. Null quotes him:

> What will ye have a man do to him that is not yet come to
> the knowledge of the truth of the Gospel... ? Shall we
> perhaps, in his journey coming towards us, by severity
> and cruel behaviour overthrow him? ... if it be a true rule
> of our Saviour Christ to do good for evil, than let such as
> are not yet come to favour our religion learn to follow the
> doctrine of the Gospel by our example in using them
> friendly and charitably.[23]

This pastoral gentleness seems to have seeped into Anglicanism. Second, Cranmer was a flawed hero. He did recant his
Protestant faith six times. He was 'redeemed' literally on the
last day, and as he held his recanting hand in the fire to be
burned first. We have already stressed how deeply this
experience of fallibility and frailty, and so dependence on
grace, has shaped Anglican consciousness.

But I want to suggest that we need to transpose Cranmer's
theology if it is to be life-giving in modern Anglicanism. Early
on in this book, I suggested that a key discipline when using
historical material for the purposes of current theology and
spirituality is to be honest when we disagree with our ancestors. Now is the time for me to come clean. The Prayer Book
and so much of Classic Anglicanism, even allowing for the
counter-examples we have found, is dominated by a sense of
sin. The experience of taking part in the Prayer Book communion service is that we are constantly reminded of our
sinfulness and of God's just anger against us. Even the first
post-Communion collect pleads with God to give us 'remission
of our sins', without 'weighing our merits' and reminds us that
we are 'unworthy' to offer God any sacrifice, even the sacrifice
of 'praise and thanksgiving'. For myself, I find the location of
this prayer in the liturgy unhelpful and its overall tone grov-
elling. (Interestingly, textual comparison shows that Cranmer
increased the severity of the wording of some of the Collects,
and altered the language to describe God more consistently in
regal terms.)

I have written in *Humane Christianity* of my passionate

belief that this overemphasis on sin and excessive use of regal imagery for God is unbalanced, untrue to Christ, and in our context, a positive hindrance to mission. However, it is possible to renew these insights in a way which is more in keeping with contemporary theological convictions and mission needs. Let me take you back to Rowan Williams' definition of Anglicanism with which we began this book. One part reads:

> It is committed to a radical criticism of any theology that sanctions the hope that human activity can contribute to the winning of God's favour... [24]

We might want to transpose even this to a positive account of how God is with humankind. The line with which we began this section is from the Collect for the Second Sunday of Trinity. It reminds us of our frailty as human beings. But instead of reading it as a threat from a God, we could, in keeping with much contemporary Anglicanism, read it as a reliable promise of God's grace to help us.

This is the key point of this section: if I am right in asserting that the *essence* of Anglicanism is the conviction that the practice of worship and the pursuit of holiness are inseparable, then that is founded on the fundamental conviction that human beings *still* need the grace of God to help them flourish, and that it is in worship that this grace is most evidently given. If we modify the Reformation focus on the 'total depravity' of human beings, so that we have a more biblical account of human frailty, then we can say that human beings are still profoundly in need of the life-giving grace of God, but without framing this within an overall message of God's punishing anger. This is a substantial change from Cranmer – though perhaps less so from Hooker – but seems to me to be one of the best examples of ecclesial evolutionary wisdom in Anglicanism. Eventually, the *enthusiastically and recklessly forgiving* God of the parable of the prodigal son has moved to be the controlling image of God in Christ for Anglicans.[25] The danger is that, when stripped of its real passion and faith, this theology can induce a sort of complacency. But Gospel love,

which is grateful for and in real relationship with the trans-
forming love of God, can not be complacent. Null's summary of
Cranmer's Gospel is still relevant for modern Anglicans: 'God's
gracious love inspired grateful human love.'[26]

Love Bade Me Welcome

Anglicans, especially English ones, are often accused of being
passionless. I hope this book may have given some indications
that this is not the whole story. But I want us to finish with a
piece of Anglican passion. We are going to listen to George
Herbert. For me, his combination of theological richness,
spiritual depth and sheer beauty makes him the best representative Anglican. Of many possibilities, I have chosen his
poem 'Love III', known from its first line, 'Love bade me welcome (which surely ought to be incorporated into Anglican
liturgy). We have already touched on some of its theological
significance but in these closing pages we will engage with it
spiritually.[27]

> Love bade me welcome: yet my soul drew back,
>   guiltie of dust and sinne.
> but quick-ey'd Love, observing me grow slack
>   from my first entrance in,
> Drew nearer to me, sweetly questioning,
>   if I lack'd anything.
>
> A guest, I answer'd, worthy to be here:
>   Love said, You shall be he.
> I the unkinde, ungratefull? Ah my deare,
>   I cannot look on thee.
> Love took my hand, and smiling did reply,
>   who made the eyes but I?
>
> Truth Lord, but I have marr'd them: let my shame
>   go where it doth deserve.
> And know you not sayes Love, who bore the blame?
>   My deare, then I will serve.

> You must sit down, sayes Love, and taste my meat:
>   So I did sit and eat.

It is at first sight a simple poem. It has a straightforward rhyme and rhythm, though of course the words flow around this rather than being constrained by it. I am most deeply moved by the utter simplicity of thought and word in the last lines: not a monosyllable out of place. The poem speaks directly to us about Christ's welcome. But whilst the metaphor of a friendly host at a banquet is typically Herbertian, the poem is richly textured.

Commentators note that we can barely count the biblical allusions in this poem. It is steeped in the language of Scripture. The poem is written by one who has spent his days with the words of the Bible so that they have become part of him. Note the words of the second line: what does it mean to be 'guiltie of dust and sinne'? This echoes the curse of Genesis 3, 'Dust shalt thou eat all the days of thy life' (v. 15) and 'dust thou art and unto dust shalt thou return' (v. 19). In Eden, humankind had the chance to be more than dust, but the consequence of sin was to have to eke a living out of dust. And in the context of a poem about a banquet, note how Adam was to 'eat' dust. It is an image of utter hopelessness and degradation.

This language was picked up in the Prayer Book (and again we cannot escape the resonances of the Prayer Book in Herbert's poetry; along with the Bible it was his book) when in words which have become part of the Anglican soul, as a body is buried so the priest says, 'earth to earth, ashes to ashes, dust to dust'. Whilst this is a recognition of human earthiness, in reality this reminds me of the gloomy and even sin-obsessed aspect of Anglicanism: the repeated confession of sin in every liturgy. Stephen Sykes explains this as the liturgical outworking of *simul iustus, simul peccator* (even when redeemed we are still sinners).

Whilst this was part of Herbert's own psyche, more powerfully, he had been touched by the gracious love of God which again and again reaches out to the bashful guilt-obsessed sinner. The deep rhythm of the poem is of Love, who is never named as Christ or God but is simply called 'Love', constantly renewing the invitation to the sinner to be welcome. The sinner arrives on the threshold, drawn by the welcome of Love (what theology of grace is at work here?), but draws back immediately. So Love gently tries to uncover the cause of the hesitation. The sinner seems consumed with self-hate. He is not even worthy to be a guest. The echoes of the Prodigal Son are strong here. The sinner then becomes more specific. He is 'unkinde' (to his fellow human beings) and 'ungratefull' (to God). So the sinner cannot even look at Love. Again, Love reaches out with profound (and theological) reassurance about the value of the sinner. But the sinner can only feel his need of punishment and wishes to be sent to where he deserves (hell?) for having marred the beautiful gift of sight. This draws from Love the most painful of the responses, which does not deny that there is 'blame' here, but takes responsibility for it. 'And know you not, who bore the blame'. We have already acknowledged this witness to the atonement.

Then, in a moment of profound insight, Herbert has the sinner try to place Love in his debt, by offering service. It is almost as if a gospel of works creeps in here. The sinner tries to justify himself by serving. As if to demonstrate Herbert's theological convictions, for the first time Love speaks sharply and does not even respond to the offer. 'You must sit down.' This is the Classic Anglican theology of the depth of human need and the total provision by the grace of God embodied in four words.

More theology is embedded in verse two. When the sinner claims that he cannot even look on Love, Love replies 'Who made the eyes but I?' We touched in chapter 1 on the evolving Anglican understanding that the same God who is active in creation is active in redemption. Here is this insight, lightly brushed in to the middle of a seventeenth-century poem. Love who made the eyes is also intent on redeeming them, even if they have been marred. The loving God who creates the delights of nature and embodied humankind is not separate from the God of the Cross.

There is of course deep sacramental spirituality here. The climax of the poem is the last couplet. The sinner is required by Love to 'taste my meat', which is an almost crude description of the Body of Christ in the eucharist. But in response to this utmost act of generosity, all the sinner can do is to 'sit and eat', to partake physically of Christ's gift.

There is perhaps an ambiguity in this poem, which may sound louder in our ears than Herbert's. When I read this poem, I often ask those present whose voice they have heard. Once they get past the question, the men often comment that they have heard a woman's voice. As I read this poem again and again, its sensuality and eroticism become ever more pressing. It is almost an account of a gentle and experienced lover helping an insecure and embarrassed man into love-making: 'Quick-ey'd Love, observing me grow slack from my first entrance in, drew nearer to me'. Trace through the poem the tangibility of Love: Love draws near and sweetly questions; Love takes the hand; Love makes eyes; Love offers 'my meat'. It is as if the doctrine of the Incarnation has taken the very tangible form of a loving, female host.

It is with the word 'Love' that we finish. This was the last poem in Herbert's collection. It was for him the climax of his work. It was his last word. I have already suggested that modern Anglican spirituality has broken through to the insight that 'God is love', with the imagery of the forgiving Father becoming dominant, moving away from the threat of an 'Almighty God'. But Herbert had got there before us. Perhaps because of his own spiritual journey, and in some tension with the theology of the Church of his day, he had come to know that God is ultimately 'love'. The vision of ever-forgiving and welcoming grace-filled Love in this poem is, I believe, the heart of Anglican spirituality.

NOTES

Introduction: passionate balancing

1. An important book has subjected this method to careful critique – Greer, *Anglican Approaches to Scripture* (see esp. p. xviii). He reminds us that it can be understood in two ways: as a method to interpret Scripture using Reason and Tradition, or as a commitment to three different theological authorities. In practice, I think both approaches have similar outcomes.

2. This is a convenient point to remind ourselves that the word 'Anglican' in its current usage is a nineteenth-century invention, ironically by Newman, intended to define a particular way of being 'Catholic'. Previously it was simply an anglicised version of the Latin word for the English. See the articles 'What is Anglicanism?' by Paul Avis and 'Anglicanism, *Ecclesia Anglicana* and Anglican: An Essay on Terminology' by J. Robert Wright in Sykes *et al., Study of Anglicanism*. To use the word 'Anglican' of the sixteenth century is highly contentious, it being argued by most historians that the term 'Anglican' can only be used with any precision from 1660 onwards. See Voak, *Richard Hooker and Reformed Theology*, pp xvi–xvii and Maltby in Platten, *Anglicanism and the Western Tradition*, p. 124.

3. These are the usual suspects in accounts of Anglicanism, and were not all accorded their current saintly status by their contemporaries. However, partly because between them there is a theological range and because they are now regarded as the shapers of Classic Anglicanism, I think it right to focus on them.

4. Canon C15. Italics mine.

5. In the Church of England the 'historic formularies' is a technical term which includes the Book of Common Prayer, the Ordinal and the Thirty-nine Articles. It is not accurate to describe these as the 'Anglican formularies' because as Philip Thomas and Evans and Wright make clear, not all Anglican Provinces enshrine all of these in their constitutions. See P. Thomas, 'A Family Affair: The Pattern of Constitutional Authority in the Anglican Communion' in Sykes, *Authority in the Anglican Communion*, p. 132; Evans and Wright, *Anglican Tradition*, section 346, p. 347, cf. 476, p. 462 and many

extracts from provincial constitutions. The Book of Common Prayer and Ordinal feature consistently, the Thirty-nine Articles less so.

6. The requirement to give 'unfeigned assent' to the Articles was removed in the 1865 Clerical Subscription Act. The status of the Book of Common Prayer is different. It is protected by Parliament and by the 1974 Worship and Doctrine Measure.

7. Avis, *Anglican Understanding of the Church*, p. 13. See also his discussion of the Declaration in 'Keeping Faith with Anglicanism' in Hannaford, *Future of Anglicanism*, pp. 8–13 and especially his phase 'dynamic orthodoxy' to describe the relationship between the given points of Anglican credal identity and the duty to 'proclaim afresh'. See also ch. 4 in Podmore, *Aspects of Anglican Identity*, which tells the story of the Declaration.

8. See the excellent discussion on the reality of development and on criteria to evaluate it – biblical, tradition-aware and reasonable – in the *Rochester Report*, s. 3.5.

9. Cameron, *Interpreting Christian History*, p. 10.

10. *Windsor Report*, para. 32, p. 20.

11. William Temple's unmistakable tones can be heard in this. Commission on Christian Doctrine (1922), *Doctrine in the Church of England* (London: SPCK; New York: Macmillan, 1938), p. 25.

12. A. Nichols, *The Panther and the Hind* (Edinburgh: T. and T. Clark, 1993), cited in R. Thompson, *Is There an Anglican Way?* (London: DLT, 1997), p. 5.

13. Cf. Countryman, *Poetic Imagination*, p. 32. A good example of confusion of thinking in this area is the otherwise stimulating booklet by Thompson, *Is There an Anglican Way?*, p. 6, where he advocates a non-foundationalist approach to Anglican theology. But his test for the Church is that it is a place of integrity where Christ 'shines'. How would we know what 'Christ shining' looks like if we did not have some foundations *already*?

14. See for example Doctrine Commission of the Church of England, *Christian Believing* (London: SPCK, 1976), ch. 6, where one of the positions on the status of the creeds was that they were 'provisional', 'inadequate', 'relative', or even irrelevant to the modern life of faith.

15. *Gift of Authority*, para. 56, p. 40: 'Is the Communion also open to the acceptance of instruments of oversight which would allow decisions to be reached that, in certain circumstances, would bind the whole Church?'

16. The threadbare nature of the language of tolerance has been sharply exposed by the current crisis. When both Liberals and Conservatives are pressing for division, Anglicans need stronger reasons and mechanisms to stay bound to each other in this part of the Body of Christ. As Archbishop Robert Runcie (hardly an authoritarian figure) stated bluntly in 1988, 'I believe the choice between independence and interdependence, already set before us as a Communion in

embryo twenty-five years ago, is quite simply the choice between unity or gradual fragmentation.' Cited in the *Windsor Report*, para. 66, p. 32.

17. Archbishops' Council, The Report from the Commission on Urban Life and Faith, *Faithful Cities* (Peterborough: Methodist Publishing House; London: Church House Publishing, 2006), esp. paras 3.42–3.45, pp. 23–5.

18. This was a phrase frequently used by Archbishop Carey. Note for example his address to the Anglican Consultative Council 11 in 1999:

> Now, some have said ... that the 'diversity' and 'comprehensive-ness' that have been our bywords can be held up as the defining characteristic of Anglicanism ... Of course we rejoice in our diversity, our openness, our blurred edges. That denotes a gen-erosity of spirit which can sometimes be lacking in other parts of the Christian family. It is also a recognition that we cannot claim the whole truth for any one part of the church. We need each part to enrich the whole ... However, we do not live by the principle 'Anything goes' ... most of us, do not accept that there are no cardinal doctrines, beliefs or limits to orthodoxy. *The Virginia Report* ... emphatically contradicts this mischievous notion and makes it clear that the limits of diversity are precisely conformity to the 'constant interplay of Scripture, tradition and reason'. So we must be very wary of any understanding of comprehensive-ness that masks doctrinal indifference. Instead we need to view it as the breadth of a Communion exploring the fullness of a faith rooted in Scripture, anchored in the creeds, expressed in faith-fulness to the Dominical sacraments and embodied in a faithful episcopally-led Church.

19. Williams, *Anglican Identities*, p. 2. Italics original.
20. Sykes, *Integrity of Anglicanism*, pp. 51–2.
21. See *Humane Christianity*, ch. 1 and *The Mystery of Salvation*.
22. Bradshaw in Hannaford, *Future of Anglicanism*, pp. 94–5. Italics mine.
23. This has been differently expressed by Morris, *F. D. Maurice and the Crisis of Christian Authority*, p. 199 (italics mine):

> It [Anglicanism] is perhaps best thought of as *an evolving but contested matrix, with certain dominant convictions remaining of central importance*, yet never defined so closely that a wide range of disagreement over their interpretation is impossible.

I warm to the phrase 'evolving but contested matrix' but affirm more strongly the role of 'certain dominant convictions'. Part of what is symbolised and actualised by the *Windsor Covenant* is precisely a clarifying of Anglican doctrinal commitments.

24. See Evans and Wright, *Anglican Tradition*, pp. 345–6 and 354–5.

25. *Windsor Report*, para. 51, p. 26, citing the Inter-Anglican Theological and Doctrine Commission. Italics original.

26. I have noted the warning about an Anglo-centric perspective on Anglicanism in Sykes *et al.*, *Study of Anglicanism*, pp. xi–xii. However, when many voices around the planet are claiming this word 'Anglican' but with a very partial dialogue with Anglican traditions, we should check our roots again.

27. 'We hold that seeing there is not any man of the *Church of England*, but the same man is also a member of the *Commonwealth*, nor any man a member of the *Commonwealth* which is not also of the *Church of England...*' (8.I.2.) Italics original. P. G. Stanwood (ed.), *Richard Hooker: Of the Laws of Ecclesiastical Polity, Books VI, VII, VIII* (Cambridge, MA/London: Harvard University Press, 1981), p. 319.

28. See Jacob, *Making of the Anglican Church Worldwide*; Sachs, *The Transformation of Anglicanism*; and especially Ward, *History of Global Anglicanism*.

29. Anglican Consultative Council, *Mission in a Broken World* (London: Church House Publishing, 1990), p. 101.

30. Wright, *Scripture and the Authority of God*, p. 21.

31. Cf. Booty, *Reflections on the Theology of Richard Hooker*, p. 153:

> I have learned from the English Reformers – and from Richard Hooker who succeeded them – to regard *The Book of Common Prayer* not just as a manual for worship but also as an instrument for the reform of society.

1. 'No monopolies here': the balancing dialogues of Anglicanism

1. Williams, *Anglican Identities*, p. 56.

2. G. White, *The Mother Church Your Mother Never Told You Of* (London: SCM Press, 1993), p. 3.

3. John Henry Newman (1801–90). Vicar of the University Church in Oxford and leader of the Oxford Movement. Converted to Roman Catholicism in 1845 and made a Cardinal in 1879.

4. Brown, *Tradition and Imagination*, p. 5.

5. See the moving extracts from letters written in the late sixteenth century by a Separatist (Congregationalist) and a Jesuit, both executed under Elizabeth I. Cited in Ives, *God in History*, p. 108; reproduced in *Humane Christianity*, p. ix.

6. See *Humane Christianity*, esp. chs 1 and 3.

7. Williams, *Why Study the Past?* p. 112. Italics original. Citing B. F. Westcott, *Lessons from Labour* (London: Macmillan, 1901), p. 148.

8. I am not alone in this. See MacCulloch, *Thomas Cranmer*, pp. 629–30.

> In an ecumenical age, and in a Western culture which honours doubt and hesitancy as a lesser evil than clear-eyed ideological

certainty, Cranmer may win admirers and sympathisers, and take his due place in the history of Anglicanism. He would not have known what Anglicanism meant, and he would probably not have approved ... but without his contribution the unending dialogue of Protestantism and Catholicism which forms Anglican identity would not have been possible.

9.   ... all speakers speak from a perspective, social and historical, and their words are *part* of the universe they claim to see as a whole. Since that is so, it will be right to suspect that the claim to understand and to speak for the global context of your own speaking is essentially a claim to power.

R. Williams, *On Christian Theology* (Malden MA/Oxford/Melbourne/Berlin: Blackwell, 2000), p. 5. Italics original.

10. E. Duffy, *The Voices of Morebath* (New Haven/London: Yale University Press, 2001).
11. Williams, *Anglican Identities*, p. 38.
12. *Ibid.*, p. 115.
13. Williams, *Why Study the Past?*, p. 10.
14. One of the puzzles for Evangelicals, when encountering the modern revisionist school of history, is that the case for interpreting Cranmer as a Protestant has to be made with such determination. It is only when one becomes aware of how much this tradition has been written out of Anglican history and that, in some circles, Cranmer is an embarrassment, that the energy drawn out of historians makes sense. McAdoo began his *Spirit of Anglicanism* in the *late* sixteenth century, *not* with Cranmer, as if the sixteenth century was too extreme and unstable to be included confidently within Anglicanism. But, my main concern is that in rediscovering Cranmer's Protestantism, the pendulum is swinging too far and the *distinctives* about Cranmer are being lost. Note the following quotation from Eamon Duffy. He is writing here explicitly about the Elizabethan Reformation, but his point is of wider relevance:

It seems to me plain that the older Anglo-Catholic account of the Reformation, as a mere clean-up operation, the creation of a reformed Catholicism which removed medieval excesses but left an essentially Catholic Church of England intact, is simply untenable. The Elizabethan reformers intended to establish a Reformed church which would be part of a Protestant international, emphatic in disowning its medieval inheritance and rejecting the religion of Catholic Europe. Its formularies, preaching and styles of worship were all designed to signal and embody that rejection. *But by the same token, it seems equally plain that Anglican self-identity was never simply or unequivocally Protestant.* Whatever the formularies and ideologues might say, the concrete reality of the Elizabethan church was always ambivalent about the Catholic past, its religious identity always troubled. *Embedded like flies in amber in its liturgy, its buildings, its ministerial orders, and in the attitudes and memories of many of its personnel, were vestiges of the past which were to prove astonishingly potent in reshaping the Church of England's future.*

In Platten, *Anglicanism and the Western Christian Tradition*, p. 63. Italics mine.

15. Martin Bucer (1491–1551) Swiss Reformer from Strasbourg, whom Cranmer invited to be Professor of Divinity at Cambridge.
16. Italics mine. For more detail on this see A. Bartlett, 'How Protestant was Cranmer's 1552 Prayer Book?' in Loades, *Word and Worship*. Cf. Duffy, who highlights precisely these points in Platten, *Anglicanism and the Western Tradition*, p. 43.
17. See the extended discussion in Null, *Cranmer's Doctrine of Repentance*, pp. 238–41. Null rightly stresses the role of repentance in forgiveness but is forced to acknowledge the strongly traditional elements in this last absolution; though he speculates that Cranmer would later have removed this.
18. Paper given at 'The Invention of Anglicanism Conference', University of Nottingham, September 2003.
19. In collaboration with Cecil of course – see Croft in Platten, *Anglicanism and the Western Christian Tradition*. The issue of Elizabeth's faith is a major area of historical controversy. See Collinson, *Elizabethans*, esp. pp. 108–18.
20. See Maltby's *Prayer Book and People in Elizabethan and Early Stuart England*, a crucial book which demonstrated the emergence of popular Prayer Book Protestantism by the 1580s.
21. The affair of the Calvinist Lambeth Articles of 1595 is an ambiguous window onto sixteenth-century Anglicanism. From one perspective, their acceptance by the episcopate indicates the dominance of Calvinism at this point in the history of the Church of England. But, that they were blocked, not least by Elizabeth herself, also reveals the constraints on Calvinism and may be taken as indicative of its increasing vulnerability. It is worth reminding ourselves of what might have become the formal theology of Anglicanism:
01. From eternity God has predestined some men to life and condemned others to death.
Bray, *Documents of the English Reformation*, p. 399. Cf. *Humane Christianity* pp. 59–60.
22. See Collinson, *Elizabethan Puritan Movement*, ch. 2. For a modern manifestation of this see P. Adam, *A Church 'Halfy Reformed': The Puritan Dilemma* (St Antholin's Lectureship Charity Lecture, 1998).
23. One of the reasons why some keep the word 'Anglican' to the post-1662 period is that they define the word in such a way as to exclude classic Protestant theology: this is both anachronistic and a deeply

partial view of Anglicanism itself. But what is unnerving when we read the disputes between these Puritans and their 'conformist' opponents is that they echo so closely some of the modern arguments between Conservative and Open Evangelicals. See A. Bartlett, 'What Has Richard Hooker to Say to Modern Evangelical Anglicanism?' in *Anvil*, 15.3, 1998, pp. 195–206.

24. See specifically on this, Lake in Platten, *Anglicanism and the Western Christian Tradition*.

25. O'Donovan, *Thirty-nine Articles*, p. 18:

> ...we must not miss the significance of the fact that they *are* the first five articles. Even if the English Reformers had nothing new to say about God and Christ, they were not to be discouraged from saying something old. We should be struck by their concern to subordinate the controversial material of the later articles, pressing and urgent as it was, to a restatement of the primitive gospel message. (Italics original.)

26. There is only space to note here that the 'martyrs' Charles I and William Laud (Archbishop of Canterbury 1633–45) are now seen by historians as having moved clearly and aggressively away from the Jacobean balance. Laudianism was innovatory. For example, it was committed to: the divine nature of episcopacy; enforced visible Catholic holiness; and active punitive hostility to Puritanism. We need to identify it clearly as a party within the Church and be careful lest Laudianism is simply equated with Anglicanism. This is another reason for *not* defining Anglicanism by 1662 standards. For a general description see D. MacCulloch, *Reformation* (London: Allen Lane, 2003), pp. 513–24.

27. McAdoo, *Spirit of Anglicanism*, pp. 12–23.

28. The older view of McAdoo, Booty *et al.* was that Hooker was simply a good typical Anglican. The two protagonists who represent the main modern strands of interpretation are Voak, *Richard Hooker and Reformed Theology* and Kirby, *Richard Hooker: Reformer and Platonist*. See Voak, pp. 1–21 and Kirby, pp. ix–x. The key issue is how far Hooker is still operating within the framework of mainstream Reformed theology (Kirby) or whether he is being innovative and thereby laying the foundations for what became known as Anglicanism (Voak). My question is to ask: how far is Hooker innovating? Or is he rather making explicit or giving a theological rationale for Cranmer and Elizabeth's Church? I would stress continuity back to Jewel and Cranmer. I think Lake and Voak undervalue the role of the theology of the Prayer Book and especially the Ordinal. See A. Bartlett, 'Cranmer, Hooker and the *Via Media*': paper given at the Invention of Anglicanism Conference, University of Nottingham, September 2003 and to be published.

29. Wright, *Scripture and the Authority of God*, p. 60.

30. Williams, *Anglican Identities*, pp. 55–6.
31. *Laws of Ecclesiastical Polity*, 5.li.3, p. 203.
32. *Ibid.*, 5.liv.5, p. 216.
33. *Ibid.*, 1.xiv.1; 3.viii.14.
34. Voak (*Richard Hooker and Reformed Theology*, pp. 251–65), in an extended, careful, complex discussion of Hooker on religious authority, argues that Hooker is indeed the originator of the three-stranded method of Anglicanism:

    ...Church of England theologians who accept the authority of Scripture, reason and tradition, in that order, may not unjustly look back to Hooker as a theological predecessor, for he mounts in the *Lawes* a classic defence of these three sources of religious authority (p. 264).

35. *Laws of Ecclesiastical Polity*, I.xiv.2, p. 216. Also *Humane Christianity*, pp. 21–3 and 63–5.
36. *Laws of Ecclesiastical Polity*, 3.iv.1, p. 303.
37. *Ibid.*, 3.ii.1, p. 298.
38. *Ibid.* (Folger edn), 7.xi.11, p. 210 and 7.v.10, p. 170. Italics mine. See the crucial article by A. S. McGrade, 'Richard Hooker on Episcopacy and Bishops, Good and Bad' in *International Journal for the Study of the Christian Church*, vol. 2, no. 2, 2002, pp. 28–46.
39. *Laws of Ecclesiastical Polity*, Preface, iv.1, p. 107.
40. *Ibid.* (Folger edn), 7.v.8, p. 168.
41. Williams, *Anglican Identities*, p. 37.
42. Cf. *Humane Christianity*, p. 64.
43. C. Chartres (ed.), *Why I Am Still an Anglican* (London/New York: Continuum, 2006), p. 110.
44. *Laws of Ecclesiastical Polity*, 3.xi.8, p. 341.
45. See the classic definition of the 1948 Lambeth Conference:

    Authority as inherited by the Anglican Communion from the undivided Church [note] of the early centuries of the Christian era, is single in that it is derived from a single Divine source, and reflects within itself the richness and historicity of the Divine Revelation ... It is distributed among Scripture, Tradition, Creeds, the Ministry of the Word and Sacraments, the witness of saints and the *consensus fidelium*, which is the continuing experience of the Holy Spirit through His faithful people in the Church.

    Cited in Sykes, *Unashamed Anglicanism*, p. 168.
46. Cited in J. Booty, 'Hooker and Anglicanism' in W. Speed Hill (ed.), *Studies in Richard Hooker* (Cleveland: Press of Case Western Reserve University, 1972), p. 218.
47. G. Cuming, *A History of Anglican Liturgy* (London: Macmillan, 1969), p. 92.

48. Herbert, *Poems*, p. 122.
49. Note More's comment on the Aristotelian mean as being 'both English and Greek' in More and Cross, *Anglicanism*, p. xxiii.
50. See Rowell, *Vision Glorious*, p. 67.
51. More and Cross, *Anglicanism*, p. xxxvii.
52. Herbert, *Country Parson*, p. 204.
53. *Ibid.*, p. 226.
54. This is well-described and framed by Avis, who sees it as the essential trigger for the beginnings of a move in Anglican ecclesiology from the erastian to an apostolic (episcopal) paradigm. See Avis, *Anglicanism and the Christian Church*.
55. I am hugely indebted to Morris's outstanding *F. D. Maurice and the Crisis of Christian Authority*. Maurice's ideas, especially about the relationship between church parties and their own theological perspectives and a dynamic way of discovering Christian truth, are still 'live'. A Mauricean approach to comprehension as the holding of opposites in tension is said to lie behind the Lambeth Conference resolutions in 1948 and 1968 and to have become virtually the official Anglican line on comprehension (Morris, p. 200 and Sykes, *Integrity of Anglicanism*, p. 18).
56. Maurice, *Kingdom of Christ*, vol. 2, p. 308.
57. *Ibid.*, p. 309.
58. *Ibid.*, p. 310. Italics original.
59. *Ibid.*, p. 310.
60. *Ibid.*, p. 311.
61. Morris, *F. D. Maurice and the Crisis of Christian Authority*, p. 70, cf. p. 91–2.
62. Sykes, *Integrity of Anglicanism*, p. 19.
63. See Morris, *F. D. Maurice and the Crisis of Christian Authority*, pp. 111–19 and 197–202:

> The seriousness of internal conflict in the modern Anglican Communion may have brought the attractiveness of Maurice's ecclesiology finally to an end. But that possibility can only serve to highlight the extraordinary influence it exercised for so long. Articulated as a defence of the role of the Church in promoting religious and social harmony, it represented the pained reaction of one sympathetic Anglican to the multiple crises his church faced in the early decades of the nineteenth century. It was, then, a thoroughly contextual ecclesiology. Yet it proved itself susceptible to translation and development, by which the consideration of one church's breadth could be turned into a general policy of promoting and containing internal church pluralism. In the process it proved an extremely adaptable tool (p. 201).

The fact that this great method is reaching breaking point is a

substantial part of the argument that Anglicanism needs more
robust methods for enabling its survival.

2 'An adequate sufficiency': theological and spiritual modesty

1. This is an echo of one of the most famous pieces of (Anglican)
   Christian apologetic, *Mere Christianity* by C. S. Lewis (first pub.
   1952). It tried to do precisely what Anglicans have often tried to do:
   express the common essential elements of Christian Faith simply.
   It has, significantly, been subject to a sharp and not entirely unfair
   critique for being both culturally conditioned and also highly
   selective by Cameron in his *Interpreting Christian History*, pp.
   231–35.
2. Cited in McAdoo, *Spirit of Anglicanism*, p. 320.
3. See for example pp. 3–16 of More and Cross, *Anglicanism*, which
   cites a range of seventeenth-century authors, including King James
   I, all affirming this.
4. McAdoo, *Being an Anglican*, pp. 12–13 and citing J. W. C. Wand,
   Anglicanism in History and Today (London: Weidenfield and
   Nicholson, 1961), p. 46.
5. Sykes, *Integrity of Anglicanism*, ch. 4.
6. McAdoo, *Being an Anglican*, p. 16.
7. O'Donovan, *Thirty-nine Articles*, p. 14. Italics mine.
8. *Laws of Ecclesiastical Polity* 3.i.3, p. 285.
9. Countryman, *Poetic Imagination*, p. 32.
10. J. E. Booty (ed.), *An Apology of the Church of England by John Jewel*
    (Ithaca, New York: Cornell University Press, 1963), p. 17. Also J. E.
    Booty, *John Jewel as Apologist of the Church of England* (London:
    SPCK, 1963).
11. More and Cross, *Anglicanism*, p. xxxvii. Italics mine.
12. *Laws of Ecclesiastical Polity*, 1.ii.2, p. 150.
13. Folger lists four theologians and two Classical authors behind this
    quotation. See W. Speed Hill and E. Grislis, *Richard Hooker: Of the
    Laws of Ecclesiastical Polity. Introductions; Commentary, Preface
    and Books I-IV* (Binghampton NY: Medieval and Renaissance Texts
    and Studies, 1993), p. 479.
14. Sermon on 'The Certainty and Perpetuity of Faith in the Elect', vol. 1
    of the Everyman edn, *Laws of Ecclesiastical Polity*, p. 3.
15. Williams, *Anglican Identities*, p. 26. Italics mine.
16. *Laws of Ecclesiastical Polity*, Preface, vi.3, p. 118.
17. *Ibid.*, Preface, ix.1, p. 143.
18. *Ibid.*, 1.xvi.5/6, pp. 228–9. Cf. Voak's summary (*Richard Hooker and
    Reformed Theology*, p. 263) of Hooker's epistemology. From top to
    bottom in order of certainty:

    1 Doctrines found in Holy Scripture 'by expresse literall mention'.

     2 (a) Doctrines deduced from Holy Scripture by demonstrative rea-
          soning; and

        (b) Natural laws and *mere natural spiritual facts* deduced by
          demonstrative reasoning.

     3 Probable reasoning and tradition licensed by a society such as a
        Church.

     4 Private probable reasoning and tradition.

19. *Laws of Ecclesiastical Polity*, 3.i.2, p. 284, cf. section 8, p. 288.

20. In this respect I am giving less weight to Hooker's sense of certainty than does Voak, who would stress Hooker's confidence in 'demonstrative reasoning' (*Richard Hooker and Reformed Theology*, p. 264), rather than the 'probable reasoning' which I am discussing.

21. Cf. Williams, *Anglican Identities*, p. 44:

> The connections are not wholly explicit in Hooker, but there is a line to be drawn from here to the pragmatic or probabilistic, historically alert accounts of human knowing characteristic of later Anglican philosophy, from Butler to Newman...

22. Cunliffe, *Joseph Butler's Moral and Religious Thought*, p. 1. Note also that Butler's importance is highlighted in A. Redfern, *Being Anglican* (London: DLT, 2004 edn), ch. 6.

23. Butler, *Analogy of Religion*, Intro., section 4, p. 5. Cf. part 2, ch. 8, s. 9, p. 320.

24. *Ibid.*, part 2, ch. 3, ss. 4, 5, p. 201. On this see T. Penelhum, 'Butler and Human Ignorance' in Cunliffe, *Joseph Butler's Moral and Religious Thought*, pp. 117–40. Also Penelhum, *Butler*, ch. 8.

25. Butler, *Analogy of Religion*, Introduction, ss. 5, 6, pp. 6–7.

26. I. Ramsey, *Joseph Butler: Some Features of His Life and Thought* (London: Dr Williams' Library, 1969), pp. 14–16.

27. C. Chartres (ed.), *Why I Am Still an Anglican* (London/New York: Continuum, 2006), p. 139.

28. Ramsey, *Joseph Butler: Some Features of His Life and Thought*, p. 20. My italics.

29. See also the discussion in Sykes, *Unashamed Anglicanism*, pp. 66ff.

30. *Laws of Ecclesiastical Polity*, 3.iii.3, p. 301.

31. *Windsor Report*, para. 88, p. 38.

32. Try S. McFague, *Speaking in Parables: A Study in Metaphor and Theology* (London: SCM Press, 2nd edn, 2002). See also 'Theological Integrity' in R. Williams, *On Christian Theology* (Malden MA/Oxford/Melbourne/Berlin: Blackwell, 2000).

33. Scott, *Sacred Tongues*, p. 3.

34. Commission on Christian Doctrine (1922), *Doctrine in the Church of England* (London: SPCK; New York: Macmillan, 1938), pp. 37–8.

35. David Scott, writing in Cluysenaar, *Henry Vaughan: Selected Poems*, p. ix.

36. See the balanced discussion of the Prayer Book in G. Mursell, *English Spirituality: From Earliest Times to 1700* (London: SPCK; Louisville KY: Westminster John Knox Press, 2001), pp. 309–14. NB by 'poetic' I do not mean in poetic form. Cranmer was notoriously bad at verse!

37. It is not certain who took the decisions about the Collect for Purity, but it is widely acknowledged to be Cranmer's work. I am deeply indebted to Dr Bridget Nicholls for guidance about this prayer.

38. See the excellent discussion of Cranmer's views of the 'heart' in A. Null, 'Thomas Cranmer's Theology of the Heart' in *Anvil*, vol. 3, no. 3, 2006.

39. From 'A Wreath', in Herbert, *Poems*, p. 189.

40. 'Jordan I', *ibid.*, p. 75.

41. 'The Quidditie' [verbal play or subtle argument], *ibid.*, p. 86.

42. Carey, *John Donne*, p. 162.

43. 'Jordan (II)', Herbert, *Poems*, p. 117.

44. Carey, *John Donne*, p. 177. One of the 'Holy Sonnets'.

45. Scott, *Sacred Tongues*, p. 8. Italics mine.

46. Countryman, *Poetic Imagination*, p. 61. See ch. 3 for a broad discussion of this theme.

47. See 'Apophatic Spirituality' in P. Sheldrake (ed.), *The New SCM Dictionary of Spirituality* (London: SCM Press, 2005), p. 117.

48. Herbert, *Poems*, p. 98.

49. Mursell, *English Spirituality*, pp. 212–15.

50. Cluysenaar, *Henry Vaughan: Selected Poems*, p. 19, citing 'The Showre' and 'The Ass'.

51. *Ibid.*, pp. 131–2.

52. 'Cock-crowing', *ibid.*, p. 136.

53. *Ibid.*, p. 154.

54. R. S. Thomas, *Later Poems* (London: Macmillan, 1984), p. 23. I am indebted to the Revd Mike Catling for wisdom on Thomas. On Thomas, see B. Rogers, *The Man Who Went into the West* (London: Aurum Press, 2006).

55. Thomas, *Later Poems*, p. 113.

56.   The collects and other prayers, the canticles and the responses both contain and imply particular doctrines. None of these, of course demand from the worshipper the same kind of assent implied in the saying of the creed. Indeed not even the creed, in the context of worship, necessarily implies that one who utters it has a conscious and definite knowledge of, and assents to, the implications of each and every clause.

   Sykes, *Integrity of Anglicanism*, p. 46.

57. Maurice, *Kingdom of Christ*, vol. 2, pp. 316–17.

58. Chartres, *Why I Am Still an Anglican*, p. 4.

59. *Windsor Report* appendix 2, p. 65.

60. Sykes, *Integrity of Anglicanism*, pp. 11ff. The reference is to the *Laws of Ecclesiastical Polity*, 3.i.4 and 5. Italics mine.
61. Sykes, *Integrity of Anglicanism*, p. 21. Italics mine.
62. Sykes, 'The Fundamentals of Christianity' in *Unashamed Anglicanism*, pp. 64ff.
63. Doctrine Commission of the Church of England, *Christian Believing* (London: SPCK, 1976), p. 41.
64. Sykes is particularly critical of this aspect of the Report. It was the trigger for his book *The Integrity of Anglicanism*, which argued that this degree of latitude lacked intellectual, institutional and moral integrity. In the opinion of many, this Report was the nadir of English Anglican public theology and it is striking that the Report was not 'received' by General Synod and that thereafter the Doctrine Commission was brought more directly under the authority of the House of Bishops.
65. Sykes, *Unashamed Anglicanism*, p. 77.
66. Sykes, *Integrity of Anglicanism*, pp. 5–6.
67. Williams, *Anglican Identities*, p. 54.
68. C. Buchanan, *Is the Church of England Biblical?* (London: DLT, 1998), pp. 266–7.
69. Anglicans cannot go with Newman's belief in the indefectibility of the Church (though he stated this very carefully), yet there is something thought-provoking about Newman's idea that the Church is required to hold the faith in full whereas individuals are allowed much greater latitude. Cf. the extracts from Newman's *Lectures on the Prophetical Office of the Church* from the 1838 2nd edn in Chadwick, *Oxford Movement*, pp. 125ff.
70. McAdoo, *Being an Anglican*, p. 32.
71. R. Williams, *Silence and Honey Cakes* (Oxford: Lion, 2003), p. 45.

3 'Always Scripture and...'

1. The 2005 English Church survey reported that only 27 per cent of Christians in England were reading the Bible 'at least weekly' in addition to hearing it at church (*Church Times*, 22 September 2006, p. 20).
2. Wright, *Scripture and the Authority of God*, chs 2 and 9 especially. He lists as key features of the current crisis: postmodernity and the questioning of 'truth'; the fluidity of personal identity; the problematic relationship between Bible and politics; the competing effects of the generic Enlightenment critique of religious knowledge and of specific postmodern critiques (e.g. Feminist); the gulf between biblical scholarship and other theological disciplines; specific ethical issues which have pressurised traditional ways of handling these issues scripturally; misinterpretations of the Bible by Conservatives and Liberals.

3. It goes on: '...so that whatsoever is not read therein, nor may be proved thereby, is not to be required of any man, that it should be believed as an article of the Faith, or be thought requisite or necessary to salvation.'

4. Note Voak: 'Throughout the *Lawes* he [Hooker] evinces a marked hostility to the Reformed (and more generally Protestant) concept of *sola scriptura*' (Voak, *Richard Hooker and Reformed Theology*, p. 320). It is not surprising that Anglicans are *not* committed to *sola scriptura* if the founder of Anglicanism wasn't. Further, *sola scriptura* in the sixteenth century was part of a fourfold statement which included 'grace alone, faith alone, and Christ alone'. The latter presupposes the Patristic inheritance. I am indebted to Professor Moberly for reminding me of this.

5. *Windsor Report*, para. 54, p. 27. Italics original.

6. Cf. Wright, *Scripture and the Authority of God*, pp. 22–3.

7. Cf. *Laws of Ecclesiastical Polity*, 3.x.7 and 3.xi.2.

8. Ramsey, *Gospel and the Catholic Church*, p. 64.

9. Lake in Platten, *Anglicanism and the Western Christian Tradition*, p. 99.

10. Article 20 – Of the Authority of the Church:

> The Church hath power to decree Rites or Ceremonies, and authority in Controversies of Faith: And yet it is not lawful for the Church to ordain any thing that is contrary to God's Word written...

11. 'A Fruitful Exhortation to the Reading and Knowledge of Holy Scripture', Homily One in *Sermons or Homilies* (first pub. 1547, this edn Lewes, Sussex: Focus Christian Ministries Trust, 1986), p. 5.

12. See 'The Order how the rest of Holy Scripture is approved to be read' in the prefatory sections to the 1549 and 1552 Prayer Books.

13. Bray, *Documents of the English Reformation*, p. 235.

14. *Laws of Ecclesiastical Polity*, Preface, iii.2, p. 95. Italics mine.

15. Of many possible examples, note the *Rochester Report*, 3.3.2, p. 79:

> ...it must always be remembered that God can and does speak through the Bible to Christians who are not biblical scholars as they study Scripture in their private devotions or hear it read and preached publicly in the context of the liturgy.

16. *Laws of Ecclesiastical Polity*, 1.xiv.4, p. 217.

17. For help with this: A. C. Thiselton, *The Two Horizons: New Testament Hermeneutics and Philosophical Description* (Carlisle: Paternoster, 1980) and R. Briggs, *Reading the Bible Wisely* (London: SPCK, 2003).

18. *Laws of Ecclesiastical Polity*, 1.xv.3, p. 222. See 3.x and xi for an extended discussion. Italics mine.

19. *Ibid.*, Preface iv. 4, p. 110.

20. 'Richard Hooker and the Ordination of Women to the Priesthood' in Sykes, *Unashamed Anglicanism*.

21. Chadwick, *Mind of the Oxford Movement*, p. 146, citing Newman, *Arians of the Fourth Century* (first pub. 1833). Cf. the discussion in Greer, *Anglican Approaches to Scripture*, pp. 97–103.

22. *Windsor Report*, para. 60, p. 30.

23. Greer, *Anglican Approaches to Scripture*, p. 30.

24. *Rochester Report*, pp. 81–4.

25. P. Trible, *Texts of Terror: Literary-feminist Readings of Biblical Narratives* (Philadelphia: Fortress, 1984).

26. See M. Nazir-Ali in Kuhrt, *Proclaim Afresh*, p. 87, where he comments specifically on the significance of Jesus' teaching on the *lex talionis* for Christian handling of biblical texts. NB this does not mean that the Old Testament is *a priori* inferior. The rediscovered and liberating 'Lament' tradition is prominent in the Hebrew scriptures, quite unlike the Christian New Testament.

27. 'Concerning the Service of the Church', as revised in 1552.

28. A. Nicolson, *Power and Glory* (London: HarperCollins, 2003), p. 193.

29. *Windsor Report*, para. 56, p. 29.

30. 'Concerning the Service of the Church'.

31. Canon C26.

32. *Laws of Ecclesiastical Polity*, 5.xxii.6, p. 85. Italics mine.

33. *Ibid.*, 5.xxii.10, p. 92.

34. *Ibid.*, 5.xxii.1, p. 80.

35. Herbert, *Country Parson*, ch. 7, p. 204.

36. Pollard, *Let Wisdom Judge*, p. 13.

37. *Ibid.*, p. 51.

38. *Ibid.*, p. 15. Simeon shared Hooker's penchant for gentle mockery: 'Of this he is sure, that there is not a decided Calvinist or Arminian in the world who equally approves of the whole of Scripture ... who, if he had been in the company of St Paul whilst he was writing his Epistles, would not have recommended him to alter one or other of his expressions' (Moule, *Charles Simeon*, p. 79, citing Simeon's preface to his *Horae Homileticae*.)

39. Note Simeon's profound love of the Book of Common Prayer and so of Holy Communion and his Classic Anglican theology of Christ's special spiritual presence at this feast. See 'The Lord's Supper' in Pollard, *Let Wisdom Judge*, p. 175. Note also Simeon's obedience to his bishop in the matter of the appointment to Holy Trinity, his general support of episcopacy and his decision to keep to Anglican order and discipline about preaching, in direct opposition to the views of Methodist and Dissenting friends. Finally, note Simeon's belief that when he pronounced a blessing he was indeed an instrument of God 'blessing'. See esp. Smyth, *Simeon and Church Order*, ch. 6.

40. Pollard, *Let Wisdom Judge*, p. 13 citing Simeon's preface to his *Horae Homileticae*. Capitals original.

41. Moule, *Charles Simeon*, p. 77. No exact reference to Simeon's work given. See also 'The Word of God precious' in Pollard, *Let Wisdom Judge*, p. 169.

42. Pollard, *Let Wisdom Judge*, p. 16, citing *Horae Homileticae*, vol. 21, p. 307. Italics original.

43. See the 'Hints on Writing Sermons' in *ibid.*, p. 22. Much of this section is based on this extract.

44. *Ibid.*, p. 15, citing Bishop Daniel Wilson.

45. 'Christ Crucified, or Evangelical Religion described' in *ibid.*, p. 103.

46. *Ibid.*, p. 19.

47. See the excellent R. T. France, 'Not One of Us' in Kuhrt, *Proclaim Afresh*, pp. 75–82.

48. Herbert, *Country Parson*, p. 201.

49. The phrase was Benjamin Jowett's in his essay 'On the Interpretation of Scripture' in *Essays and Reviews*. See J. R. Moore (ed.), *Sources* (Manchester/New York: Manchester University Press, 1988), p. 29.

50. Greer, *Anglican Approaches to Scripture*, ch. 4.

51. Williams, *Anglican Identities*, p. 81.

52. Moore, *Sources*, p. 36. Italics original.

53. Williams, *Anglican Identities*, p. 75.

54. Wright, *Scripture and the Authority of God*, pp. 89–93.

55. See the many examples in Wingate *et al.*, *Anglicanism: A Global Communion* and in Sugden and Samuel, *Anglican Life and Witness*.

56. J. Allen, *Rabble-rouser for Peace* (London: Rider, 2006), p. 116.

57. *Ibid.*, p. 139.

58. *Ibid.*, p. 169.

4 'It works but don't ask me how': Anglican Tradition

1. J. H. Newman, *Lectures on the Prophetical Office of the Church* (2nd edn, 1838), cited in Chadwick, *Mind of the Oxford Movement*, p. 123. Italics mine.

2. J. Keble, *Sermons Academic and Occasional* (first pub. 1847), cited in Chadwick, *Mind of the Oxford Movement*, p. 130.

3. Even Laud, despite distinguishing between the very influential Apostolical Tradition and the less influential Tradition of the later Church, stressed the primacy of Scripture: 'For the Scripture doth infallibly confirm the authority of Church traditions truly so called: but tradition doth but morally and probably confirm the authority of Scripture.' From the published record of the *Conference* between Laud and Fisher (as published in 1639), p. 63, cited in McAdoo, *Being an Anglican*, p. 15.

4. Our interpretation of the Oxford Movement has been substantially altered by the ground-breaking work of Peter Nockles. See both his *Oxford Movement in Context* and his essay in Platten, *Anglicanism*

and the Western Tradition. Nockles has demonstrated how much the Movement consciously distanced themselves from previous and especially contemporary Anglican traditions whilst convincing themselves about their interpretation of Anglican history.

5. See the excellent discussion in the *Rochester Report*, paras 3.4.1 to 3.4.16.

6. This is brilliantly expressed by Euan Cameron: 'Individual Christians, according to the leading reformers, are simultaneously sinful and justified. Even as grace works within us, we experience unruly passions and unworthy desires. The reformers said the same, though not always so stridently, about the Church' (*Interpreting Christian History*, p. 238).

7. One of the difficulties (and gifts) for Anglicans is that Cranmer did not leave detailed commentaries on, for example, the Articles. Despite fine historical work, we often have to hypothesise as to his or his successors' intentions. To demonstrate the complexity of working with the Articles as *definitive* statements of doctrine, try reading two different commentaries on them, one Catholic the other more Evangelical: E. J. Bicknell, *A Theological Introduction to the Thirty-nine Articles* (London: Longmans, first pub. 1919, 2nd edn 1925); W. H. Griffith Thomas, *The Principles of Theology* (London: Church Book Room Press, first pub. 1930, 3rd edn 1945).

8. This example reveals why it is such nonsense for some Anglicans to appeal to the Articles or the wider English Reformation as the basis for a semi-congregational policy. Cf. D. Holloway, *Finance, Centralism and the Quota*, Reform Discussion Paper No. 6, 1994, p. 15 or C. Green, *An Oversight?* Reform Discussion Paper No. 3, 1993, p. 15. The Church of England in its reformed state has always had a relatively strong central authority. Reform must be justified on different and honest historical grounds.

9. MacCulloch, *Thomas Cranmer*, pp. 232–4.

10. P. Thomas, 'Some Principles of Anglican Authority' in Sykes, *Authority in the Anglican Communion*, p. 25, citing the 1948 Lambeth Conference. The key text reads:

> It is thus a dispersed rather than a centralized authority having many elements which combine, interact with, and check each other ... Where this authority of Christ is to be found mediated not in one mode but in several we recognize in the multiplicity God's loving provision against the temptations to tyranny and the dangers of unchecked power.

Cited in Sykes, *Unashamed Anglicanism*, p. 168. Stephen's essays in the section 'The Anglican Doctrine of the Church' are foundational for my discussion.

11. Thomas in Sykes, *Authority in the Anglican Communion*, p. 23.

12. *Laws of Ecclesiastical Polity*, 3.i.13, p. 295.

13. *Ibid.*, 3.i.9, p. 289.
14. *Ibid.*, 3.i.7, p. 288.
15. *Ibid.*, 3.i.14, p. 296.
16. Bradshaw in Hannaford, *Future of Anglicanism*, p. 96.
17. Ramsey, *Gospel and the Catholic Church*, p. 66. Italics original.
18. *Ibid.*, p. 80.
19. *Ibid.*, ch. 6.
20. *Ibid.*, p. 219. Italics mine.
21. *Ibid.*, p. 220.
22. Williams, *Anglican Identities*, p. 26.
23. If this argument about the simple organic nature of Anglican conceptions of the Church is right, then we need to recognise that even if Anglicans split, the universal Church of Christ continues – more visibly maimed – and as Hooker would remind us, there *will be* Christians in each of the broken parts. This might temper some of the current rush to separate, especially if we believe our unity really does flow from Christ. As the *Windsor Report* reminds Anglicans sharply: 'Communion is, in fact, the fundamental limit to autonomy'. *Windsor Report*, para. 82, p. 36.
24. *Windsor Report*, para. 5, p. 12. See also Avis, *Anglicanism and the Christian Church* for the argument in favour of baptism as the ecclesial foundation of Anglicanism.
25. Bradshaw in Hannaford, *Future of Anglicanism*, p. 94.
26. Williams. *Anglican Identities*, p. 8.
27. See France in Kuhrt, *Proclaim Afresh*, pp. 80–1.
28. *Laws of Ecclesiastical Polity*, 5.lxxvi.10, p. 416.
29. *Ibid.*, 5.lxxvii.1, p. 417.
30. I am also following Classic Anglicanism in focusing on the *two* dominical sacraments, though I can conceive of other 'sacramental actions' within the sacramentality of the Church and the world.
31. *Defence of the True and Catholic Doctrine of the Sacrament*, published in 1550, followed by his *An Answer to a Crafty and Sophistical Cavillation Devised by Stephen Gardiner*, published in 1551.
32. G. Dix, *The Shape of the Liturgy* (London, A. and C. Black, 2nd edn, 1960 reprint), p. 672. Cf. the excellent detailed comment on this in Null, *Thomas Cranmer's Doctrine of Repentance*, pp. 242–5.
33. Brightman, *English Rite*, vol. II, p. 698.
34. B. Spinks, 'Cranmer's Methods of Liturgical Compilation' in P. Ayris and D. Selwyn (eds), *Thomas Cranmer: Churchman and Scholar* (Woodbridge: Boydell, 1993), p. 179. Cf. Collinson's robust rejection of the charge of Zwinglianism against Cranmer in his preface to P. N. Brooks' *Thomas Cranmer's Doctrine of the Eucharist* (London: Macmillan, 2nd edn, 1992).
35. MacCulloch, *Thomas Cranmer*, p. 392.
36. *Laws of Ecclesiastical Polity*, 5.lvii.5, p. 236.
37. See Stevenson, *Covenant of Grace Renewed*, p. 30 for detailed

discussion. He too regards Hooker's sacramental theology as profoundly balanced and Anglican.

38. *Laws of Ecclesiastical Polity*, 5.lxvii.12, p. 328. Italics original.

39. *Ibid.*, 5.lxvii.6, p. 322.

40. *Ibid.*, 5.lxvii.3, p. 320.

41. *Ibid.*, 5.lxvii.12, p. 331.

42. *Ibid.*, 4.i.3, p. 361.

43. L. Andrewes, *Ninety-Six Sermons. Vol. II: Sermons preached in Lent, on Good-Friday, and on Easter-Day* (Oxford: Library of Anglo-Catholic Theology, Parker, 1841), p. 402.

44. This quotation is from an unpublished paper, Kenneth Stevenson's Michael Vasey Lecture in 2005, 'Worship and Theology: Lancelot Andrewes in Durham Easter 1617'.

45. L. Andrewes, *Ninety-Six Sermons. Vol I: Sermons on the Nativity* (Oxford: Library of Anglo-Catholic Theology, Parker, 1854), p. 7. I am indebted to Jeffrey Steel for this reference and for much education about Andrewes. See his article 'Eucharistic Celebration in the Nativity Sermons of Lancelot Andrewes' in *The Anglican*, vol. 34, no. 2, April 2005, pp. 19–23.

46. Stevenson, *Covenant of Grace Renewed*, p. 52.

47. *Ibid.*, p. 52.

48. From the *Reply*, cited in *ibid.*, p. 45.

49. This is not to deny the serious historical debate about whether the Anglo-Catholics were *specially* effective. See Yates, *Anglican Ritualism in Victorian Britain*.

50. From a report, cited in Palmer, *Reverend Rebels*, p. 168:

> We have put into the army 39 young men, into the navy 57 young men. We have emigrated to Australia, America and elsewhere 63. We have started in life over 100 young men who lived with us. We have reformed 25 thieves just out of gaol. We have sent into service and into shops about 100 girls ... We have turned many drunkards into self-respecting, church-going people. We have rescued 144 fallen women, and got in preventive Homes 124 children, snatched from the brink of ruin. We have shut up in the district over 50 brothels ... We house 6 old couples free of rent ... We feed for a halfpenny a meal 180 children ... We teach over 500 children in our Sunday-schools, and 600 in our Day-schools ... We have a nigger-troupe *(sic)*, an acrobatic troupe, dancing-class, and glee club; a sewing-class; a large temperance society and Band of Hope a lending library, and three penny savings banks.

Allowing for the exaggeration in fund-raising reports and for the problematic language of the nineteenth century, this was both significant work and also entirely typical of the best Victorian urban clergy, of all traditions. It is worth reading them in their own words. See Dolling's *Ten Years in a Portsmouth Slum* (first pub. 1896).

51. Palmer, *Reverend Rebels*, p. 176.
52. In *Robert William Radclyffe Dolling* (London: Catholic Literature Association, 1933, p. 21). Available at 'The Canterbury Project' http:// anglicanhistory.org/bios/rwrdolling.html
53. J. Keble, *The Christian Year*, p. 59. (First published 1827). Cited from London: Bickers, 1880).
54. J. H. Newman, *Parochial and Plain Sermons* (Sermon for the Feast of the Circumcision of our Lord), cited in Rowell, *Vision Glorious* from the 1873 edn, p. 8.
55. From his 1850 *Sermons III*, cited in Rowell, *Vision Glorious*, p. 15.
56. 'Holy Communion' in Keble, *Christian Year*, p. 275.
57. Ramsey, *Christian Priest Today*, p. 36.
58. R. Williams, 'Sacraments of the New Society', p. 93, in Brown and Loades, *Christ: the Sacramental Word*.
59. Ramsey, *Christian Priest Today*, p. 16.

5 'God-given Reason'

1. See J. Saxbee, *Liberal Evangelism* (London: SPCK, 1994) for a passionate advocacy of the Liberal perspective. On the other hand, encountering dogmatic or complacent Anglican Liberalism is a deeply unpleasant experience and, from my perspective, *some* Liberals have gone far too far in 'rethinking' the faith. Evangelicals may know they are right with God, Catholics may be snobby about liturgy, but Liberals know they are the clever people...
2. See the discussion in Greer, *Anglican Approaches to Scripture*, pp. xixff. Note also McGrade's lovely irony: 'No Church claims irrationality as an identifying mark, nor do Anglicans claim that they alone are reasonable.' I wonder... See A. S. McGrade, 'Reason', p. 115, in Sykes *et al.*, *Study of Anglicanism*.
3. This is more associated with Methodist theological method but has also been adopted by some Anglicans. See Greer, *Anglican Approaches to Scripture*, p. xviii citing Booty.
4. Greer, *Anglican Approaches to Scripture*, p. xx.
5. There is of course controversy both as to who should be included in this movement and also about its convictions and value. It has been criticised for reducing Christian faith to a set of moral regulations inspired chiefly by Natural Law and at its worst, for a tendency to Socinianism (anti-Trinitarianism). For a classic account of the movement see McAdoo, *Spirit of Anglicanism*, chs 5 and 6.
6. See the succinct article by D. A. Palin, 'Rational Religion in England...' in S. Gilley and W. J. Sheils (eds), *A History of Religion in Britain* (Oxford: Blackwell, 1994).
7. See the most recent study, Jones, *Broad Church*.
8. See the excellent discussion in D. Brown, *Tradition and Imagination*, pp. 32–44.

9. *The Westminster Confession*, section 6, article 2. Bray, *Documents of the English Reformation*, p. 492. Italics mine.

10. There is a highly complex discussion underlying this about Hooker's views on Reason and sin. Is he really a neo-Thomist believer in the power of Reason or a good Reformed theologian believer in total depravity? Voak tries to solve this Gordian knot by positing a doctrine of 'common grace' which is available to Christian and non-Christian. The problem is that Hooker is not very explicit on this topic. See Voak, *Richard Hooker and Reformed Theology*, pp. 163ff.

11. *Ibid.*, pp. 97ff.

12. From his essay 'Faith and Evidence' (1964) in A. Loades and R. MacSwain (eds), *The Truth Seeking Heart: Austin Farrer and His Writings* (Norwich: Canterbury Press, 2006), p. 172.

13. From 'Emptying Out the Sense' (1970) in *ibid.*, p. 205.

14. From 'Does God Exist?' (1947) in *ibid.*, p. 215.

15. All the quotations in this next section come from Hooker, *Laws of Ecclesiastical Polity* (Folger edn), 7.xi.10, pp. 210–11. Italics mine.

16. Voak, *Richard Hooker and Reformed Theology*, p. 238.

17. *Ibid.*, p. 239 and p. 265.

18. *Ibid.*, p. 256.

19. *Laws of Ecclesiastical Polity* (Folger edn), 7.xi.10, pp. 210–11.

20. Traditionally taken from Proverbs 20:27. Whichcote was vice-Chancellor of Cambridge during the Commonwealth and suffered demotion at the Restoration. See the extract from his *Discourses* (published 1751) in More and Cross, *Anglicanism*, p. 213.

21. Butler, *Analogy of Religion*, Conclusion, ch. 9, s. 7, p. 334.

22. Butler, *Analogy of Religion*, Part 2, ch. 3, s. 3, p. 200.

23. Patrick, *Miners' Bishop*, p. 61, citing Westcott's *Essays in the History of Religious Thought in the West* (1891), pp. 380–4. I am indebted to my colleague Gavin Wakefield for this reference.

24. O. Chadwick, *The Victorian Church*, Part I (London: A. and C. Black, 3rd edn 1971), p. 551.

25. H. Chadwick, 'Reception' in Sugden and Samuel, *Anglican Life and Witness*.

26. *Windsor Report*, para. 68, p. 33.

27. Sykes, *Unashamed Anglicanism*, p. 168.

28. *Ibid.*, p. 169. Italics original.

29. *Ibid.*, p. 175. Italics original.

30. *Windsor Report*, para. 157, p. 60.

31. Sykes, *Integrity of Anglicanism*, p. 22, citing Ramsey, *Gore to Temple*, p. 14.

32. Technically this is a theological opinion rather than a doctrine, but it is a long-standing one (back to Augustine) and has had profound pastoral consequences.

33. Ramsey, *Gore to Temple*, p. 164, cited in Patrick, *Miners' Bishop*, p. 224.

34. Williams, *Anglican Identities*, p. 97.
35. See Dormer *et al.*, *Anglicanism*.
36. Crowther's is both an inspiring and a sobering story. A converted freed slave, he was trained and sent back to Nigeria as a missionary bishop. But his authority was undermined by the reluctance of the white missionaries to accept him.
37. See succinctly T. E. Yates, 'Anglicans and Mission' in Sykes *et al.*, *Study of Anglicanism*, p. 488. For fuller accounts of Venn and how he was 'updated' into the twentieth century, see the work of Max Warren and Stephen Neill.
38. See *Windsor Report*, paras 71–86, pp. 34–8.
39. Responsibility for co-ordinating Anglican liturgy rests with the International Anglican Liturgical Commission. See their page on http://www.aco.org.
40. The 1888 Lambeth Conference took a hard line against polygamous marriage. The 1988 Lambeth Conference, resolution 26, allowed a polygamist to keep his existing wives but promise to marry no more. Anglican Consultative Council, *The Truth Shall Make You Free: The Lambeth Conference 1988* (London: Church House Publishing, 1988), p. 221.
41. Inge, *Thomas Traherne*, p. 17.
42. *Ibid.*, p. 111.
43. *Ibid.*, p. xxiii.
44. *Ibid.*, p. xiii.
45. *Ibid.*, p. 108.
46. Patrick, *Miners' Bishop*, p. 225, citing *Christian Aspects of Life* (1897), p. 32.
47. *Being Human*, p. 2. For a rich account of the nature of wisdom see S. Barton (ed.), *Where Shall Wisdom Be Found?* (Edinburgh: T. and T. Clark, 1999).
48. See for example chs 2 and 3 in Williams, *Anglican Identities*.
49. See a summary of this perspective in E. Graham, H. Walton, and F. Ward, *Theological Reflection: Methods* (London: SCM Press, 2005), ch. 5 or Hardy, *Finding the Church*, ch. 2.
50. B. Kaye, *A Church Without Walls* (Victoria: HarperCollins, 1995), p. 120.
51. *Ibid.*, p. 220.
52. Williams, *Anglican Identities*, p. 45. My italics.
53. *Ibid.*, p. 26.
54. *Ibid.*, p. 55.
55. Hardy, *Finding the Church*, p. 3. Italics original.

6 The 'beauty of holiness': worship as the heart of Anglicanism

1. Ford and Hardy, *Living in Praise*, p. 11.
2. For an excellent account of how this was true in the Tudor and Stuart

periods see Maltby in Platten, *Anglicanism and the Western Christian Tradition*, p. 128.

3. *Laws of Ecclesiastical Polity*, 5.xxiv.2, p. 107.
4. Maltby in Platten, *Anglicanism and the Western Christian Tradition*, p. 132.
5. Croft in Platten, *Anglicanism and the Western Christian Tradition*, p. 85.
6. See the vols. by Brown and Loades. Also J. Inge, *A Christian Theology of Place* (Aldershot: Ashgate, 2003).
7. C. Chartres (ed.), *Why I Am Still an Anglican* (London/New York: Continuum, 2006). See also Lewis and Platten, *Flagships of the Spirit*.
8. MacCulloch, *Thomas Cranmer*, pp. 629–30.
9. *Laws of Ecclesiastical Polity*, 5.xxxviii.1, p. 146.
10. *Ibid.*, 5.xxxviii.3, p. 149. Citing Basil, *Homilia in Psalmum Primum*, ch. 1 in the 1551 *Opera*.
11. Ford and Hardy, *Living in Praise*, p. 13.
12. Williams, *Anglican Identities*, p. 30.
13. Ford and Hardy, *Living in Praise*, p. 14.
14. The obvious candidate for inclusion here would be Jeremy Taylor (1613–67), whose book *Holy Living* (1650) encompasses the whole sweep of this chapter from personal and social holiness to its roots in daily prayer and the eucharist. But this book is too long already and I have covered him, a little, elsewhere. See *Humane Christianity*, pp. 149–56.
15. Collinson, 'Thomas Cranmer' in Rowell, *English Religious Tradition and the Genius of Anglicanism*, p. 98. That Cranmer intended to create a genuinely comprehensive church is the thrust of Collinson's book *From Cranmer to Sancroft* (London: Hambledon, 2006).
16. Collinson, 'Thomas Cranmer', p. 99.
17. This is another highly technical debate but we must note as well as Null's detailed work on Cranmer's personal documents (*Thomas Cranmer's Doctrine of Repentance*, pp. 195–204) the very odd shape of Article 17. O'Donovan makes great play of this. He stresses the relative location of Cranmer's views on predestination: 'It does not come at the beginning, with the doctrines of God and creation, but is among the Articles on salvation. For Cranmer this doctrine is about our salvation, and not part of the general theistic understanding of how a transcendent God directs contingent events.' He goes on to stress that the Article does not speak of the fearful 'double decree'. Certainly it reads a little oddly, as if the negative is missing. It may look as if this is simply the political care of a wily pastor, who does not want the unsaved falling into despair or recklessness, but O'Donovan argues that it is because 'Cranmer will not say that there is such a thing as foreordination to damnation, but only that belief in such does exist…': whereas 'predestination to life is the everlasting

purpose of God' (O'Donovan, *Thirty-Nine Articles*, pp. 85–6). On Cranmer's private views Null is convincing but he also notes that Cranmer's presentation of the Reformed view is 'pastoral' (p. 223) and that he kept his views on predestination 'hidden from view in the prayer book' (p. 252). Why? Most crucially, Null writes: 'Cranmer's liturgy remained vulnerable to being understood as stressing salvation contingent on human response' (p. 253).

18. P. Collinson, *The Elizabethan Puritan Movement* (London: Jonathan Cape, 1967), p. 120, citing John Field in the 1572 *Admonition to the Parliament*.

19. W. Temple, *Christianity and Social Order* (Harmondsworth: Penguin, 1942), p. 44. For insights into Temple's thinking and work see A. Suggate, *William Temple and Christian Social Ethics Today* (Edinburgh: T. and T. Clark, 1987) and S. Spencer, *William Temple: A Calling to Prophecy* (London: SPCK, 2001).

20. Temple, *Christianity and Social Order*, p. 74.

21. A. Null, 'Thomas Cranmer's Theology of the Heart' in *Anvil*, vol. 3, no. 3, 2006, p. 212.

22. Again I stress my gratitude to Dr Bridget Nicholls for the detailed guidance that lies behind this section.

23. Null, *Anvil*, p. 211 citing J. G. Nichols (ed.), *Narratives of the Days of the Reformation* (London: Camden Society, 1859), p. 244.

24. Williams, *Anglican Identities*, p. 2.

25. A bold claim perhaps! But notice that Williams' list of 'successors to Westcott' (*Anglican Identities*, p. 83) includes Vanstone, the archetypal theologian of this perspective. See *Love's Endeavour, Love's Expense: the Response of Being to the Love of God* (London: DLT, 1977). From within Evangelicalism note John Stott, with his recognition of the breadth of Anglicanism and sensitive commendation of the theology of the Cross. See *The Cross of Christ* (Leicester: IVP, 1986) and (with David Edwards) *Essentials* (London: Hodder and Stoughton, 1988).

26. Null, *Thomas Cranmer's Doctrine of Repentance*, p. 252.

27. 'Love III', Herbert, *Poems*, p. 192. For detailed background and very helpful insights I am indebted to 'Love Bade Me Welcome' in Sykes, *Unashamed Anglicanism*.

SELECT BIBLIOGRAPHY

General Recommended Reading

Of the making of books on the meaning of Anglicanism there is no end, especially during periods of crisis. Books which I have found especially helpful in my teaching and writing include: P. Avis, *The Anglican Understanding of the Church: an Introduction* (London: SPCK, 2000) and *Anglicanism and the Christian Church: Theological Resources in Historical Perspective* (London: T. and T. Clark, 2nd edn, 2002); I. Bunting (ed.), *Celebrating the Anglican Way* (London/Sydney/Auckland: Hodder and Stoughton, 1996); S. W. Sykes, *Unashamed Anglicanism* (London: DLT, 1995) and R. Williams, *Anglican Identities* (London: DLT, 2004). See also A. Redfern, *Being Anglican* (London: DLT, 2004 edn). I would give more weight to Anglicanism's doctrinal core than Bishop Alastair but his selection of Anglicans to celebrate is exhilarating and very close to my own. See also R. Giles, *How to Be an Anglican* (Norwich: Canterbury Press, 2003), the funniest book on being an Anglican.

No one writing in this field will wish to bypass the monumental work of Archbishop Henry McAdoo, especially *The Spirit of Anglicanism* (London: A. and C. Black, 1965) and *Being an Anglican* (Dublin/London: SPCK, 1977) but I fear it is beginning to show its age. The same can be said of Bishop Stephen Neill's book, *Anglicanism* (first pub. 1958), however crucial it was for Evangelical Anglicans in a former generation.

Well-informed readers will remember that a previous volume in this series also considered the Anglican Tradition: L. William Countryman, *The Poetic Imagination* (London: DLT, 1999). My own book takes a different line (more confident of a doctrinal core to Anglicanism), and a different method (historical theology rather than poetry), but readers are very strongly encouraged to read Countryman's book because it is an exquisite exploration of the best of 'Anglican' poetry with stimulating theological comment.

The most valuable book on the new historical study of the history of the Church of England and its impact on our understanding of Anglicanism is S. Platten (ed.), *Anglicanism and the Western Christian Tradition* (Norwich: Canterbury Press, 2003). Anyone wishing to dig into the history behind my book must read it.

There are two treasures which I encourage all my students to buy: P. E. More and F. L. Cross (eds), *Anglicanism* (London: SPCK, 1935 and later editions), a wonderful if not entirely balanced compendium of quotations from Classic Anglicanism; and also G. Rowell, K. Stevenson and R. Williams (eds), *Love's Redeeming Work* (Oxford/New York, OUP, 2001). S. W. Sykes, J. Booty and J. Knight (eds), *The Study of Anglicanism* (London: SPCK; Minneapolis: Fortress, 2nd edn, 1998) is also very valuable.

Other General Works on Anglicanism

G. R. Evans and J. R. Wright (eds), *The Anglican Tradition* (London: SPCK; Minneapolis: Fortress, 2001)

R. A. Greer, *Anglican Approaches to Scripture* (New York: Herder and Herder, 2006)

R. Hannaford (ed.), *The Future of Anglicanism* (Leominster: Gracewing, 1996)

K. Hylson-Smith, *Evangelicals in the Church of England 1734–1984* (Edinburgh: T. and T. Clark, 1989)

—*High-Churchmanship in the Church of England from the sixteenth century to the late twentieth century* (Edinburgh: T. and T. Clark, 1993)

D. Loades (ed.), *Word and Worship* (Oxford: The Davenant Press, 2005)

C. Podmore, *Aspects of Anglican Identity* (London: Church House Publishing, 2005)

G. Rowell (ed.), *The English Religious Tradition and the Genius of Anglicanism* (Wantage: Ikon, 1992)

S. W. Sykes, *The Integrity of Anglicanism* (London/Oxford: Mowbray, 1978)

S. W. Sykes (ed.), *Authority in the Anglican Communion* (Toronto: Anglican Book Centre, 1987)

Key Modern Reports and Documents

Anglican Consultative Council and the Pontifical Council for Promoting Christian Unity, ARCIC, *The Gift of Authority: Authority in the Church III* (London: Catholic Truth Society; Toronto: Anglican Book Centre; New York: Church Publishing Incorporated, 1999)

Archbishops' Council, *Mission-shaped Church* (London: Church House Publishing, 2004)

Canons of the Church of England (Church House Publishing, London, 6th edn, 2000, incl. 1st Supplement, 2005)

Church of England Council for Christian Unity, *Together in Mission and Ministry: the Porvoo Common Statement* (London: Church House Publishing, 1993)

Doctrine Commission of the General Synod of the Church of England, *The Mystery of Salvation* (London: Church House Publishing, 1995)

—*Being Human* (London: Church House Publishing, 2003)

General Synod, House of Bishops, *Women Bishops in the Church of England?* (*The Rochester Report*) (London: Church House Publishing, 2004)

The Lambeth Commission on Communion, *The Windsor Report* (London: Anglican Communion Office, 2004)

Other Books with Specific Relevance to Issues within Anglicanism Cited in This Book

A. Bartlett, *Humane Christianity* (London: DLT, 2004)

G. Bray (ed.), *Documents of the English Reformation* (Cambridge: James Clarke, 1994)

D. Brown, *Tradition and Imagination* (Oxford/New York: OUP, 2004)

—*Discipleship and Imagination* (Oxford/New York: OUP, 2004)

D. Brown and A. Loades (eds), *Christ: the Sacramental Word* (London: SPCK, 1996)

—*The Sense of the Sacramental* (London: SPCK, 1995)

J. Carey (ed.), *John Donne* (Oxford/New York: OUP, 1990)

A. Cluysenaar (ed.), *Henry Vaughan: Selected Poems* (London: SPCK, 2004)

D. Dormer, J. MacDonald and J. Caddick, *Anglicanism: the Answer to Modernity* (London/New York: Continuum, 2003)

D. F. Ford and D. W. Hardy, *Living in Praise* (Grand Rapids, MI: Baker Academic, 2005)

D. W. Hardy, *Finding the Church* (London: SCM Press, 2001)

D. Inge (ed.), *Thomas Traherne: Poetry and Prose* (London: SPCK, 2002)

G. Kuhrt (ed.), *To Proclaim Afresh* (London: SPCK, 1995)

C. Lewis and S. Platten, *Flagships of the Spirit: Cathedrals in Society* (London: DLT, 1998)

M. Oakley (ed.), *John Donne: Verse and Prose* (London: SPCK, 2004)

G. A. Patrick, *The Miners' Bishop: Brooke Foss Westcott* (Peterborough: Epworth, 2nd edn, 2004)

D. Scott, *Sacred Tongues: the Golden Age of Spiritual Writing* (London: SPCK, 2001)

K. Stevenson, *Covenant of Grace Renewed* (London: DLT, 1994)

N. T. Wright, *Scripture and the Authority of God* (London: SPCK, 2005)

God and History

For a recent and very important book, also reflecting theologically on church history, though using a different methodology to mine, focusing on the theological connectedness of Christians as members of the Body of Christ over time, see R. Williams, *Why Study the Past?* (London: DLT, 2005). I find it striking that Williams feels able to draw much fuller theological lessons from the past than Euan Cameron in *Interpreting*

Christian History (Malden MA/Oxford/Victoria: Blackwell, 2005), precisely because of this richer theological engine. The key work on the relationship between historical study and spirituality remains P. Sheldrake, *Spirituality and History* (London: SPCK, 2nd edn, 1995). For other important discussions on the relationship between history and Christian faith by Christians who are historians see H. Butterfield, *Christianity and History* (first pub. 1949), D. Bebbington, *Patterns in History* (Leicester: Inter-Varsity Press, 1979) and E. Ives, *God in History* (Tring: Lion, 1979).

Further Reading by Topic

Cranmer

C. Frederick Barbee and P. Zahl, *The Collects of Thomas Cranmer* (Grand Rapids MI/Cambridge: Eerdmans, 1999)

P. N. Brooks (ed.), *Cranmer in Context* (Cambridge: Lutterworth, 1989)

D. MacCulloch, *Thomas Cranmer* (New Haven/London: Yale University Press, 1996)

A. Null, *Thomas Cranmer's Doctrine of Repentance* (Oxford: OUP, 2000)

O. O'Donovan, *On the Thirty-nine Articles* (Exeter: Paternoster, 1986)

For the Prayer Books I used F. E. Brightman, *The English Rite* (London: Rivingtons, 1915); the Everyman edition of the 1549 and 1552 books and a standard copy of the 1662, which is readily available.

Elizabeth

P. Collinson, *The Elizabethan Puritan Movement* (London: Jonathan Cape, 1967)

—*Elizabethans* (London/New York: Hambledon, 2003)

J. Maltby, *Prayer Book and People in Elizabethan and Early Stuart England* (Cambridge: CUP, 1998)

Hooker

Currently the most straightforward way to read Hooker is to find a second-hand Everyman edition of Books I–V of the *Laws of Ecclesiastical Polity*, which were first published in the 1590s. The outstanding critical edition of all eight volumes (three volumes were published posthumously) and other writings is the recent Folger Edition. My quotations are normally taken from the Everyman edition, but checked against Folger. It is also possible to read both a biography of Hooker and some translations of Hooker edited by Philip Secor. References in the *Laws* are to the Book (5), the chapter (iv) and the sub-section (3).

N. Atkinson, *Richard Hooker and the Authority of Scripture, Tradition and Reason: Reformed Theologian of the Church of England?* (Carlisle: Paternoster, 1997)

J. Booty, *Reflections on the Theology of Richard Hooker* (Sewanee, TN: University of the South Press, 1998)

W. J. Torrance Kirby, *Richard Hooker, Reformer and Platonist* (Aldershot/Burlington, VT: Ashgate, 2005)

N. Voak, *Richard Hooker and Reformed Theology* (Oxford/New York: OUP, 2003)

Andrewes

M. Dorman, *Lancelot Andrewes, 1555–1626: a Perennial Preacher in the post-Reformation English Church* (Tucson: Fenestra Books, 2004)

N. Lossky, *Lancelot Andrewes: the Preacher* (Oxford: Clarendon Press, 1991)

P. McCullough (ed.), *Lancelot Andrewes: Selected Sermons and Lectures* (Oxford: OUP, 2005)

D. Scott (ed.), *Lancelot Andrewes: the Private Prayers* (London: SPCK, 2002)

P. Welsby, *Lancelot Andrewes* (London: SPCK, 1964)

Herbert

G. Herbert, *The English Poems of George Herbert*, ed. C. A. Patrides (first pub. 1633; London: J. M. Dent, 1974)

—*The Country Parson*, ed. A. Pasternak Slater (first pub. 1652; London: Everyman, 1974)

E. Clarke, *Theory and Theology in George Herbert's Poetry* (Oxford: Clarendon, 1997)

W. Cope, *George Herbert: Verse and Prose* (London: SPCK, 2002)

P. Sheldrake, *Love Took My Hand: The Spirituality of George Herbert* (London: DLT, 2000)

Butler

J. Butler, *The Analogy of Religion* (first pub. 1738; cited from the version edited by W. E. Gladstone, Oxford: OUP, 1896, in the World Classics reprint, 1907)

C. Cunliffe (ed.), *Joseph Butler's Moral and Religious Thought* (Oxford: OUP, 1992)

T. Penelhum, *Butler* (London/Boston/Henley: Routledge and Kegan Paul, 1985)

Simeon

H. E. Hopkins, *Charles Simeon: Preacher Extraordinary* (Bramcote: Grove Books, 1979)

H. Moule, *Charles Simeon* (first pub. 1892, 2nd edn London: Inter-Varsity Fellowship, 1948).

A. Pollard (ed.), *Let Wisdom Judge: University Addresses and Sermon Outlines by Charles Simeon* (London, Inter-Varsity Fellowship, 1959)

C. Smyth, *Simeon and Church Order* (Cambridge: CUP, 1940)

Anglo-Catholicism

O. Chadwick (ed.), *The Mind of the Oxford Movement* (London, A. and C. Black, 1960)

P. Nockles, *The Oxford Movement in Context* (Cambridge/New York/ Melbourne: CUP, 1994)

B. Palmer, *Reverend Rebels* (London: DLT, 1993)

J. S. Reed, *Glorious Battle* (Nashville/London: Vanderbilt University Press, 1996)

G. Rowell, *The Vision Glorious* (Oxford: OUP, 1983)

N. Yates, *Anglican Ritualism in Victorian Britain 1830–1910* (Oxford: OUP, 1999)

Maurice

F. D. Maurice, *The Kingdom of Christ* (first pub. 1842, 2nd edn). I am citing the Everyman edition, ed. E. Rhys (London/New York: J. M. Dent, n.d).

Tod E. Jones, *The Broad Church: A Biography of a Movement* (New York: Lexington Books, 2003)

J. Morris, *F. D. Maurice and the Crisis of Christian Authority* (Oxford/ New York: OUP, 2005)

A. Vidler, *The Theology of F. D. Maurice* (London: SCM Press, 1947)

Ramsey

M. Ramsey, *The Gospel and the Catholic Church* (London: Longman, 1936)

—*The Christian Priest Today* (London: SPCK, revised edn 1987)

—*From Gore to Temple* (London: Longman, 1960)

O. Chadwick, *Michael Ramsey: a Life* (Oxford: OUP, 1990)

R. Gill and L. Kendall (eds), *Michael Ramsey as Theologian* (London: DLT, 1995)

Anglican Communion

W. M. Jacob, *The Making of the Anglican Church Worldwide* (London: SPCK, 1997)

W. L. Sachs, *The Transformation of Anglicanism* (Cambridge: CUP, 1993)

C. Sugden and V. Samuel (eds), *Anglican Life and Witness* (London: SPCK, 1997)

K. Ward, *A History of Global Anglicanism* (Cambridge: CUP, 2006)

A. Wingate, K. Ward, C. Pemberton and W. Sitshebo (eds), *Anglicanism: a Global Communion* (London: Mowbray, 1998)